# Macromedia® Director® 8

## *Creating Powerful Multimedia*

AGAINST THE CLOCK
PERFORMANCE SUPPORT & TRAINING SYSTEMS

**PRENTICE HALL**
Upper Saddle River, NJ 07458

Library of Congress Cataloging-in-Publication Data

Macromedia Director 8 : creating powerful multimedia
Against The Clock
p. cm. — (Against The Clock series)
ISBN 0-13-032523-6
1. Director (Computer file) 2. Multimedia systems
I. Against The Clock (Firm) II. Series
QA76.575 .M313 2001
006.7'869—dc21

00-061967

**Executive Editor**: Elizabeth Sugg
**Developmental Editor**: Judy Casillo
**Supervising Manager**: Mary Carnis
**Production Editor**: Denise Brown
**Director of Manufacturing and Production**: Bruce Johnson
**Manufacturing Buyer**: Ed O'Dougherty
**Editorial Assistant**: Lara Dugan
**Formatting/Page Make-up**: Against the Clock, Inc.
**Prepress:** Photoengraving, Inc.
**Printer/Binder**: Press of Ohio
**Cover Design**: Joe Sengotta
**Icon Design**: James Braun
**Creative Director**: Marianne Frasco



Prentice Hall International (UK) Limited, London
Prentice Hall of Australia Pty. Limited, Sydney
Prentice Hall Canada Inc., Toronto
Prentice Hall Hispanoamericana, S.A., Mexico
Prentice Hall of India Private Limited, New Delhi
Prentice Hall of Japan, Inc., Tokyo
Pearson Education Asia Pte. Ltd., Singapore
Editora Prentice Hall do Brasil, Ltda., Rio de Janeiro

---



Prentice Hall

10 9 8 7 6 5 4 3 2

ISBN 0-13-032523-6

# Preface

## Purpose

The Against The Clock series has been developed specifically for those involved in the field of graphic arts and now — video and multimedia production. Many of our readers are already involved in the industry in advertising and television production companies, in multimedia, and in the world of Internet web design. Others are just now preparing themselves for a career somewhere in these professions.

This series of courses will provide you with the skills necessary to work in this fast-paced, exciting, and rapidly expanding business. While many people feel that they can simply purchase a computer and the appropriate software and begin designing and producing high-quality presentations, the real world of multimedia production and professional communications requires a far more serious commitment.

## The Series

The applications presented in the Against The Clock series stand out as the programs of choice in professional graphic arts environments.

We've used a modular design for the Against The Clock series, allowing you to mix and match the drawing, imaging, and page-layout applications that exactly suit your specific needs.

Titles available in the Against The Clock series include:

*Macintosh: Basic Operations*
*Windows: Basic Operations*
*Adobe Illustrator: Introduction and Advanced Digital Illustration*
*Macromedia FreeHand: Introduction and Advanced Digital Illustration*
*Adobe InDesign: Introduction and Advanced Electronic Mechanicals*
*Adobe PageMaker: Introduction and Advanced Electronic Mechanicals*
*QuarkXPress: Introduction and Advanced Electronic Mechanicals*
*Microsoft Publisher: Creating Electronic Mechanicals*
*Microsoft PowerPoint: Presentation Graphics with Impact*
*Microsoft FrontPage: Designing for the Web*
*Macromedia Painter: A Digital Approach to Natural Art Media*
*Adobe Photoshop: Introduction and Advanced Digital Images*
*Adobe Premiere: Digital Video Editing*
***Macromedia Director: Creating Powerful Multimedia***
*File Preparation: The Responsible Electronic Page*
*Preflight: An Introduction to File Analysis and Repair*
*TrapWise and PressWise: Digital Trapping and Imposition*

We've designed our courses to be cross-platform. While many sites use Macintosh computers, there is an increasing number of graphic arts service providers using Intel-based systems running Windows (or WindowsNT). The books in this series are applicable to either of these systems.

All of the applications that we cover in the Against The Clock series are similar in operation and appearance whether you're working on a Macintosh or a Windows system. When a particular function does differ from machine to machine, we present both.

## ICONS AND VISUALS

**Pencil** icon indicates a comment from an experienced operator. Whenever you see the pencil icon, you'll find corresponding sidebar text that augments or builds upon the subject being discussed at the time.

**Bomb** icon indicates a potential problem or difficulty. For instance, a certain technique might lead to pages that prove difficult to output. In other cases, there might be something that a program cannot easily accomplish, so we might present a workaround.

**Pointing Finger** icon indicates a hands-on activity — whether a short exercise or a complete project. Note that sometimes this icon will direct you to the back of the book to complete a project.

**Key** icon is used to point out that there is a keyboard equivalent to a menu or dialog-box option. Key commands are often faster than using the mouse to select a menu option. Experienced operators often mix the use of keyboard equivalents and menu/dialog box selections to arrive at their optimum speed.

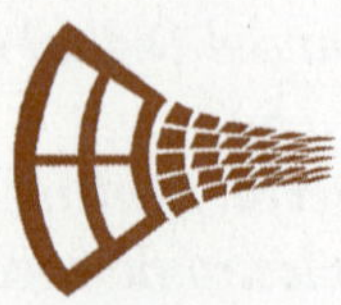

If you are a Windows user, be sure to refer to the corresponding text or images whenever you see this **Windows** icon. Although there isn't a great deal of difference between using these applications on a Macintosh and using them on a Windows-based workstation, there are certain instances where there's enough of a difference for us to comment.

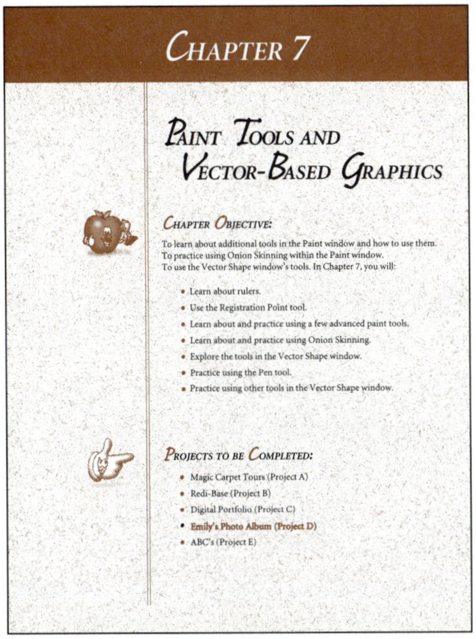
CHAPTER 7

PAINT TOOLS AND VECTOR-BASED GRAPHICS

CHAPTER OBJECTIVE:

To learn about additional tools in the Paint window and how to use them. To practice using Onion Skinning within the Paint window. To use the Vector Shape window's tools. In Chapter 7, you will:

- Learn about rulers.
- Use the Registration Point tool.
- Learn about and practice using a few advanced paint tools.
- Learn about and practice using Onion Skinning.
- Explore the tools in the Vector Shape window.
- Practice using the Pen tool.
- Practice using other tools in the Vector Shape window.

PROJECTS TO BE COMPLETED:

- Magic Carpet Tours (Project A)
- Redi-Base (Project B)
- Digital Portfolio (Project C)
- **Emily's Photo Album (Project D)**
- ABC's (Project E)

***Chapter openers*** *provide the reader with specific objectives.*

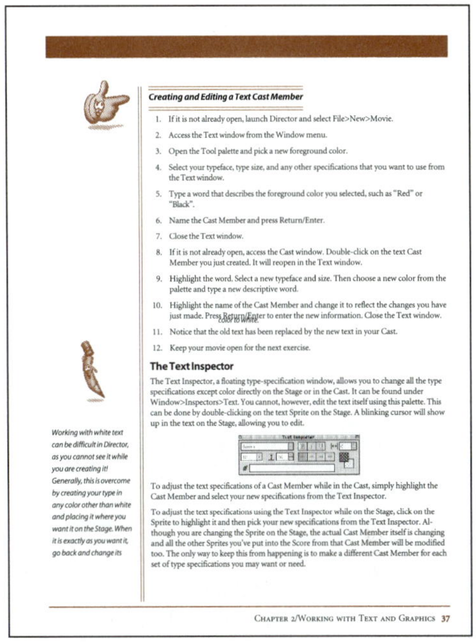
*Creating and Editing a Text Cast Member*

1. If it is not already open, launch Director and select File>New>Movie.
2. Access the Text window from the Window menu.
3. Open the Tool palette and pick a new foreground color.
4. Select your typeface, type size, and any other specifications that you want to use from the Text window.
5. Type a word that describes the foreground color you selected, such as "Red" or "Black".
6. Name the Cast Member and press Return/Enter.
7. Close the Text window.
8. If it is not already open, access the Cast window. Double-click on the text Cast Member you just created. It will reopen in the Text window.
9. Highlight the word. Select a new typeface and size. Then choose a new color from the palette and type a new descriptive word.
10. Highlight the name of the Cast Member and change it to reflect the changes you have just made. Press Return/Enter to enter the new information. Close the Text window.
11. Notice that the old text has been replaced by the new text in your Cast.
12. Keep your movie open for the next exercise.

**The Text Inspector**

The Text Inspector, a floating type-specification window, allows you to change all the type specifications except color directly on the Stage or in the Cast. It can be found under Window>Inspectors>Text. You cannot, however, edit the text itself using this palette. This can be done by double-clicking on the text Sprite on the Stage. A blinking cursor will show up in the text on the Stage, allowing you to edit.

To adjust the text specifications of a Cast Member while in the Cast, simply highlight the Cast Member and select your new specifications from the Text Inspector.

To adjust the text specifications using the Text Inspector while on the Stage, click on the Sprite to highlight it and then pick your new specifications from the Text Inspector. Although you are changing the Sprite on the Stage, the actual Cast Member itself is changing and all the other Sprites you've put into the Score from that Cast Member will be modified too. The only way to keep this from happening is to make a different Cast Member for each set of type specifications you may want or need.

*Working with white text can be difficult in Director, as you cannot see it while you are creating it! Generally, this is overcome by creating your type in any color other than white and placing it where you want it on the Stage. When it is exactly as you want it, go back and change its*

CHAPTER 2/WORKING WITH TEXT AND GRAPHICS 37

***Sidebars and hands-on activities*** *supplement concepts presented in the material.*

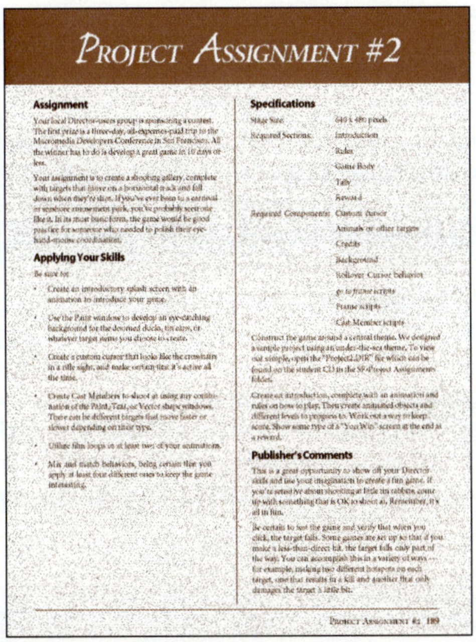
PROJECT ASSIGNMENT #2

**Assignment**

**Applying Your Skills**

**Specifications**

Stage Size: 640 x 480 pixels

Required Sections: Introduction, Rules, Game Body, Tally, Reward

**Publisher's Comments**

PROJECT ASSIGNMENT #2 189

***Step-by-step projects*** *result in finished artwork — with an emphasis on proper file construction methods.*

# The Projects You Will Work On

In addition to explantory text and illustrations, Against The Clock course materials have been constructed with two primary building blocks: exercises and projects. Projects always result in a finished piece of work — digital imagery typically built from the ground up, utilizing photographic-quality images; vector artwork from illustration programs; and type elements from the library supplied on your student CD-ROM.

This course, *Macromedia Director: Creating Powerful Multimedia*, uses several step-by-step projects on which you will work during your learning sessions. (There are also open-ended project assignments immediately preceding the two reviews.) You will find images of the step-by-step projects that you will complete by the end of the course displayed on the inside front and back covers of the book. Here's a brief overview of each:

## Project A: Magic Carpet Tours

Designed to provide a "tour" through a typical Director production, this project was specifically created to familiarize you with a working Director file. This particular production makes use of sound and various graphics and transitions. Although you will not be doing much to "create" this file, it is important to browse around and become familiar with the parts and pieces that were used to make it all come together.

## Project B: Redi-Base

This project assumes that the student has been hired by their client to create a presentation that could be used by sales representatives to market the Redi-Base product. Redi-Base will be featured and sampled at an upcoming food festival. During the creation of the production the student will work with Keyframes using Director's timeline. Additionally they will practice moving and extending Sprites.

## Project C: Digital Portfolio

One of the most important aspects of a student's career path is the creation or compilation of a dramatic and compelling portfolio of work. This portfolio kiosk, developed by Elizabeth Beecher, a student from Allentown Business School, displays some of her work and certainly portrays Elizabeth as a competent and professional artist. Students may wish to substitute their own work to develop their personal portfolio.

## Project D: Emily's Photo Album

An interactive photo album is the basis for this project. Although we have provided images, video, and sound files for the creation, students may wish to use their own components to complete the production. The specifications for the project call for various screens that display photographs of the first three years of Emily's life. The final production will have an introductory screen followed by imagery that shows Emily as she is maturing.

## Project E: ABC's

The ABC presentation is an example of using multimedia for educational purposes. This project is designed to provide practice assembling an animation and turning the pieces into Film Loops.

## FOR THE STUDENT

On the CD-ROM you will find a complete set of the Against The Clock (ATC) fonts, as well as a collection of data files used to construct the various exercises and projects.

The ATC fonts are solely for use while you are working with the Against The Clock materials. These fonts will be used throughout both the exercises and projects.

A variety of student files have been included. These files are necessary to complete both the exercises and the step-by-step projects.

## FOR THE INSTRUCTOR

The Instructor Kit consists of an Instructor's Manual and an Instructor's CD-ROM. It includes various testing and presentation materials in addition to the files that come standard with the student books.

- **Overhead Presentation Materials** are provided and follow along with the course. These presentations are prepared using Microsoft PowerPoint and are provided in both native PowerPoint format as well as Acrobat Portable Document Format (PDF).
- **Extra Projects Assignments** are provided along with the data files required for completion. These projects may be used to extend the course, or may be used to test the student.
- **Finished artwork (in PDF format)** for all projects that the students complete is supplied on the CD-ROM.
- **Test Questions and Answers** are included on the instructor CD-ROM. These questions may be modified, reorganized, and administered throughout the delivery of the course.

# Acknowledgments

I would like to give special thanks to the writers, illustrators, editors, and others who have worked long and hard to complete the Against The Clock series. Foremost among them are Robin McAllister, Dean Bagley, Terry Graybill, Toni Toomey, and Don Poyssick.

Thanks to the dedicated teaching professionals whose comments and expertise contributed to the success of these products, including Brian Williams of Manatee Community College, Steve Wrobles of Schoolcraft Community College, Julie Bath of Wichita Technical College, and Martin Wnuk of The University of Houston.

A special thanks to the Allentown Business School students including Elizabeth Beecher, Jill Hantz, Sally Behler, Jeanie Dietrich, and Nick Gathagan who created some of the projects and exercises used in this book.

Thank you to my family: Jason, Jo Ann, Ted, Michele, and Emily Lyn — the coolest and most understanding four-year old I know. And a special thanks to Jill Clayman, my best friend in the whole world.

And a big thanks to David Grodis, copy editor and final link in the chain of production, for his help in making sure we said what we meant to say.

A big thanks to Judy Casillo, developmental editor, and Denise Brown, production editor, for their guidance, patience, and attention to detail.

A final thanks to Frank Romano — who taught me everything I know.

*—Tara Holod, July 2000*

## Our History

Against The Clock (ATC) was founded in 1990 as a part of Lanman Systems Group, one of the nation's leading systems integration and training firms. The company specialized in developing custom training materials for such clients as *L.L. Bean, The New England Journal of Medicine, Smithsonian,* the *National Education Association, Air & Space Magazine, Publishers Clearing House,* The *National Wildlife Society, Home Shopping Network,* and many others. The integration firm was among the most highly respected in the graphic arts industry.

To a great degree, the success of Lanman Systems Group can be attributed to the thousands of pages of course materials developed at the company's demanding client sites. Throughout the rapid growth of Lanman Systems Group, Founder and General Manager Ellenn Behoriam developed the expertise necessary to manage technical experts, content providers, writers, editors, illustrators, designers, layout artists, proofreaders, and the rest of the chain of professionals required to develop structured and highly effective training materials.

Following the sale of the Lanman Companies to World Color, one of the nation's largest commercial printers, Ellenn embarked on a project to develop a new library of hands-on training materials engineered specifically for the professional graphic artist. A large part of this effort is finding and working with talented professional artists, writers, and educators from around the country.

The result is the ATC training library.

## About the Author

Tara Holod attended Rochester Institute of Technology in the early nineties and received her B.F.A in graphic design with a concentration in psychology. She then went for her M.S in electronic publishing with a concentration in interactive media design. After leaving Rochester, Tara cut her teeth in the wonderful world of print media working for two of the finest color printers in the country, World Color Press and Webcraft Technologies.

In addition to teaching and running the evening Graphic Design program at the Allentown Business School, Tara is currently developing multimedia projects and an e-commerce web site. She also occasionally moonlights as a subject specialist evaluator for the ACICS (Accreditation Council for Independent Colleges and Schools) and the PA Department of Education evaluating multimedia, web, computer animation and video programs at various institutions of higher education for accreditation by the aforementioned organizations.

# Getting Started

## Platform

The Against The Clock series is specifically designed to apply to both Macintosh and Windows systems — this course will work for you no matter which environment you find yourself in. There are some slight differences between the two, but when you're working in an actual application, these differences are limited to certain functions and actions. As a result, there are almost no cross-platform incompatibilities with which to be concerned.

## Naming Conventions

In the old days of MS-DOS systems, file names on the PC were limited to something referred to as "8.3," which meant that you were limited in the number of characters you could use to an eight-character name (the "8") and a three-character suffix (the "3"). Text files, for example, might be called *myfile.txt*, while a document file from a word processor might be called *myfile.doc* (for document). On today's Windows systems, these limitations have been, for the most part, overcome. Although you can use longer file names, suffixes still exist. Whether you see them or not is another story.

When your system is first configured, the Views are normally set to a default that hides these extensions. This means that you might have a dozen different files named *myfile*, all of which may have been generated by different applications and consist of completely different types of files.

You can change this view by double-clicking on *My Computer* (the icon is on your desktop). This will open the file. Select View>Folder Options. From Folder Options, select the View tab. Within the Files and Folders folder is a checkbox: "Hide file extensions for known file types." When this is unchecked, you can see the file extensions. It's easier to see what you're looking at if they're visible. While this is a personal choice, we strongly recommend viewing the file extensions. All the files used in this course have been named using the three-character suffix.

To ensure that the supplied student files are fully compatible with both operating systems, we've named all the files using the three-character suffix — even those on the Macintosh.

## Key Commands

There are two keys generally used as *modifier* keys — they do nothing when pressed, unless they are pressed in conjunction with another key. Their purpose is to alter the normal functions of the key which is pressed simultaneously.

Key commands are fairly consistent between the Macintosh and the Windows versions of this software. The major difference lies in the names of special function keys. The Macintosh has a key marked with an Apple and an icon that resembles a clover leaf. This is the Command key. The key with equivalent functions on the Windows platform is the Control key.

The Command/Control key is generally used when taking control of the computer. When combined with the "S" key, it functions to save your work. When combined with "O" it opens a file; with a "P" it prints the file. In addition to these functions, which work with most Windows programs, the Command/Control key may be combined with other keys in Director to take control of specific functions.

Another special function key is the Alt (for Alternate) key or the Option key (for the Mac). It too is a modifier key, and you must hold it down along with whatever other key (or keys) is required for a specific function.

The keys on the top row of the keypad, F1–F12 also accomplish specific tasks in conjunction with the computer. F1 will bring up the Help menu. F6 and Shift-F6 will move elements to the front or the back of a "stack" of text and graphic objects.

## The CD-ROM and Initial Setup Considerations

Before you begin using your Against The Clock course book, you must set up your system to have access to the various files and tools to complete your lessons.

### Student Files

This course comes complete with a collection of student files. These files are an integral part of the learning experience — they're used throughout the course to help you construct increasingly complex elements. Having these building blocks available to you for practice and study sessions will ensure that you will be able to experience the exercises and complete the project assignments smoothly spending a minimum of time looking for the various required components.

In the Student Files folders, we've created sets of data. Locate the **SF-Director** folder and drag the icon onto your hard disk drive. If you have limited disk space, you may want to copy only the files for one or two lessons at a time.

We strongly recommend that you work from your hard disk. However, in some cases you might not have enough room on your system for all the files we've supplied. If this is the case, you can work directly from the CD-ROM.

### Creating a Project Folder

We strongly recommend that you work from your hard disk. Director will run as much as three to five times slower if it must access a CD-Rom.

Throughout the exercises and projects you'll be required to save your work. Since the CD-ROM is "read-only," you cannot write information to it. Create a Work in Progress folder on your hard disk and use it to store your work. Create this folder while looking at your desktop. This will create the folder at the highest level of your system, where it will always be easy to find. Name it "**Work in Progress**".

## Fonts

Although we have included a set of ATC fonts on this CD-Rom, for this particular book you may elect to use your own as none of the exercises *require* a specific selection. Instructions for installing fonts are provided in the documentation that came with your computer. In general, drag them into your System>Fonts folder on the Macintosh, or, under Windows, from your Start>Settings>Control Panel>Fonts, select File>Install New Font. Navigate to the Fonts folder on the CD, select the fonts, and click OK.

## System Requirements

The following hardware and software is the minimum required to author Director movies.

If you are running a Windows operating system, you will need an Intel Pentium II 200 processor running Windows 95/98 or NT version 4.0 or later; 32 MB of available RAM plus 100 MB of available disk space; a color monitor, and a CD-ROM drive.

For the Macintosh you will need a PowerPC Macintosh running System 8.1 or later; 32 MB of available RAM; plus 100 MB of available disk space; a color monitor, and a CD-ROM drive.

## Prerequisites

This book assumes that you have a basic understanding of how to use your system.

You should know how to use your mouse to point and click, and how to drag items around the screen. You should know how to resize a window, and how to arrange windows on your desktop to maximize your available space. You should know how to access pull-down menus and how checkboxes and radio buttons work. Lastly, you should know how to create, open, and save files.

If you're familiar with these fundamental skills, then you know all that's necessary to utilize the Against The Clock courseware library.

**Notes:**

# Introduction

Macromedia Director has long been a powerhouse in the Multimedia world. Director was initially created in the 1980's as a two-dimensional animation program, but has evolved into an almost universal editor and layout tool for media of all types. With Director you can incorporate text, images, sounds, digital videos, 3D animations and its own 2D animations into complex multimedia experiences.

Director is commonly used to create projects which include educational CD-ROMs, games, instructional presentations, interactive encyclopedias, the interactive portions of DVD's and enhanced CD's, corporate presentations, and informational kiosks such as those found in your local music or book store. It is a powerful program that doesn't limit your creative vision.

One advantage that Director has over most competitive offerings is Lingo — a powerful built-in scripting language — Lingo. Using Lingo you can write scripts for customized and advanced tasks that aren't available from the standard Director interface. Though the language is quite robust, and as a result can be intimidating, you'll find that with a few simple commands you can accomplish some pretty impressive results. Through exercises provided in this course, you'll learn how to use Lingo to make your materials more intuitive and interesting.

Additionally, the Library palette — a feature new to Director 7.0 — provides you with a large variety of pre-written Lingo Behavior scripts from which to choose. This greatly broadens your interactive options without having to know complex Lingo coding. It also provides you with some pre-written Java and Internet scripts which are very helpful if you are going to convert your Director movie into a Shockwave file and post it on the Internet.

With the new Java and Internet behaviors, Macromedia is making a strang committment to making Director more web-friendly. The new Vector Shape window also enhances this ability. You can now create compact vector graphics right within the Director environment.

Lastly, be aware that learning how to use Director does not make a good multimedia artist. There are many other aspects of designing and developing a compelling project — creativity and imagination not the least of them.

Like all design work, multimedia projects should be planned down to the finest detail before picking up a mouse. It is far easier to create a project correctly the first time than it is to try to take it apart, fix it, and put it back together. A multimedia project consists of various elements tied together; remove one of them and the rest (typically) will not work right. With a complex project, sometimes finding the problem is as — or more — difficult than fixing it once you do.

Many successful multimedia designers follow a basic list of tasks when approaching a new project or a major update to one that already exists. Here's a sample:

- Meet with client to define the project's goals and audience.
- Create thumbnail sketches and storyboards.
- Refine sketches and create a flowchart diagram of how a person will navigate through the project.
- Create detailed layouts, screen by screen, explaining exactly what will be on each screen and where these items will be placed.
- Create a prototype of the project.
- Present the prototype to the client for last minute changes and additions.
- Create the final project.

By following these guidelines and checking with your client every step of the way, you have a good chance of avoiding costly mistakes that may be nearly impossible to repair.

Throughout the process, the basic elements of design must be applied. Good design sense can go by the wayside quite easily when you get excited about Director and start playing with every possible video, sound, and special effect. Lack of grace and balance in a project is one clear difference between projects done by experienced designers and ones slapped together by a novice.

Good luck and we hope you enjoy the book.

# Chapter 1

# Getting Acquainted with Director

## Chapter Objective:

To begin to understand how Director 8.0 works by examining its interface and the theater metaphor it employs. In Chapter 1, you will:

- Launch the program and work through a full-length, hands-on project.
- Gain an understanding of Director's terminology.
- Learn about the Stage.
- Learn about the Cast.
- Learn about the Property Inspector.
- Learn about importing and creating Cast Members.
- Gain an understanding of the differences between and the advantages of linking and embedding files.
- Learn about Scores and how they are used.
- Learn about the Playback Head, frames, and channels.
- Gain an understanding of how to use the Control Panel.
- View the Toolbar and all of its options.

## Projects to be Completed:

- **Magic Carpet Tours (Project A)**
- Redi-Base (Project B)
- Digital Portfolio (Project C)
- Emily's Photo Album (Project D)
- ABC's (Project E)

# Getting Acquainted with Director

Director's interface may seem intimidating because of its numerous palettes and dialog boxes. Although there are a lot of each, the good news is that they are at least set up logically. A theater metaphor is used for the names and actions of Director's most common palettes. For example, the blank area shown in the graphic below is called the Stage. The Stage is where your creations will unfold.

The Cast is used to assemble your characters for display on the Stage. The Cast can contain video, images, text, sounds, and props. The Cast is similar to the backstage area of a theater — the place where the actors wait until they are needed.

Next is the Score. Here, you tell your cast members where to go, how to behave, and when to do what. It essentially contains the directions and cues for your actors.

The Control Panel, not shown, is just what its name implies. It offers tools for controlling your movie. Play, Stop, and Rewind, among many other options, are on this palette.

Finally, the Property Inspector, shown in the bottom-right corner, is new to Director 8.0. You can use it to change the properties, or attributes, of any aspect of your presentation, regardless of what type of media it is.

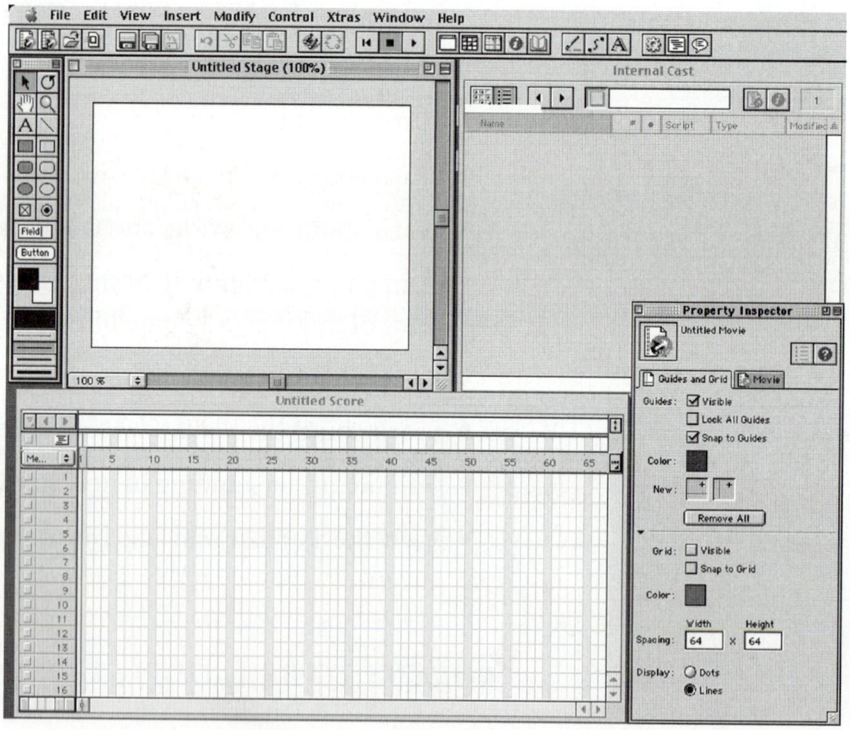

## The Stage

The blank expanse in the middle of your monitor is the Stage. As previously stated, your creations unfold here. When the curtain goes up, or you click the Play button, this is where the objects appear and interact.

There are different Stage sizes available for your movie. The general suggestions and information listed below might help you with your decisions regarding Stage size.

The Stage may be accessed by going to Window>Stage, but it is usually already open. The Stage size usually defaults to 320 x 240 pixels. This size is fine if you are going to be creating something interactive for the Internet; however, it is a bit small for creating traditional multimedia. For such projects it is recommended that you work in 640 x 480 pixels, which simulates the size of a 14″ monitor. Until you have some experience working in Director, this is the maximum Stage size you should use. Anything larger might cause technical difficulties.

You may adjust the Stage size at any time by clicking on the Stage to make it active, going to the Property Inspector, and then choosing a size. There are a few issues to consider when deciding to choose a Stage size larger than 640 x 480 pixels:

- Who is your audience?
- Will they have monitors larger than 14″?
- Will they have a machine powerful enough to run the software?
- Will complex video, sound, and graphics slow down your system?
- Do you know how to streamline your project if it does slow to a crawl?

Once these questions are answered satisfactorily, you can safely increase the Stage size. For now, let's stay with Director's default settings.

The Stage can be moved around your monitor by dragging it by the Title bar at the top. Moving the Stage may be necessary when trying to fit many of Director's palettes on the screen.

You can add a color to or change the color and/or size of the Stage using the Property Inspector. However, once you change the Stage color, the Stage remains that color for your entire movie unless you utilize Director's scripting language, Lingo (in which case, you could change the Stage color for each frame). If you want more than one color, you have the option of creating various colored backgrounds in the Paint window. We will address the Paint window later.

## *Getting Started*

1. Launch Director by double-clicking on the Director 8.0 icon. That empty white box in the center of your monitor is the Stage. If it does not appear automatically, you can access it from the Window menu. Alternately, you can use the keyboard shortcut Command/Control-1.
2. Click on the Stage to make it active. Make certain the Property Inspector is open. If it is not, go to Window>Inspectors>Property and it will open.
3. In the Property Inspector, click on the Movie tab, at the top. Make certain that your screen size is set to 640 x 480 pixels. If it is not, change the setting.

*There really is no way to close a Director movie without closing Director itself. The only exception is to open a new movie (or another movie that you are working on) in its place by selecting File>Open. This allows the current movie to close and the new movie to take its place.*

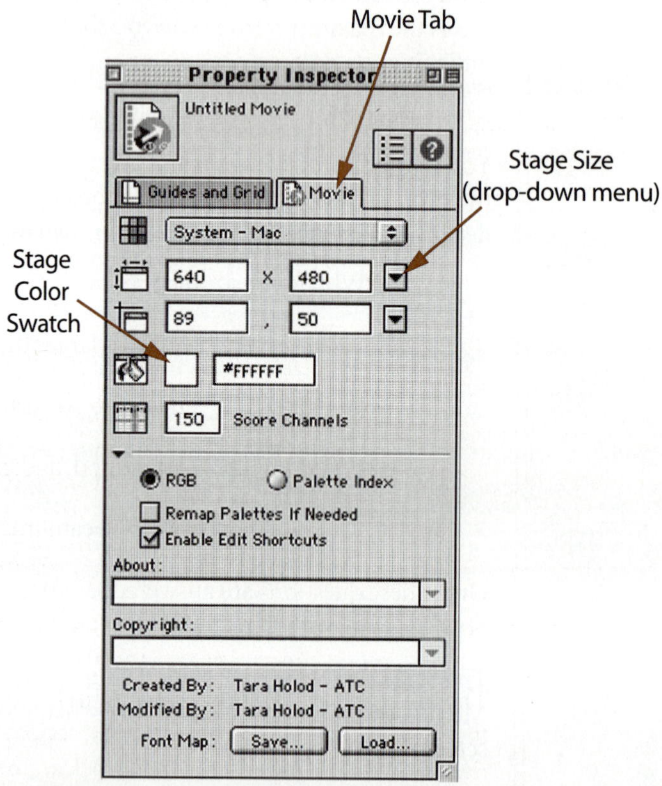


4. Click on the Stage Color Swatch. In the Color palette that appears, select the color of your choice. You'll notice that the Stage color has changed.
5. Select File>Quit to close the movie (and Director) without saving your changes. See the note in the margin about closing Director movies.

## The Cast

The Cast is not just where you keep the actors, or graphics; it is also where you will place, view, and store all of your backgrounds, sounds, videos, behaviors, scripts, images, and text. It can be viewed in list form or in thumbnail form, whichever you prefer. Many of you will find the thumbnail form to your liking because you can actually see the graphics. Those who are more used to lists and are comfortable not seeing their graphics will probably prefer the list form.

Each item occupies its own line in the list or thumbnail slot and is identified as a Cast Member. Additionally, you can easily give Cast Members names in order to better identify them. Naming your Cast Members is recommended since it gets difficult to keep them straight as your project becomes more intricate.

The Cast window can be accessed from the Window menu. The Cast's width and height can be adjusted by dragging the bottom-right corner of the Cast window, making it flexible for those working with monitors of all sizes.

Each variety of Cast Member, such as text or video, appears in the thumbnail Cast with a small icon depicting its file type on the bottom-right corner of each thumbnail. In the list Cast, the icon is the first item you see on each line. A Cast Member with a Paint Brush icon is a graphic and can be edited in Director's Paint window. A Cast Member with an "A" icon is editable text and can be edited in Director's Text window.

A single Cast Member can be used many times in a movie. The actual Cast Member located in the Cast slot/list is the source for any of the multiple versions you create. If you alter the original in the Cast, it alters all the versions that you have created throughout your movie.

The image below shows the Cast in thumbnail form. To toggle between thumbnail and list form, click on the second button from the left.

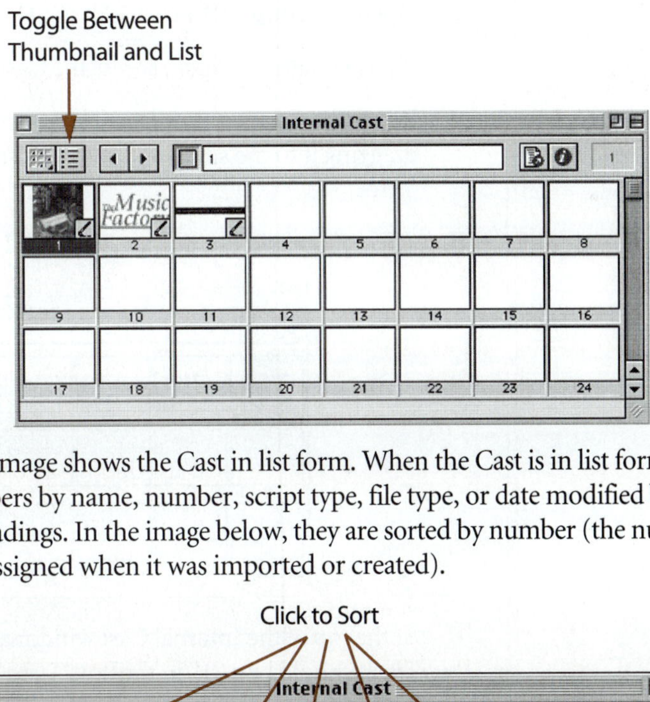


The following image shows the Cast in list form. When the Cast is in list form, you can sort the Cast Members by name, number, script type, file type, or date modified by clicking on the column headings. In the image below, they are sorted by number (the number the Cast Member was assigned when it was imported or created).

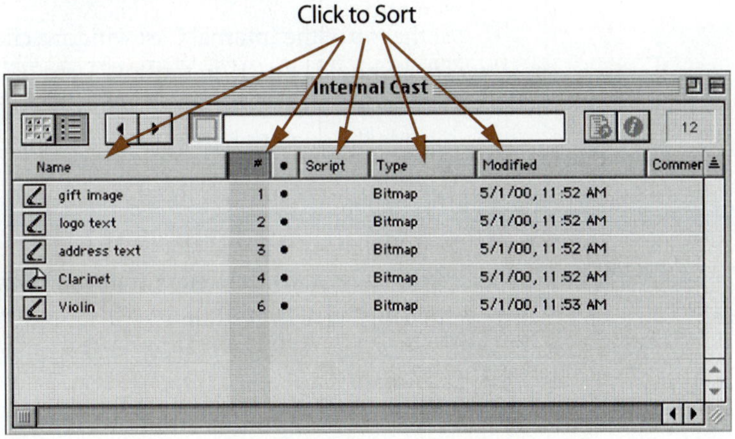

Either type of Cast can be sorted by highlighting all Cast Members, going to Modify>Sort, and then choosing the method by which you wish to sort your Cast.

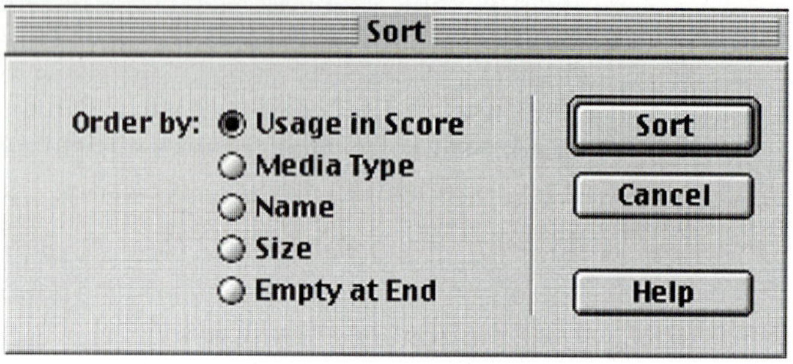


### *Manipulating the Cast*

If you wish to see the final version of this project, navigate to the **SF-Director>Finished Exercises** folder and open the **Finchap1.DIR file.** Otherwise, start with step 1.

1. Double-click on the Director icon to launch the application.
2. Open the **Chap1.DIR** movie in the **SF-Director** folder.
3. If it is not already open, access the Cast by selecting it from the Window menu.
4. Resize the Cast window by clicking on the lower-right corner of the palette and dragging it to the size you desire. For this exercise, make sure the Cast is in thumbnail form.
5. Click on the picture of Cast Member 1 to highlight it.

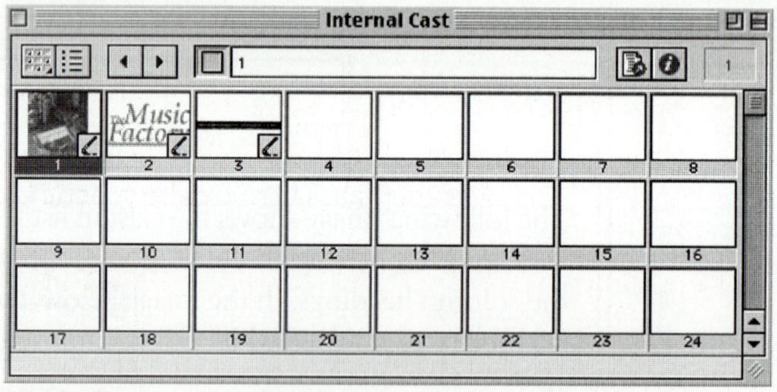


6. At the top of the Internal Cast window, click inside the Text box in the top center. There should be a "1" in the box. Type "Gift Image" and press the Return/Enter key on your keyboard. The Cast Member's name is now Gift Image. Be certain not to include the quotation marks when naming your Cast Members.
7. Rename Cast Member 2 "Logo Text", and Cast Member 3 "Address Text".
8. Select File>Save As and change the name of the document to "Practice.DIR". Be certain to save your document in your **Work in Progress** folder. Keep this movie open for the next exercise.

## The Cast Palette Buttons

You can navigate forward or backward through your Internal Cast window by using the arrow buttons at the top left of the window. The circle with the "i" is the Cast Member Properties button, or the shortcut to the Property Inspector. When the button is clicked, information on the Cast Member currently selected is displayed. The button to the left of the Cast Member Properties button is the Cast Member Script button, which is discussed later in this book.

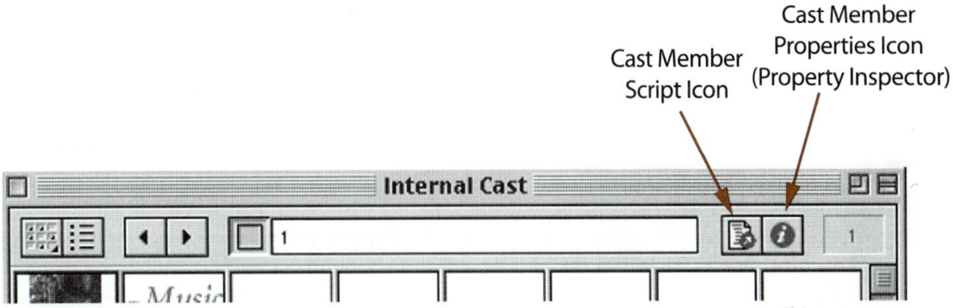

### *Checking out the Buttons*

1. Continuing with the **Practice.DIR** file you created in the last exercise, click on the "Gift Image" Cast Member to select it.

2. Click twice on the Right Arrow button (next Cast Member) at the top of the Cast window and then click twice on the Left Arrow button (previous Cast Member) to get back to the first Cast Member (Gift Image). Using the arrow buttons is one way to navigate through the Cast.

3. Click on the Cast Member Properties button at the top of the Cast window. "Gift Image" is a bitmap graphic, thus the Property Inspector displays the Bitmap properties of the Cast Member, as shown in the following image. The Property Inspector displays the properties of whichever type of Cast Member you have highlighted.

   Every Cast Member has Member properties, which can be adjusted by clicking on the Member tab. There are also generic Cast properties listed under the Cast tab.

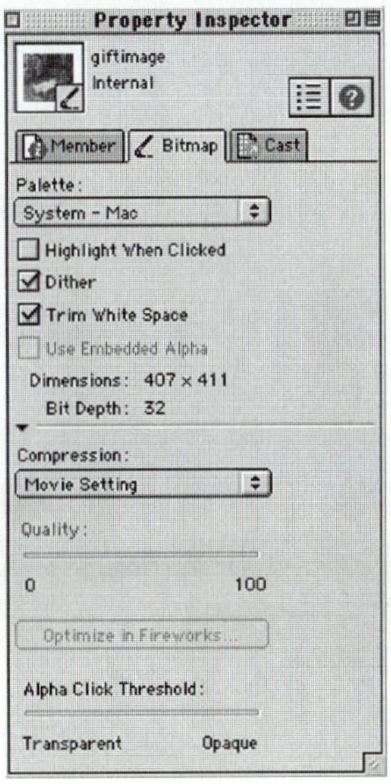

4. To edit a Lingo script, click on the Cast Member Script button at the top of the Internal Cast window. Each Cast Member can be scripted to perform various actions. We'll learn more about writing scripts in Chapter 5.

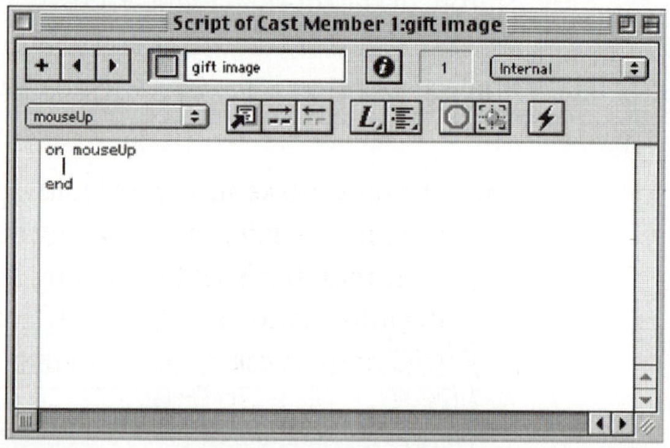


5. Click the little square on the top-left corner of the Title bar to close the dialog box (click on the "X" in the upper-right corner if you are using Microsoft Windows). Save your changes and keep this file open for the next exercise.

*The keyboard shortcut to import Cast Members is (Command/Control-R)*

## Imported Cast Members

You can import Cast Members created in a number of outside applications into your multimedia project. Although Director has Paint and Vector Graphics windows suitable for creating basic graphics, Adobe Photoshop is currently the raster-based graphics creation program of choice for most designers. There are currently three ways to import Cast members:

- The drag-and-drop method. You can click on a file, drag it from its current location on your hard drive, and drop it in the next open thumbnail slot or at the bottom of the list in your Cast.
- The File>Import method. You can select File>Import to display the Import Files window, as shown below. Here, you select the files you desire, click Add, and then Import.
- The Lingo method. You can write custom scripts to import new Cast Members.

*The Import dialog box for the Windows version looks a little different. It doesn't have the Options button; however, it does have Move Up and Move Down buttons, which are a nice addition.*

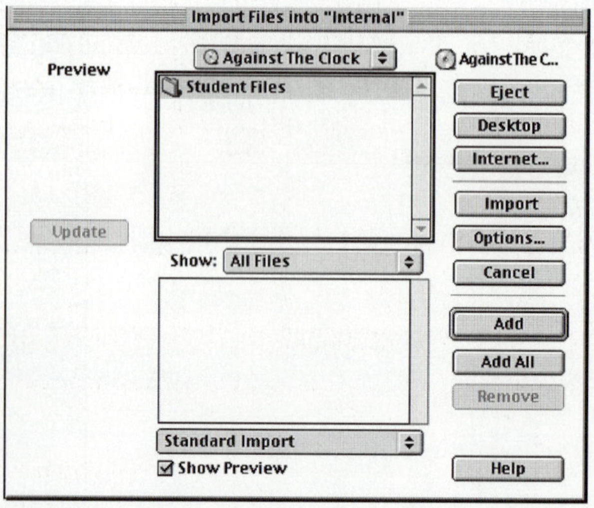


For now, we will be using the File>Import method.

*Director supports most common file formats currently used to save animations, images, sounds, videos, color palettes, and Web image and text files. For a current list of accepted file types, look at the last page of this Chapter.*

*Director automatically links files that are too large to be embedded, so that your movie does not become unmanageable. It typically links all video files and some larger sound files. Be sure to keep an eye on your Cast so that you know which files are linked — it is easy to throw them away by accident.*

### *Importing Cast Members*

1. With the **Practice.DIR** file open, click on Cast slot 6 (your Cast should be in thumbnail form for this exercise). Select File>Import to display the Import Files window.
2. Navigate to and select the **Violin.PCT** file from the **SF-Director** folder. Click the Add button to move the file into the bottom box.
3. For now, make sure the Media Option box at the bottom displays Standard Import, not Link to External File or any other option. Click the Import button. You may, if your monitor is set to anything less than millions of colors, see a dialog box requesting information about color bit depth. You can use either 32 or 16 bit; however, 16 bit will, in most cases, produce smaller files without a noticeable loss of image quality.
4. The new file is now Cast Member 6. If you had not highlighted a specific empty slot in the Cast before importing the new file, the file would have been placed into the next available slot, rather than this specific slot. Director has automatically given the Cast Member a name. If you had been using the Cast in list form, you would not have been able to specify where the new file would go before you imported it. You would have to rearrange your Cast Members afterward.
5. Save your changes and keep this movie open for the next exercise.

## Linked vs. Embedded Cast Members

You have just now successfully imported and embedded a Cast Member. Embedded means that you actually pasted an exact copy of your file into Director permanently. You don't need your original file any longer.

You can also create a Linked Cast Member. The original file of a linked Cast Member resides outside your Director project and is merely linked to the project. You need to keep all linked files forever, and they must be stored in the same folder as your movie or else your movie will not work. In the image below, notice the Paintbrush icon on Clarinet.PCT has a dog-eared top-right corner, indicating that the file is linked, rather than embedded.

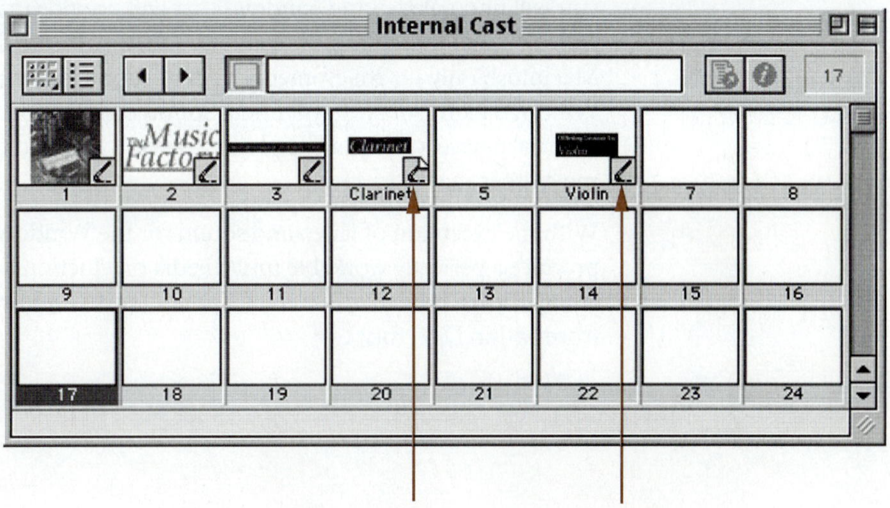


Linked Paint Graphic (dog-earred page)

Embedded Paint Graphic

You can manually link files rather than embed them. Expert developers pick and choose what they want embedded and what they want linked. However, for our purposes, you can embed everything except digital video files, which Director will link automatically.

If you do want to experiment with linking various files, change the Media Option box in the Import Files window from Standard Import to Link to External File before importing. Just make sure to set the option back when you are done so that some other Director user doesn't end up linking all of his/her imported files by accident.

### *Linking a File Manually*

1. With the **Practice.DIR** file still open, highlight the "Violin" Cast Member if it is not already highlighted.
2. You will now select File>Import and import the **Clarinet.PCT** file as a linked file. To do this, change the Standard Import option to Link to External File in the Import dialog box. Click Add and then click Import. Director automatically places the file in Cast Member slot 7.
3. Notice that you have linked a small graphic icon that normally would not have been linked. Also note that it was put into slot 7 of your Cast. This is because the violin graphic in Cast slot 6 was the last item you had highlighted in your Cast, and the next open Cast slot is 7.
4. Highlight Cast slot 4 and then import the following images (be sure to reset the import option to Standard Import): **Fiddle.PCT**, **Flute.PCT**, **Guitar.PCT**, and **Oboe.PCT**. These images are located in your **SF-Director** folder and may be placed anywhere in the Cast. If you highlighted Cast slot 4 correctly before importing, they should have filled up slots 4, 5, 8 & 9.
5. Save your changes and keep this movie open for the next exercise.

## Creating Cast Members in Director

You can create a variety of Cast Members from within Director. Under the Window menu, you will find palettes and windows that will provide the tools necessary to create paint graphics, vector graphics, and text. By selecting Insert>Media Elements>Sound (on Macintosh only— Macromedia doesn't support capturing sound internally for the Windows platform) you will find a Sound palette capable of recording sound from an external device, such as a CD player. Capturing sound this way requires less memory than most other methods.

With the exception of video and sound for the Windows 98 and NT platforms, you can produce a perfectly workable multimedia production from within Director. In Chapter 2, you will learn how to utilize the Paint and Text windows to begin creating Cast Members from within Director.

## The Score

It may be helpful to think of the Score in musical terms. Your Cast holds all of your notes, i.e., Cast Members. The Score is where you put the notes together to form music. Until you compose your multimedia production, it is nothing more than a group of Cast Members waiting to be used, like notes waiting to be turned into music.

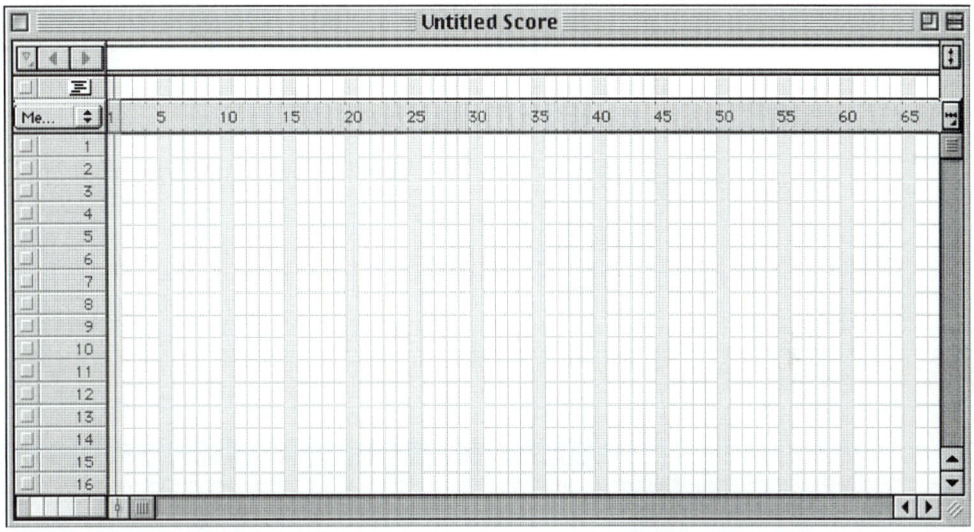

### *Opening the Score*

1. Continuing with the **Practice.Dir** file, select the Score window from the Window menu. If necessary, reposition the Cast and Score windows until they both fit on your screen.
2. Resize the Score window by dragging its bottom-right corner until you are comfortable with your working environment. It is advisable to keep your Score window relatively small and use the scroll bars along the bottom and right sides to navigate.
3. Go to File>Save to save your changes. Keep the file open for the next exercise.

### Frames

You will notice several numbers across the top of the Score. These are Frames. Each column of cells is a frame. A movie starts at frame 1 and continues across the frames until it is finished. It could be 50 or 5,000 frames long, depending on the content.

You can add frames any time you wish by going to Insert>Frames and indicating how many you need. Be careful, though, because Director inserts the new frames right after the one you are currently on. If you are on frame 1 and ask for 10 new frames, they will be inserted between frames 1 and 2. If you are on frame 30, the new frames will be inserted between frames 30 and 31.

Rest assured, you can remove frames, but only one frame at a time. To do so, go to Insert>Remove Frame. Whatever frame you are currently on will be deleted.

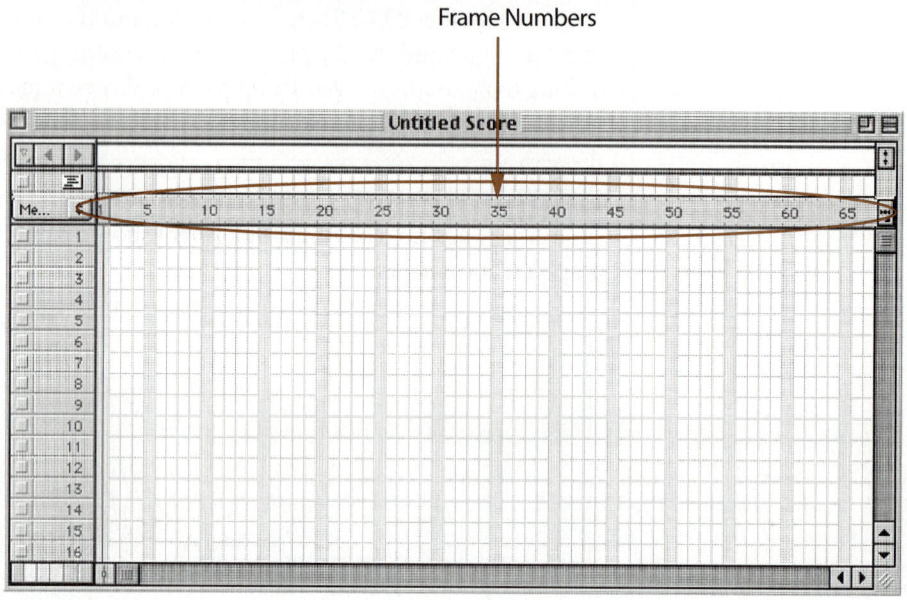

### *Placing a Cast Member in the Score*

1. Continuing with the **Practice.Dir** file, drag the "Gift Image" Cast Member to the Stage. This graphic will be the background for our movie. Notice the new object that is now displayed in the Score (if it doesn't start at frame 1, drag it back to frame 1). Once a Cast Member is placed in the Score, it is called a Sprite. We'll discuss more about Sprites in Chapter 3. On the Stage, drag the image to the top-right corner so that the top and right edges of the image are touching the top and right edges of the Stage.

*Sprites in Director typically default to a length of 28 frames. This is an arbitrary number which can be easily changed to suit your own personal work habits. This can be changed by going to File>Preferences>Sprite, which will be reiterated in a later chapter.*

2. The movie will be 50 frames long, so take the right side of the Sprite in the Score and drag (or Option/Alt-drag if the Sprite only covers one frame) the Sprite out to frame 50. The Sprite should now span frames 1-50.

   You can make a Sprite occupy any number of Frames by dragging it from either end.

3. Save your changes and keep the document open for the next exercise.

### Channels

Channels, the rows of the Score, hold Cast Members. The numbered rows are called Visual Channels. They hold anything that might show up on the Stage, including video, text, graphics, and images.

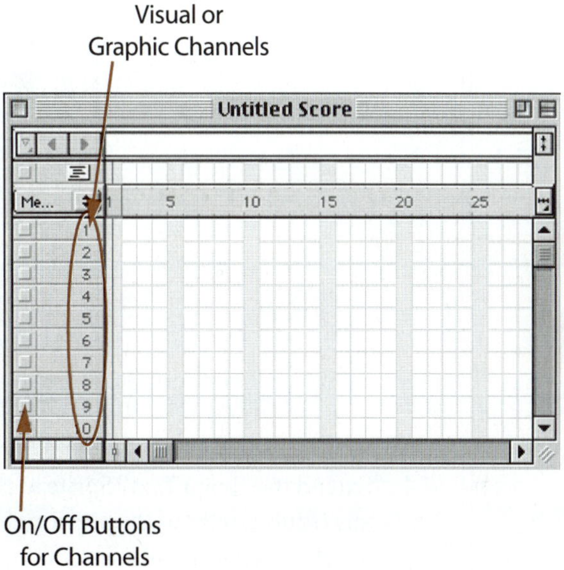


Upon opening a new movie, Director defaults to 150 available channels, but there are up to 1,000 channels available for any Director movie. To make more channels available, click on the Movie tab in the Property Inspector and adjust the box with "150"in it to whatever number you need. It is recommended by Macromedia that you keep the number of channels used to a minimum because of memory constraints.

You can also turn off any channel you don't wish to see by clicking on the little square to the left of each channel number. This is similar to turning on and off layers in Photoshop.

#### *Placing Cast Members in Different Channels*

1. Let's continue with the **Practice.DIR** file. Your first Sprite should be in channel 1 of the Score. If it is not, click on the middle of it and drag it up until it rests in channel 1.

2. Drag the "Logo Text" Cast Member down to frame 1, channel 2 (directly under the first Sprite). When you drag Cast Members straight to the Score, you will see that they are placed exactly in the center of the Stage. Place the logo text in the black area in the top-left corner of the Stage. Center it between the left edge of the Stage and the left edge of the gift image.

At this point you will see red text with a white background. You will get rid of the white background in the next step.

3. Highlight the "Logo Text" Sprite in the Score. While the Sprite is still highlighted, click on Copy in the Property Inspector and drag down to select Background Transparent. Your white background should now disappear.

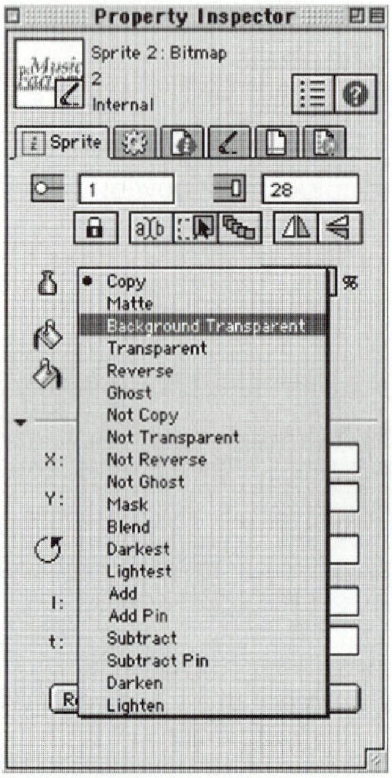


4. Extend the "Logo Text" Sprite so that it covers frames 1-50 in channel 2. (If you have any trouble, refer to the previous exercise). This ensures that the logo text stays on the Stage throughout the entire 50 frames of the movie.

5. Save your changes and keep this movie open for the next exercise.

## The Playback Head

As you look at the Score, you will notice a red rectangle with a vertical red line coming out from the top and bottom. This is called the Playback Head. Notice the red rectangle is on top of a particular frame. The frame it is on is what is currently displayed on the Stage. Anything under that red line, from the top of the Score to the bottom, will be visible.

You can drag the Playback Head right and left to see the progression of your movie, or you can drag it to a particular frame.

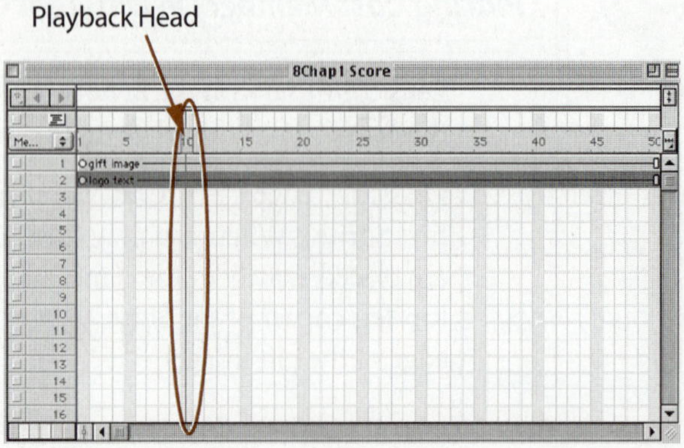

## *Adding Sprites to the Score*

1. Continuing with the **Practice.Dir** file, drag the Playback Head to frame 1 if it is not already there.
2. Drag "Address Text" from the Cast to the Stage (not the Score). Center it in the black area across the bottom of the Stage. Notice that when you drag something directly to the Stage, you can place it anywhere; it is not automatically centered.
3. Your new Sprite should have ended up in frame 1, channel 3 of your Score. If it did not, fix it now by dragging it to the correct location. Extend this Sprite to cover frames 1- 50.
4. Drag your Playback Head to frame 4 or click on Frame 4 and your Playback Head jumps to this location. This is where you want your next Sprite to start when you drag it to the Stage.
5. Drag "Violin" to the Stage and place it under the line in the Music Factory logo. Make certain it is in channel 4 in the Score and extends from frame 4-50.
6. Drag your Playback Head to frame 10 and then drag a copy of "Fiddle" to the Stage and place it, left-aligned, under the word "violin". Make certain it is in channel 5 and extends from frame 10-50.
7. Drag your Playback Head to frame 16 or click on frame 16. This is where you want your next Sprite to start when you drag it to the Stage.
8. Drag a copy of "Guitar" to the Stage and place it, left-aligned, under the word "fiddle". Make certain it is in channel 6 and extends from frame 16-50.

9. Drag your Playback Head to frame 22 or click on frame 22. This is where you want your next Sprite to start.

10. Drag a copy of "Flute" to the Stage and place it, left-aligned, under the word "guitar". Make certain it is in channel 7 and extends from frame 22-50.

11. Drag your Playback Head to frame 28 or click on frame 28.

12. Drag a copy of "Oboe" to the Stage and place it, left-aligned, under the word "flute". Make certain it is in channel 8 and extends from frame 28-50.

13. Drag your Playback Head to frame 34 or click on frame 34.

14. Drag a copy of "Clarinet" to the Stage and place it, left-aligned, under the word "oboe". Make certain it is in channel 9 and extends from frame 34-50.

Feel free to go back to any of the Sprites if necessary and readjust the spacing between them to make them all fit. Be careful to highlight the whole Sprite in the Score before moving the Sprite on the Stage because if you do not, it will create unwanted motion/animation. Until you learn how to deal with animated Sprites in Chapter 3, should this happen, it is best to delete the Sprite and do that step over.

15. Save your changes and keep this file open for the next exercise.

## Special Channels

There are various special channels that contain objects that are not graphic in nature. These might include sound files, color palettes, Frame Scripts, Transitions, and the Tempo Channel. These channels are not numbered; rather, they are denoted by icons. You will learn about these special channels one at a time as we use them in upcoming chapters. To view these channels if they are hidden, click on the button with the double arrow located on the right edge of the Score just above the frames.

*Remember where the Special Channels Hide/Show button is located on the Score. Many newcomers repeatedly forget where this button is located.*

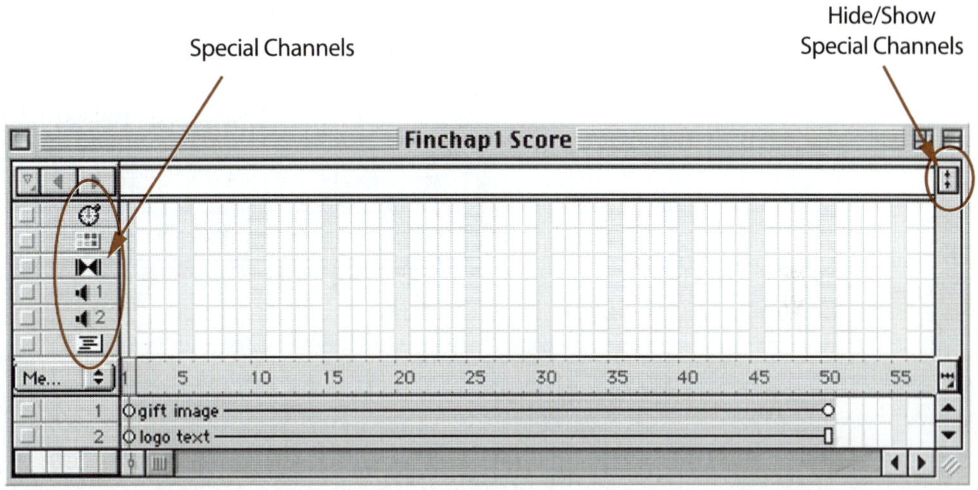


# The Control Panel

The Control Panel is a small window that holds the buttons for controlling your movie, such as Play, Stop, and Rewind. The Control Panel looks similar to the front of a VCR. Access the Control Panel from the Window menu.

On the top right of the Control Panel is the Loop button, which causes your movie to replay continuously until you click Stop. The two buttons on the top left are the Step-Forward and Step-Backward buttons. They step you through the movie frame by frame.

The box in the center displays the frame number you are on. You can navigate to other frames in your movie by typing the frame number that you want to go to and pressing the Enter key.

The button on the bottom left controls the sound level. If you drag down, you can adjust the volume of your movie. You can also mute the sound.

Under the Loop button is the Play Selected Frames Only button. This one is self-explanatory. You can highlight several frames in your movie, click this button, and then click Play. Director will play only the frames you have highlighted.

The number in the box on the right (as seen in the image that follows) determines the Preferred Frame Rate of your movie. This is the speed at which you want your movie to run. It is typically set to 15 frames per second. The number directly below displays the Actual Frame Rate of your movie. As you play your movie, watch this box. This indicates the speed at which the movie is actually running.

Under the Frames Per Second drop-down menu, on the bottom half of the Control Panel, you will find options for Running Total and Estimated Total. If you choose either of these and play your movie, the Control Panel will display the length of your presentation (in the Actual Frame Rate area) in seconds.

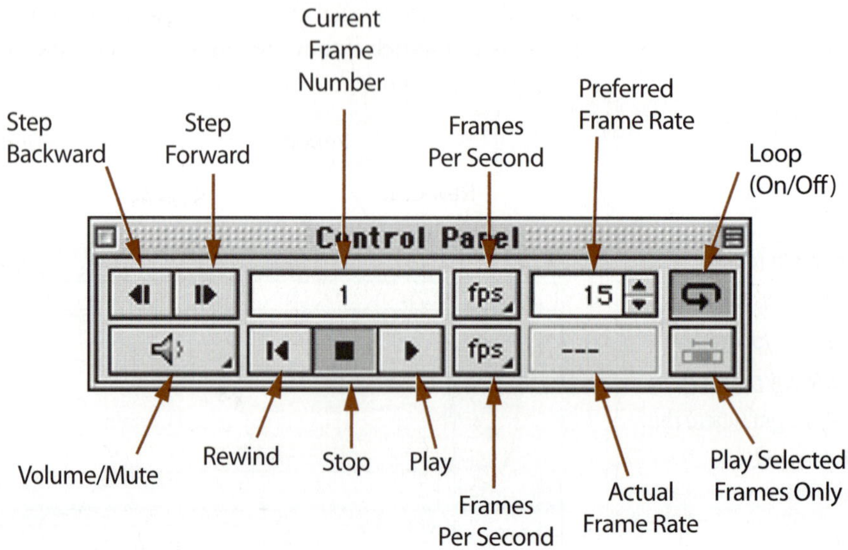

## *Using the Control Panel*

1. With the **Practice.DIR** file open, select Window>Control Panel to access the Control Panel if it is not already open.
2. Rewind the movie by clicking the Rewind button.
3. Click the Play button to play the movie.
4. Click the Stop button to stop the movie.
5. The movie is short, so let's loop it and try again. Just click the Loop button.

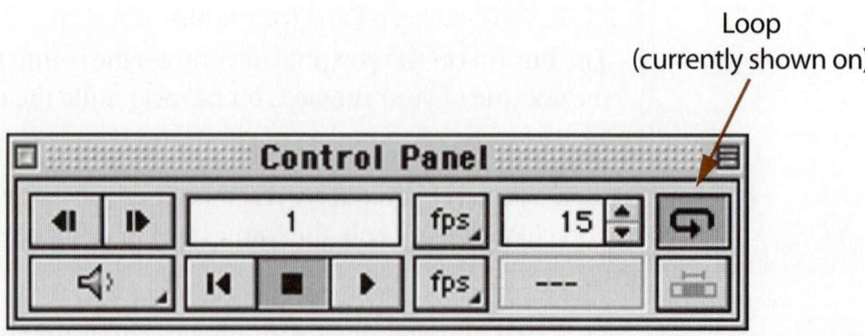

*Director must always have a file open for the application to continue running.*

6. Watch the frame rate — do the numbers match? Is the actual speed matching the preferred speed?
7. Select File>New>Movie to close the current movie.

## The Toolbar

The Toolbar, which may be accessed from the Window menu, is a panel of shortcut controls. If you can spare the screen space, the Toolbar can help make working easier and more efficient. For example, you can click on the Paintbrush button and go right to the Paint window, or click on the "A" and it will open the Text window. If you let your cursor linger on a button for a moment, the name of the tool will pop up for you to see. You can turn the Toolbar on or off from the Window menu.

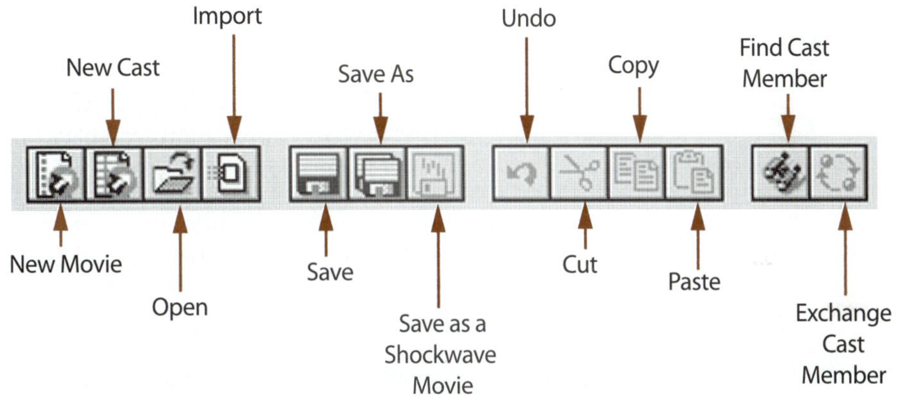


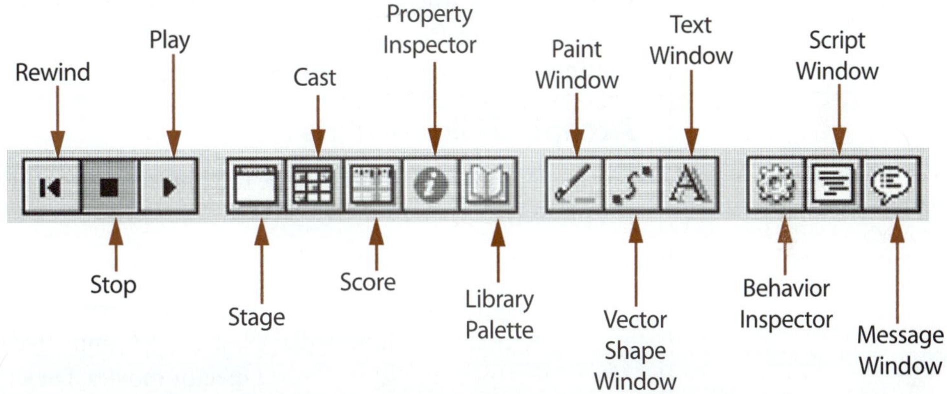


## Maximizing Performance of Your Director Project

It is not easy to keep Director running smoothly. To help your future projects as much as possible, follow the tips given below. Please try to remember to implement them whenever possible, as it will only make your Director experience better.

### File Sizes

Keep image-file sizes, actually all file sizes, to a minimum. When creating images with any program, remember that vector-based image or graphic files are smaller than comparable raster-based image or graphic files. Most illustration programs are vector-based. Photoshop is raster-based. Director itself has palettes for creating either type of image or graphic file.

Compressing any video or sound will help tremendously. Director now offers JPEG compression for individual Cast Members and/or the whole movie if/when you are ready to publish to the Web. There will be more on this in the Preparation and Delivery Chapter at the end of this book.

### Working from the Hard Drive

Work from your hard drive, not a CD-ROM or removable medium. This does two things:

- First, it reduces the risk of file corruption, which occurs quite easily with most removable media.
- Second, the transfer rate is not nearly as fast from removable media as it is from your hard drive, so your movie will play much faster and better if you run it from your hard drive.

### Memory Issues

If possible, quit all other applications while you are working in Director. Director likes to use a lot of RAM, so the fewer applications you have open, the better.

If you are a Macintosh user and are getting messages stating that Director does not have enough memory to run, increase your memory in Director's Get Info box. To do this, quit the application, highlight the Director icon, and then select File>Get Info. Make certain Show is set to Memory and then modify the Minimum and Preferred Size options to maximize the application's performance.

Windows users shouldn't have to worry about increasing memory since it tends to use virtual memory when necessary to ease the burden. If you get any virtual memory errors while using Director on Windows, it probably means that your hard drive is too full to continue. Try removing some files.

## Accepted File Formats

The highlighted formats tend to be used most often in real-world projects, usually without any problems.

| Type of File | Supported Formats |
| --- | --- |
| Animation/ Multimedia | Flash movies, animated GIF, PowerPoint presentations, Director movies, Director external cast files |
| Image | BMP, GIF, JPEG, LRG (xRes), Photoshop 3.0 or later, MacPaint, PNG, TIFF, PICT, Targa |
| Multiple-image file | Windows only: FLC, FLI |
| | Macintosh only: PICS, Scrapbook |
| Sound | AIFF, WAV, MP3 audio, Shockwave Audio, Sun AU, uncompressed and IMA compressed |
| Video | Quicktime 2, 3, and 4; AVI |
| Text | RTF, HTML, ASCII (text only), Lingo scripts |
| Palette | PAL, Photoshop CLUT |

***Complete Project A: Magic Carpet Tours***

# CHAPTER 2

# WORKING WITH TEXT AND GRAPHICS

## CHAPTER OBJECTIVE:

To create a new movie, adjust the Stage to your liking, and create your own Cast Members using the Paint and Text windows. In Chapter 2, you will:

- Practice setting up a new movie.
- Adjust the Stage color and size.
- Learn about the Paint window.
- Use the filled and outline shape tools.
- Learn what a gradient is and how to apply one.
- Practice using the Air Brush, Paint Brush, and line tools.
- Create bitmap text in the Paint window.
- Learn how to use the Text window to create editable text.
- Learn about and how to use the Text Inspector.

## PROJECTS TO BE COMPLETED:

- Magic Carpet Tours (Project A)
- Redi-Base (Project B)
- Digital Portfolio (Project C)
- Emily's Photo Album (Project D)
- ABC's (Project E)

# Working with Text and Graphics

Two of the most commonly used windows in Director are the Paint and Text windows. These two windows are a good place to begin creating Cast Members for Director projects. As you become experienced in Director, you will likely create your graphics, complex text treatments, and illustrations in other graphics applications, such as Adobe Illustrator, Macromedia FreeHand, and Adobe Photoshop.

## The Paint Window

The Paint window is a bitmap-based image-creation window that is used for the following tasks:

- Creating bitmap graphics or text.
- Making adjustments to imported bitmap graphics.
- Rotating, skewing, and distorting any bitmap graphics currently in your Cast.

For those of you who have used Adobe Photoshop or an illustration program such as Illustrator or FreeHand, most of the tools in the Paint window will look familiar.

The top row of items in the Paint window is identical to the top row of items in the Cast. It contains a Text box for naming your graphic, the Forward, Backward, and Next buttons, and the Cast Member Script and Cast Member Properties icons.

In this chapter you will experiment with all the tools displayed on the left side of the window except the Registration tool. You will work with the other tools, including the Registration tool, later in this book.

## Filled Shape Tools

There are three filled shape tools — the Filled Rectangle, the Filled Ellipse, and the Filled Polygon. When creating these shapes, use the color in the foreground. You may choose a new color for your tool at any time.

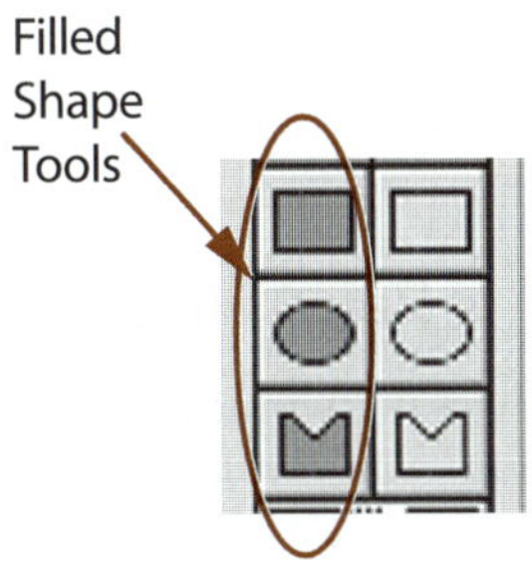

### *Working with Filled Shapes*

*The steps listed in the exercise on this page are the first steps to be taken when creating any Director movie. Your Stage size, however, will typically be 640 x 480 pixels or smaller, not necessarily the size listed here.*

1. If it is not already open, launch Director 8.0.
2. Director creates an untitled movie upon opening. If you currently have another Director movie open, select File>New>Movie.
3. Pick a Stage color from the Property Inspector and change your Stage size to 512 x 342 pixels (for this exercise only).
4. If they are not already open, access the Stage and Cast windows. Close all other windows for now.
5. Select File>Save As and name your movie "Graphics.DIR". Save this file in your **Work in Progress** folder.
6. Open the Paint window from the Window menu.
7. Click on the Foreground Color box and select a color.

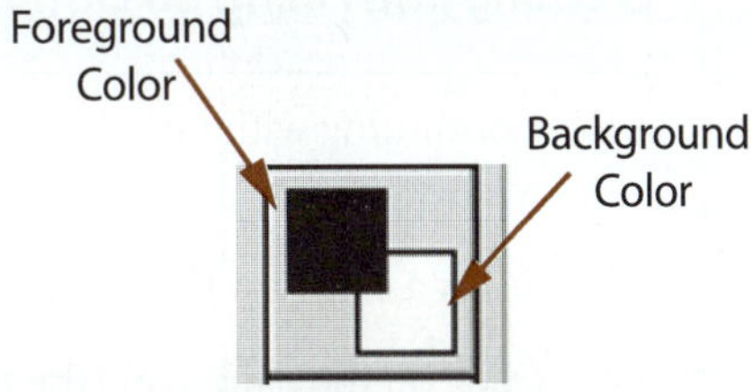


8. Click on the Filled Rectangle tool and draw a rectangle on the canvas in the Paint window. You must make certain that the Ink Effects drop-down menu, at the bottom of the Paint window, says "Normal" (see image below). The rectangle automatically fills with the color identified in the Foreground Color box.

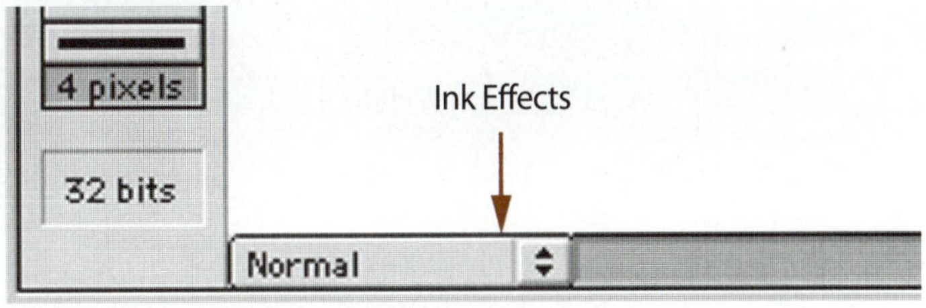

9. Click inside the Text box at the top of the Paint window and type in a descriptive name for this Cast Member. Press Return/Enter on your keyboard and the rectangle becomes your first Cast Member.

10. Click on the "+" sign at the top of the Paint window to display a new blank canvas. Notice that in the Cast, Cast Member 2 is now highlighted.

11. Save your changes and keep this document open for the next exercise.

*If you want to make a perfect square or circle, hold down the Shift key, then draw using your Rectangle or Ellipse tool.*

## Outlined Shape Tools

The same three tools are available for the outlined shapes — the Rectangle, the Ellipse, and the Polygon. When using the outlined shape tools, remember that the outline color is the color of the foreground.

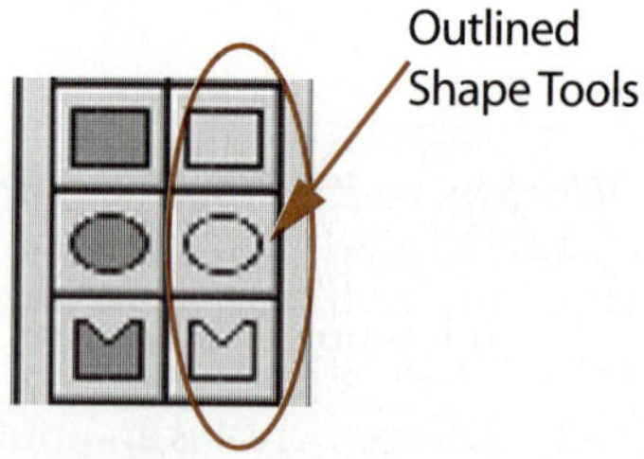


The thickness or weight of the outline may be changed by selecting a different line width from the area under the Color box. You can make the line any width you want by double-clicking on the last line-width option. A box appears that allows you to customize the width.

If you don't want any line, for example if you are using a filled shape tool to create a gradient, select the top line width — it will set it to "no line".

### *Creating and Filling an Outlined Shape*

1. Continuing with Graphics.DIR, click the outlined Ellipse Shape tool in the Paint window and draw a circle while holding down the Shift key.

2. Select a color for the inside of the circle from the Foreground Color box.

3. Click on the paint can (the Fill tool), then click inside the circle and it will fill the area with the Foreground color you have selected.

4. Name the object and then click the "+" in the upper-left corner of the Paint palette for the next piece of empty canvas in your Cast. Keep the document open for the next exercise.

## Gradients

A gradient blends the color within your object from 100% of one color to another, or from black to white. To create a gradient, you must first select two colors. These choices, however, are not selected from the Foreground and Background Color boxes but from two smaller boxes located side by side directly above them. The one on the left is the starting color; the one on the right is the ending color. When you click on either box, color choices appear.

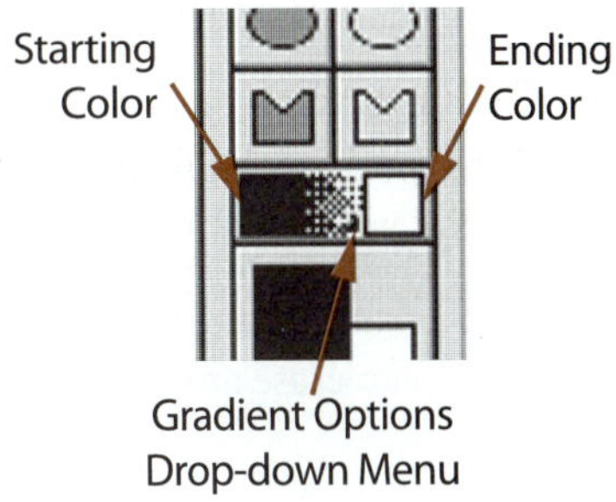


If you click between the two gradient color boxes, various gradient options — such as sunburst, top to bottom, left to right, and more — will become available. The Gradient Settings option will display a dialog box where you can manipulate various properties relevant to your gradient. Once you make a selection, you can select any filled shape tool.

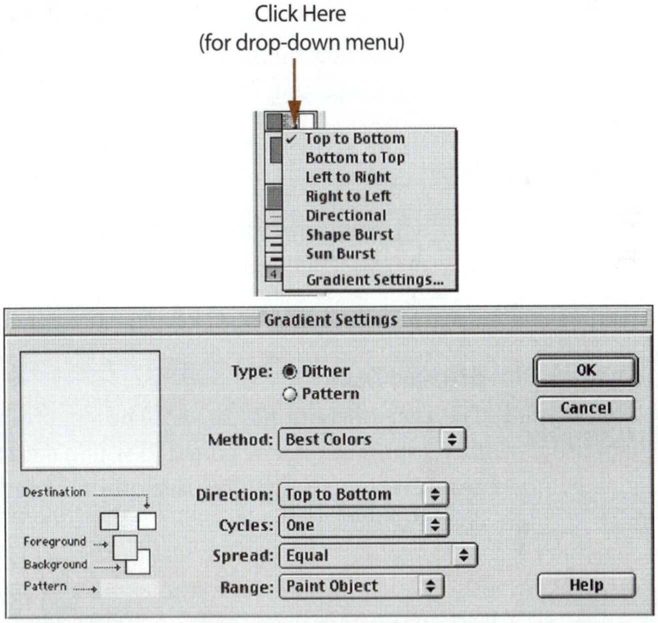


Before drawing your shape, you will need to change from the Normal option to the Gradient option in the Ink Effect menu located along the bottom of the Paint window. As the shape is drawn, it automatically takes on the gradient you selected. Each tool can have a different ink effect, so you must be sure which ink effect you want to use before you use each tool because they do not carry over to the next tool.

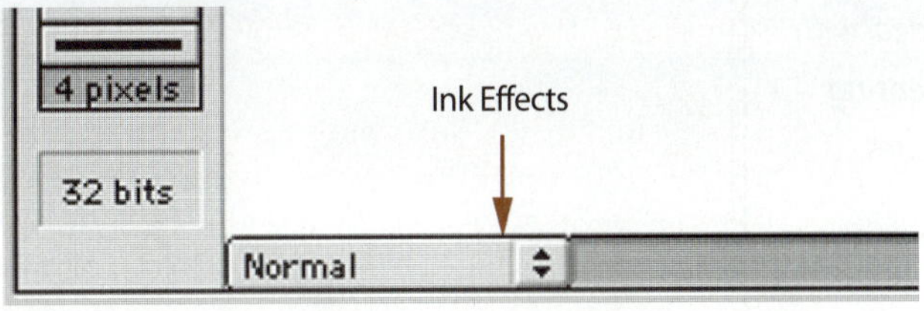

### *Creating a Gradient-filled Polygon*

1. With Graphics.DIR open, select two gradient colors in the Paint window. Remember, the box on the left will be the starting color and the box on the right the ending color.
2. Pick the style of gradient you desire from the drop-down menu between the gradient starting- and ending-color boxes.
3. Click on the Polygon Filled Shape tool. Practice making a few solid-color filled shapes before turning on the gradient setting.
4. When you are ready to continue, double-click on the Eraser tool to erase the entire paint area. Clicking once on the Eraser tool allows you to select the eraser so that you can erase any items you choose.

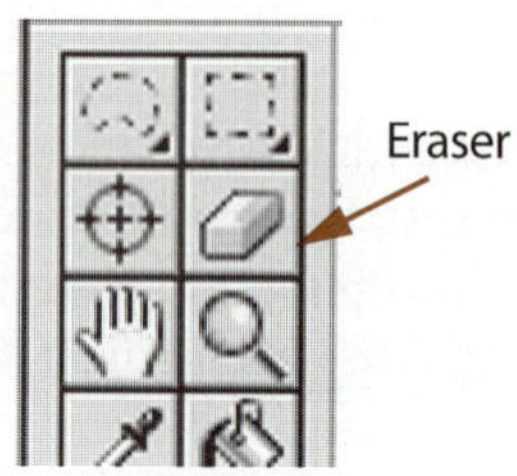

*Double-clicking will automatically close any shape you are creating with the polygon tool. Be careful because it will choose the shortest distance between the two points to close the polygon - make sure that the two points are close enough together as to not create an unwanted straight edge.*

5. Click back on the Polygon Filled Shape tool. Change the Ink Effect drop-down menu, on the bottom-left side of the Paint window, from Normal to Gradient.
6. Draw your shape. It automatically takes on the gradient colors and style you have selected.
7. Give the object a descriptive name and then click the "+" in the Paint window for the next available piece of canvas in your Cast.
8. Save your work and keep the file open.

### Bitmap Text

The Text tool button is an "A". The text produced with this tool is strictly bitmap text; therefore, it can not be edited. If you make a mistake, you must erase the text and start again. This tool should be used only for headlines or other text that will not need to be changed regularly.

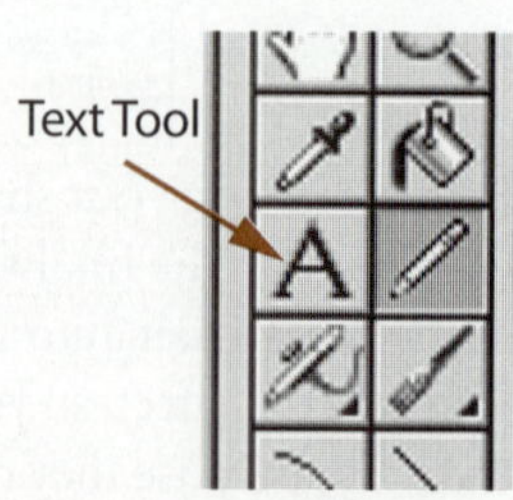

*Using bitmap text is a simple way to create type if you don't want to deal with the purchasing, licensing, and distributing issues.*

### *Creating Bitmap Text*

1. Double-click the Text tool in the Paint window. The Font dialog box should pop up.

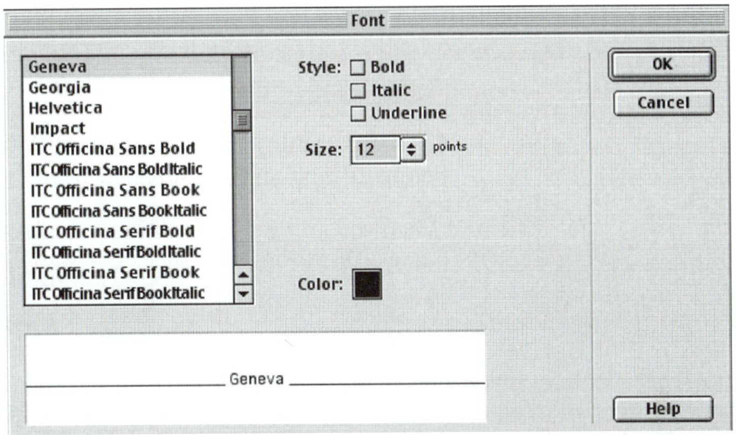


2. Select a Font, Style, Color, and Size (a minimum of 9 pt.) and then click OK.

3. Click on the white area of the Paint window and type your first name.

4. Give the object a descriptive name in the Text box at the top of the Paint window and then click the "+" button for the next empty Cast slot. Save the file and keep it open.

## The Air Brush

The Air Brush tool in Director is similar to the one in Adobe Photoshop with the exception of the anti-aliasing feature within Photoshop's airbrush. It works based on pressure. If you click in the Paint window canvas and hold down the mouse button, the tool will spray more and more paint until you let go.

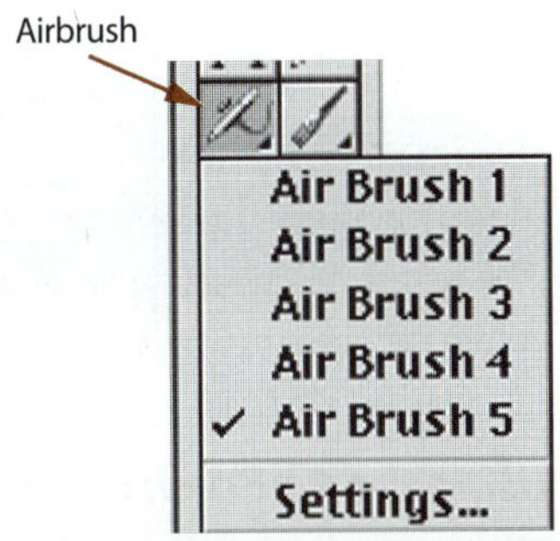


If you click on the Air Brush button and drag down, you will see six additional options: Air Brushes 1 through 5, as well as a Settings option. Air Brushes 1 through 5 have preset brush sizes and pressure settings. You can either use these or edit them to suit your taste. To edit a brush, simply choose one and select the Settings option. This displays a dialog box where you can change the Flow Rate, Spray Area, Dot Size, and more.

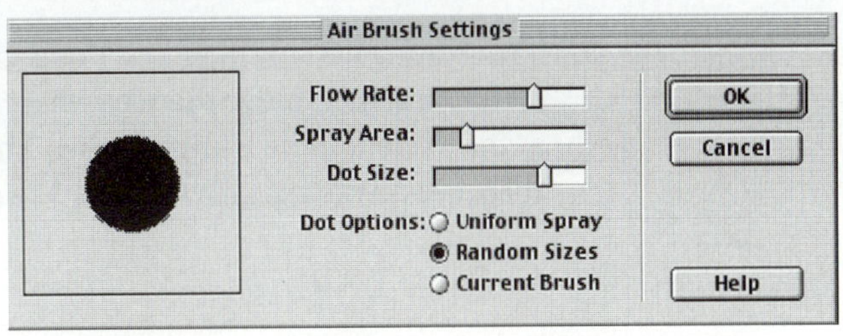

## The Paint Brush

The Paint Brush also is similar to the one in Adobe Photoshop. It, however, paints in strokes of 100% color, and the opacity cannot be altered. If you want a lighter shade of the current color, you must select a lighter color in your Foreground Color box.

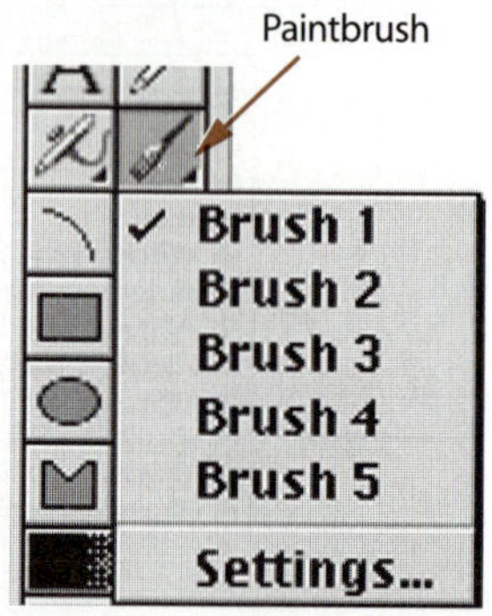


If you click on the Paint Brush button and drag down, you will see six additional options: Paint Brushes 1 through 5 and a Settings option. Paint Brushes 1 through 5 are preset brush sizes. You can use these or edit them to suit your taste.

To edit a brush, choose one and then select the Settings option. This displays the Brush Settings dialog box, where you can choose from a standard set of brushes. If you want to create a custom brush, you must change the option from Standard to Custom and make your selection. Your selection is displayed in the large edit box to the right of the brushes. You can then click on the black pixels to make them disappear (turn white) or click on the white ones to turn them black, thus making them visible.

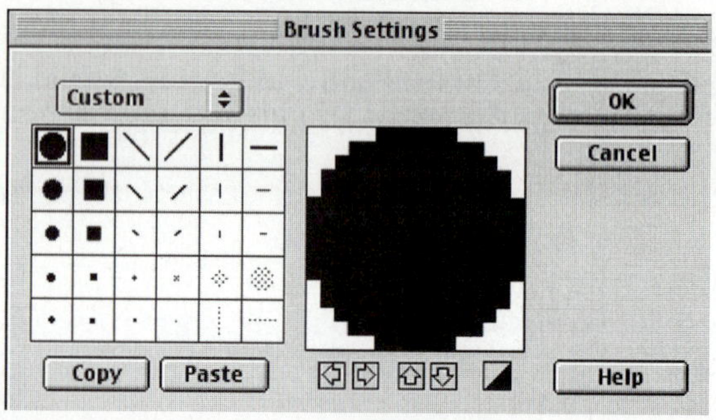

### *Using the Air Brush and Paint Brush Tools*

1. With Graphics.DIR open, experiment with a variety of the Air Brushes and Paint Brushes in the Paint window until you feel comfortable using and adjusting them.
2. Using a combination of the two, create a new Cast Member. Try to make it somewhat realistic, either an object or an animal.
3. Try creating designs in pieces. Put each piece in different areas of the Paint window canvas and then move them to where they belong by using the selection tools located at the top left of the Paint window. There is a Lasso tool on the left and a rectangular marquee on the right. To use the Marquee tool, select it and drag it from the top left

to the bottom right of your object. You will see a selection box around your object. Now drag your object to its destination. Try using the Lasso tool as well.

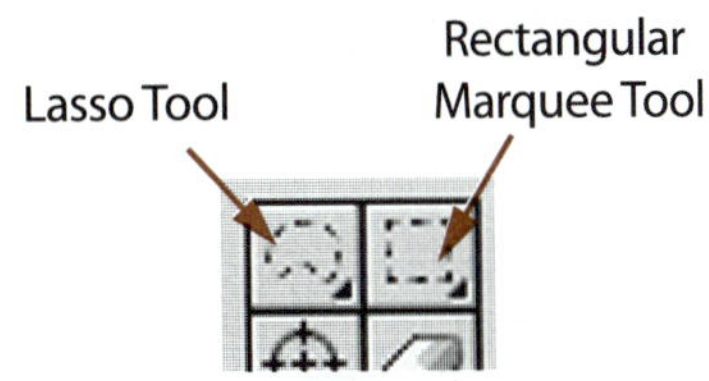


4. Experiment with the Zoom tool, which is the one with a magnifying glass icon. This tool is typically used when you need to examine or refine the details of a graphic. Select the tool and then click on your object. An inset showing your object at actual size will appear in the top-right corner of the Paint window. To Zoom out, hold the Shift key down and click on your object. To turn the magnification off, click on the inset in the upper-right corner of your canvas.

*Changing the ink effects on the bottom of the Paint window while using the Paint Brush and Air Brush tools can create interesting effects, such as cool transparencies and gradations.*

5. When finished, name your object with a descriptive name. Next, go to the next empty slot in your Cast by clicking on the "+" in your Paint window.

6. You are done with this Cast and movie; however, you may wish to keep the file open for experimentation. If not, Save and go to File>New>Movie to open a blank movie for the next exercise.

## Line Tools

In the Paint window, there are two useful line tools, the Arc tool and the (diagonal) Line tool.

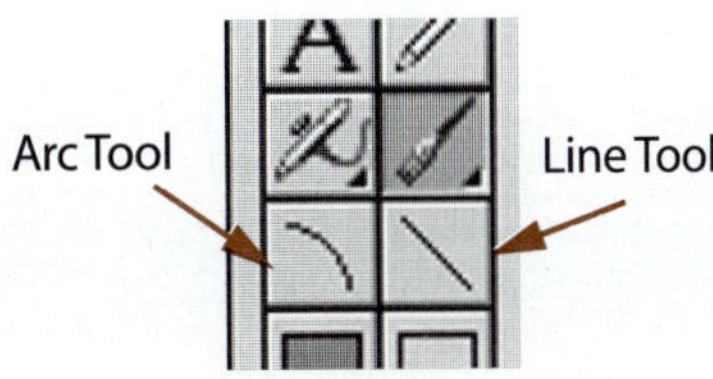


*The Arc tool can make perfect quarter-circles if you hold down the Shift key while drawing. The Line tool can make perfectly horizontal or vertical lines if you by hold down the Shift key while drawing.*

The line weight, or pixel width, can be altered. You can choose from the options under the color boxes in the Paint window. If you double-click on the bottom option, it displays the Paint Window Preferences dialog box, where you can change the width (64 pixel maximum). After you have chosen your line width, as well as your foreground color from the Foreground Color box, just click in the canvas area of the Paint window and start drawing.

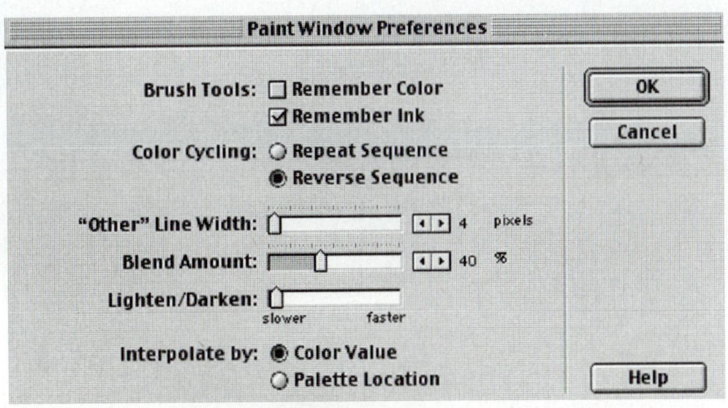

## The Text Window

You'll find that the Text window in Director is similar to most word processing programs. Here, you can create text that can be edited. If you create a text Cast Member and find a misspelled a word, you can easily correct it.

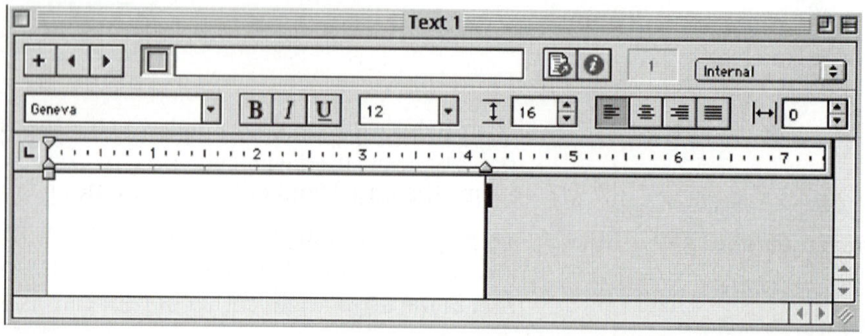


The top row of the Text window is similar to the top row of the Cast. It contains the Forward, Backward, and Next buttons, the Text box for naming Cast Members, and the Cast Member Script and Cast Member Properties buttons.

The second row contains the basic specification options necessary to create text. Here, you can select a typeface, point size, alignment, style, leading, and tracking. It also contains rulers to help determine the correct size of your text. By dragging the arrows on the ruler, you can adjust the width and indents of the text.

If you want your type to be a particular color, first open the Tool palette. The Tool palette and Text window can both be found under the Window menu. Next, pick a foreground color other than black from the Foreground Color box located at the bottom of the Tool palette. Type your text in the Text window and it becomes the new color. The Tool palette is shown below.

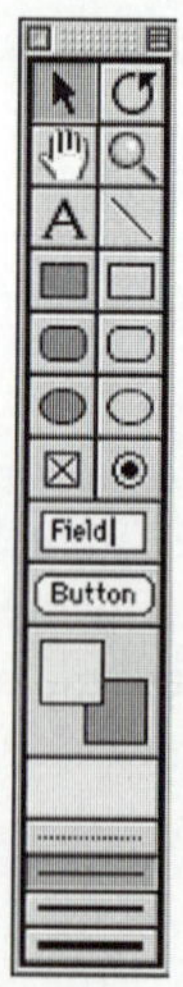

*Another way to include fonts without violating licensing agreements, according to Macromedia, is to use the Insert>Media Elements>Font option, which will embed the fonts of your choice into your Director project permanently so that they travel with your project and can be called upon at any time. This will allow you to use the editable text you create in the Text window.*

### *Creating and Editing a Text Cast Member*

1. If it is not already open, launch Director and select File>New>Movie.
2. Access the Text Editor from the Window menu.
3. Select your typeface, type size, and any other specifications that you want to use from the Text Editor.
5. Type a word that describes a color such as "Red" or "Black".
6. Name the Cast Member the same name and press Return/Enter.
7. Close the Text Editor.
8. If it is not already open, access the Cast window. Double-click on the text Cast Member you just created. It will reopen in the Text Editor.
9. Highlight the word. Select a new typeface and size. Then choose a new color from the tool palette that reflects the name of the color you typed.
10. Highlight the name of the Cast Member and change it to reflect the changes you have just made. Press Return/Enter to enter the new information. Close the Text Editor.
11. Notice that the old color of the text has been replaced by the new color text in your Cast.
12. Keep your movie open for the next exercise.

## The Text Inspector

The Text Inspector, a floating type-specification window, allows you to change all the type specifications except color directly on the Stage or in the Cast. It can be found under Window>Inspectors>Text. You cannot, however, edit the text itself using this palette. This can be done by double-clicking on the text Sprite on the Stage. A blinking cursor will show up in the text on the Stage, allowing you to edit.

To adjust the text specifications of a Cast Member while in the Cast, simply highlight the Cast Member and select your new specifications from the Text Inspector.

To adjust the text specifications using the Text Inspector while on the Stage, click on the Sprite to highlight it and then pick your new specifications from the Text Inspector. Although you are changing the Sprite on the Stage, the actual Cast Member itself is changing and all the other Sprites you've put into the Score from that Cast Member will be modified too. The only way to keep this from happening is to make a different Cast Member for each set of type specifications you may want or need.

*Working with white text can be difficult in Director, as you cannot see it while you are creating it! Generally, this is overcome by creating your type in any color other than white and placing it where you want it on the Stage. When it is exactly as you want it, go back and change its color to white.*

### *Using the Text Inspector*

1. Select Window>Inspectors>Text to display the Text Inspector.
2. Highlight the text.
3. Make some alterations to the specifications on the Text Inspector. Because the Cast slot windows are so small, changes made to Cast Members are often not visually obvious in the Cast. If you are not sure whether a Cast Member has changed, drag a copy to the Stage to view it more carefully.
4. Drag a copy of the Cast Member to the Stage if you didn't already do so in the last step.
5. Select the type on the Stage by clicking on it once.
6. Alter the specifications using the Text Inspector and watch the changes take place.
7. Double-click on the text on the Stage and change the text to read, "I've completed Chapter 2 today."
8. You are now finished with the exercises in this chapter. Quit the movie and the application without saving.

# CHAPTER 3

# ANIMATING SPRITES

## CHAPTER OBJECTIVE:

To work with the placement of Sprites using grids, guides, tweaking, and aligning and to learn about Sprite Overlays. To gain an understanding of how to change Sprite preferences and use the Property Inspector to alter Sprite properties and settings. To use Sprites in along with key-frames and tweening to produce an animation sequence. In Chapter 3, you will:

- Learn to place Sprites on a Stage or in a Score.
- Work with Sprite Overlays.
- Learn to set Sprite preferences.
- Review how to extend Sprites across frames.
- Gain an understanding of grids and guides and their use in the digital design world.
- Learn about and use the tweak feature.
- Learn about and use the align feature.
- Gain an understanding of keyframes, where they are located, and how to add or delete them.
- Work with the tweening feature.
- Work with animating in space, animating in time, and real-time recording.
- Use the Property Inspector to change Sprite properties.
- Learn about reversing animations.

## PROJECTS TO BE COMPLETED:

- Magic Carpet Tours (Project A)
- **Redi-Base (Project B)**
- Digital Portfolio (Project C)
- Emily's Photo Album (Project D)
- ABC's (Project E)

# Animating Sprites

Sprites are Cast Members that have been placed in the Score or on the Stage. A Sprite is a single instance of a Cast Member. For instance, if an image is dragged to the Stage and takes up frames 1 through 10 in the Score, that particular Sprite is 10 frames in length. If a copy of the same image is placed in frames 11 through 20, the copy might seem identical, but it is actually a separate Sprite, with its own set of specifications.

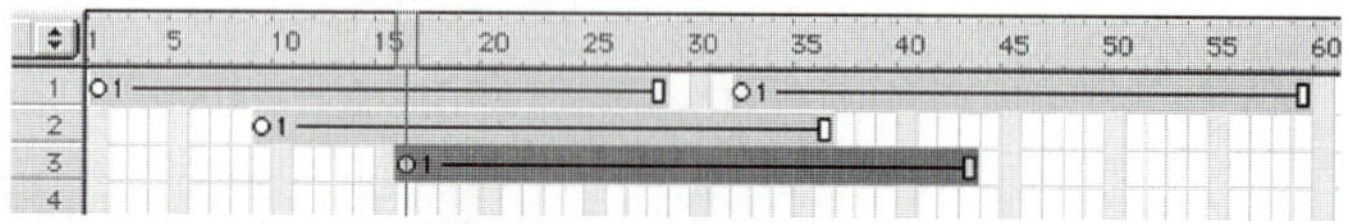

## Placing Sprites on the Stage or in the Score

In Chapter 1, you placed a Sprite in the Score and it automatically appeared centered on the Stage. This technique is useful when you have backgrounds or other items that need to be centered on the Stage. This option also allows you to easily put the Sprite in a specific location in the Score.

If you place a Sprite directly onto the Stage, however, the Sprite will appear in the next available opening in the Score. Alternatively, if you highlight a particular square or cell in the Score before dragging a Cast Member to the Stage, the Sprite will start there.

### Sprite Overlays

Each Sprite has its own properties, such as location on the Stage or opacity. When you have a hundred or so Sprites in the Score, you may have difficulty remembering the settings for specific Sprites. That's why each Sprite has its own Sprite Overlay, containing shortcut buttons used to pull up Sprite information quickly.

The Sprite Overlay is accessible from the View menu. Here, you will find three options: Show Info, Show Paths, and Settings....

- Show Info must be checked for an Overlay box to show up next to the Sprite on the Stage.
- Sprite Paths should be checked if your Sprite is animated. Checking Show Paths displays a line showing the animation path that the Sprite follows during its animation.
- Settings... displays the Overlay Settings dialog box, containing several options. Changing the color of the type in the Overlay is one of the options. If you have a black background, you don't want your text to be black because you won't be able to see it. Clicking on the current color will display a Color palette.

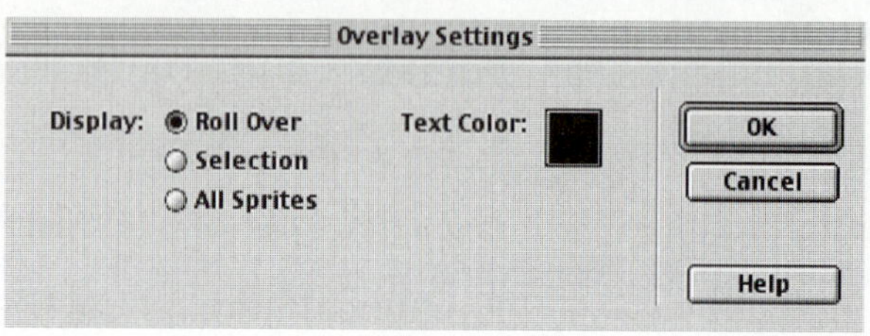

The options available in the Overlay Settings dialog box include:

- Rollover — Displays Overlays and/or animation paths for Sprites as you move the cursor over them. When you move away, the overlay disappears.
- Selection — Displays the Overlay and/or animation paths for a selected Sprite.
- All Sprites — Displays Overlays and/or animation paths for all the Sprites in the Cast. This can be confusing if you have a lot of objects in the Cast.

Below is an example of the Sprite Overlay info box and an animation path.

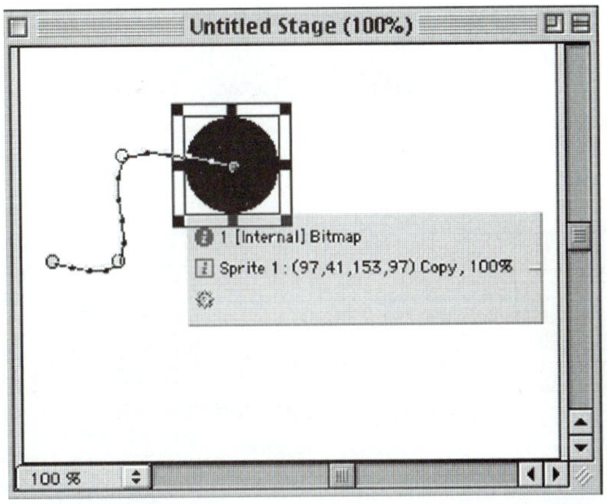


The Overlay display provides important information about the Sprite to which it's attached. The three icons inside the Overlay are links to certain tabs in the Property Inspector. For example, if you click on the Cast Member Properties icon, the top one, it displays the Sprite's basic file information in the Property Inspector. The middle icon displays the selected Sprite's options and specifications in the Property Inspector. The bottom icon displays the Behavior Inspector within the Property Inspector. We will discuss the Behavior Inspector later in this book.

## Sprite Preferences

The Sprite Preferences dialog box is accessible from the File menu. Most of the options will become self-explanatory after a few more chapters of this book, but for now we're going to focus on Span Duration.

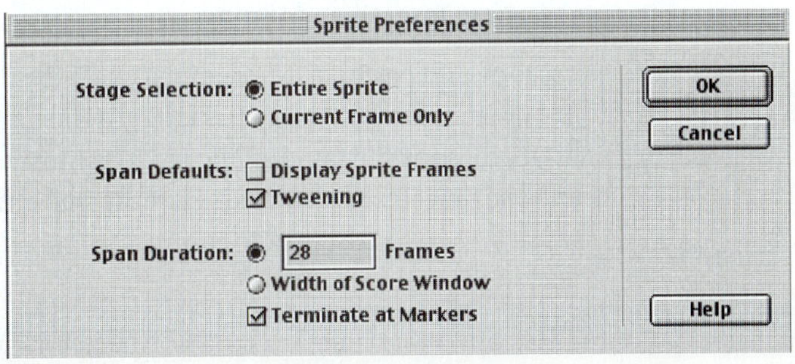


Span Duration is the number of frames over which a Sprite is spread. The default is 28 frames, meaning that each time a Sprite is placed in the Score, it will take up 28 frames unless the duration is otherwise adjusted. If the majority of work that you produce is two or three frames or if you have a monitor smaller than 14 inches, it would be best to shorten the Span Duration to maximize space and reduce scrolling time.

### Extending Sprites

Earlier, we discussed the shortcut for extending a single-frame Sprite across a number of frames: holding down the Option/Alt key while dragging the right side of the Sprite. With multiple-frame Sprites, there is no need to hold the Option/Alt key while dragging.

There are two additional ways to extend a Sprite in a Score once a Cast Member has been placed in the Score. The first is to highlight the Sprite in the Score. While holding down the Shift key, click on the frame in the Score to which you want the Sprite extended. Then select Modify>Extend Sprite, or press Command/Control-B as noted in the sidebar. The Sprite will extend or collapse to wherever the Playback Head is currently located.

*The key command to extend a Sprite is Command/Control-B. You must first Shift-click on the frame that you want the Sprite to extend out to and then press Command/Control-B.*

Alternately, you can change the numbers in the 2 fields of the Sprite tab in the Property Inspector. One is the beginning frame of a Sprite and one is the ending frame. Here, you can enter the exact frame numbers you want the Sprite to begin and end on.

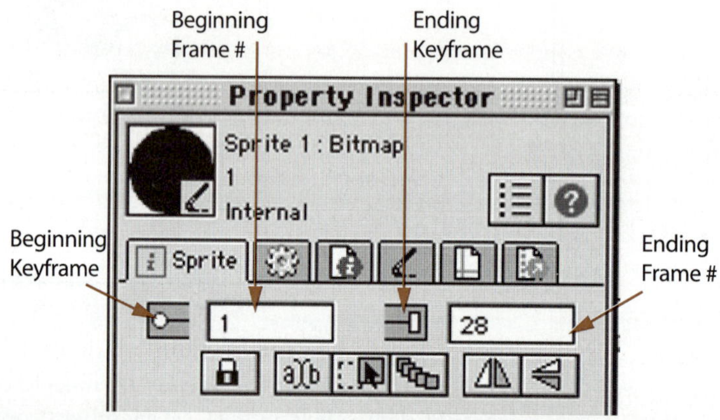


## Copying and Pasting Sprites and Cast Members

Copying and pasting Sprites and Cast Members is just like copying and pasting objects in every other desktop application. Beginners tend to underuse the Copy/Paste function. However, it can save you time. You can copy and paste whole sections of Director projects by copying and pasting whole groups of Sprites.

If you have an animation that you want to duplicate, don't redo it. For example, if you want rain, make one drop, animate it, and then copy and paste it a few times, changing the drops' size and position. Finally, grab the whole group and copy and paste it over and over again, changing position and timing.

To copy and paste a Cast Member while the Cast is in thumbnail form, simply highlight the member in the Cast, copy it, highlight the empty Cast slot, and then paste it. If the Cast is in list form, copy the same as above. To paste, however, make certain nothing is selected first, and the new item will be placed at the bottom of the list. If an item on the list is selected, when you go to paste another one, this new item will be pasted on top of the selected item, deleting it.

The Copy/Paste function could be used for a variety of tasks that would normally require repetitive steps. If you have one yellow flower and you want a red and a pink one, too, copy and paste the yellow flower twice and then go back into the Paint window and, using the Paint Bucket, change the color of the flower.

Copying and pasting Sprites is done the same way. Highlight the whole Sprite in the Score, copy it, select a frame to place it in, and then paste it.

## Using Sprite Overlays and Extending Sprites

1. If it is not already open, launch Director 8.0. If you would like to view the final version of this exercise before you begin, navigate to the **SF-Director** folder and access the **Finchap3.DIR** file in the **Finished Exercises** folder. Otherwise, begin with step 2.
2. To begin this exercise, navigate to the **SF-Director** folder and open the Chap3.DIR file.
3. Select File>Preferences>Sprite and change your Span Duration to one frame in length. Click OK. Eventually, we will be working with longer Sprites in this exercise, but for now we will practice extending Sprites.
4. From the Cast window, drag a copy of "Cloud" to the Score and place it in frame 1, channel 1. Extend the Sprite out to frame 50 by holding the Option/Alt key down and dragging the Sprite (in the Score) to the right until you reach frame 50.
5. Click the "Cloud" Sprite in the Score. Go to the Stage and move the cloud completely off the top-left edge of the Stage. This is where the clouds start. For now, only a big white box is visible, but step 9 unveils the clouds. If you click on a flower by accident, try highlighting the "Cloud" Sprite in the Score and using the Arrow keys on your keyboard to move the "Cloud" Sprite off the Stage.
6. Click on frame 50 of the "Cloud" Sprite and drag your clouds totally off the right edge of the Stage. As you drag your Sprite, you will see an elastic-like line appear with dots on it. This is the animation path. If you don't see the path, select View>Sprite Overlay>Show Paths and it will appear. Now the Sprite is set to be positioned off the right end of the Stage on frame 50 when the movie ends.

*For ease of use, this version of Director has implemented a pasteboard around the Stage area so that you can move Sprites completely on and off the Stage without having to resort to using Lingo.*

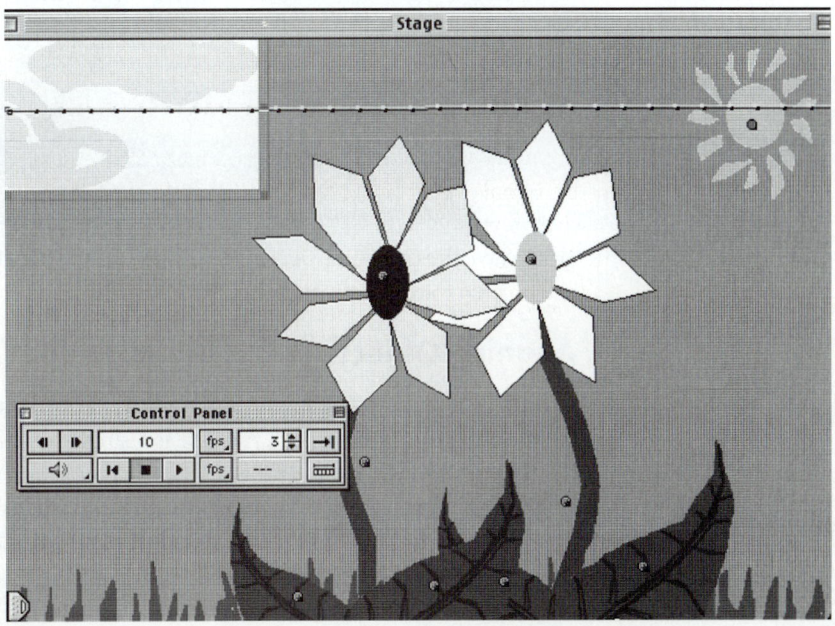

*The key command to undo a step is Command/ Control-Z. Remember to use this if necessary. Keep in mind that it will only reverse the last step that you completed - there are no unlimited undos in Director.*

7. Open the Control Panel if it is not already displayed. Rewind and play the movie. Is it too fast? Change the Preferred Frame Rate in the Control Panel to 3 fps (frames per second) if it is not already set at that rate.

8. Notice how the clouds rolled across the Stage behind the other graphics. That's because it was put in channel 1. Channels act like layers. The items in channel 13 (Daisy) will be much closer to the front than the items in channel 1 (Cloud). In this example the stems were put in the lower numbered channels and the flowers in the higher numbered channels since the flowers were meant to be viewed in front of the stems.

9. Click on the whole "Cloud" Sprite in the Score. In the Property Inspector, click on the drop-down menu that currently says Copy and select Background Transparent. You will notice that anything that was white in your clouds is now transparent. If you were to choose the Matte option, the white around the edges of the image would turn transparent, but the white within the image would not change. Use whichever option you prefer.

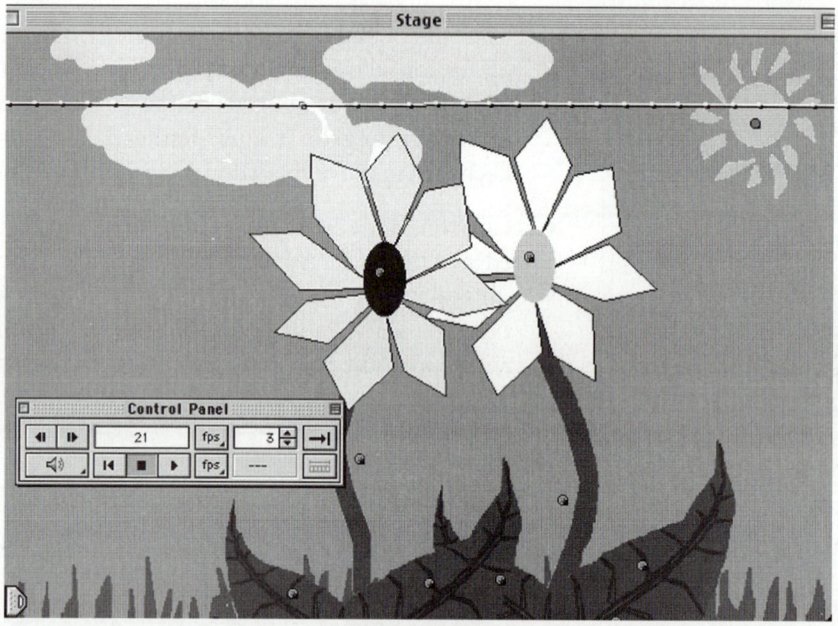


10. Save the movie as "Animation.DIR" in the **Work in Progress** folder. Keep the movie open for the next exercise.

## Aligning Objects

Guides, grids, and other alignment tools help produce well-balanced results for any page-layout or illustration project. A guide is a single horizontal or vertical line that can be used to align things visually. A grid is a set of horizontal and vertical lines that create a gridlike structure and are also used on each page as a guide to align text and graphics. These and other alignment tools will be discussed in the next few sections.

## Guides

Guides are a new and welcome addition to Director. They can be created in any color and are easily adjustable once on the Stage — just grab and go. They, along with the Grid information, can be found in the Property Inspector under the Guides and Grid tab.

To create a guide, just drag one off the Property Inspector next to where it says "New:" and drop it on the Stage. To move the guide, grab it and drag it to its new location.

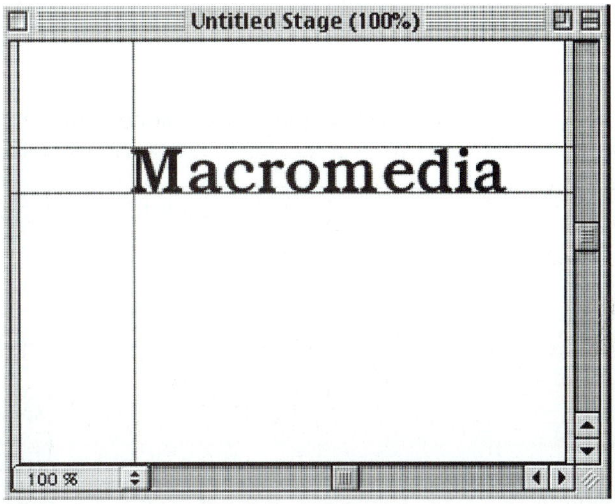


## Grids

As you can see in the image below, a grid divides the Stage into squares. As an item is placed, it doesn't need to fit exactly within a specific square. Grids also are used to help evenly space or align items.

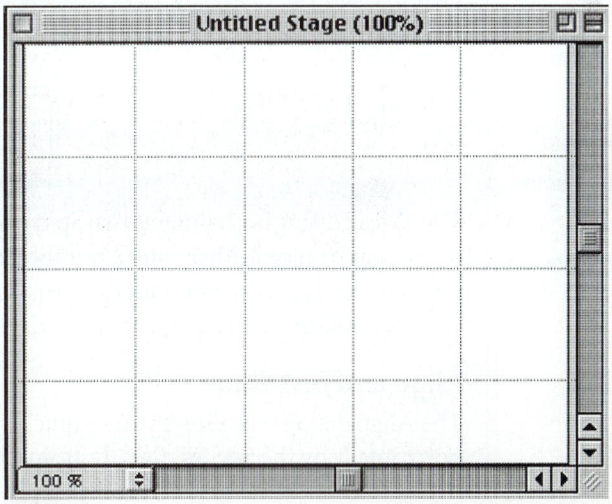


Grids in Director offer a Snap To option. If you place a Cast Member close to a grid line, the edge of it will snap right up to the edge of that line. This is useful for some projects but not all. This feature can be turned on or off by selecting Snap To Grid on the Guides and Grid tab in the Property Inspector.

In the Property Inspector, you can also select the color of your grid and dictate whether the lines of the grid are solid or dotted. Additionally, the width and height between the lines can be adjusted to display different square sizes. The width and height are in pixels, not inches.

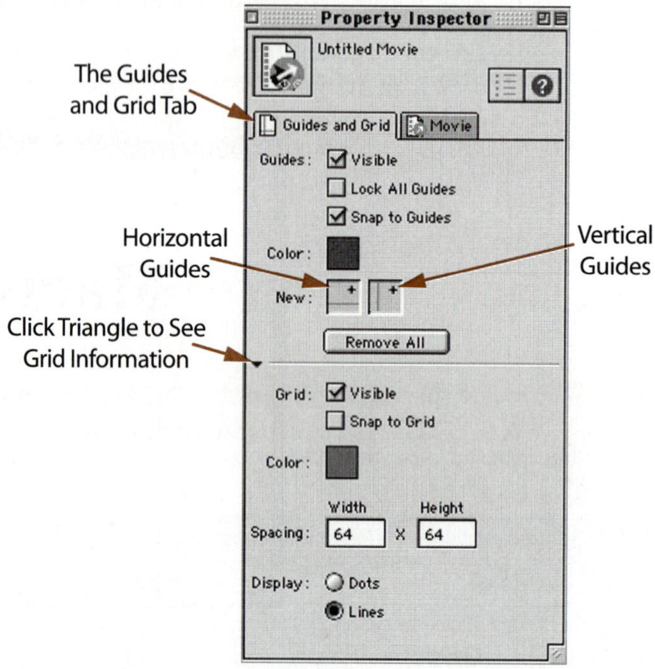


## Tweak

It is often necessary to move Sprites on a Stage in small and precise increments. The Tweak dialog box may be accessed from the Modify menu. If you have various items that need to be moved and aligned, you can move the first item and then enter the same number for the rest of the items. They will be moved the same distance, one at a time.

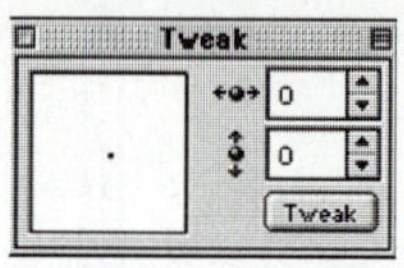


*Remember that you must enter a negative number to move left or up and a positive number to move right or down.*

The Tweak dialog box contains two Spin boxes, one for vertical movements and one for horizontal. You can either enter a number in the boxes and press the Enter key or click on an arrow in the direction you want the Sprite to move and watch it move until you are satisfied with its position. With the Sprite selected, you can also use the Arrow keys on your keyboard.

## Align and Distribute

The Align dialog box allows you to quickly align Sprites. Sprites can be aligned vertically or horizontally by the Sprites' tops, bottoms, right sides, left sides, or registration points.

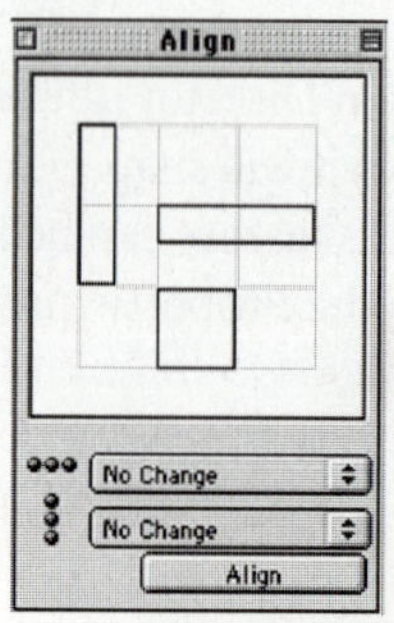

You can align several different Sprites or align a Sprite to itself over several frames by first highlighting the Sprites you want to align. Next, either click on the grid square that represents your horizontal and vertical choices for alignment or choose them individually from the two drop-down menus and click the Align button.

This dialog box also allows you to distribute Sprites across an area. You have the option of distributing them by their left sides, centers, right sides, registration points, the width of the object, or across the Stage. To do this, highlight the Sprites that you want to distribute and then choose the distribution methods individually from the two drop-down menus and click the Align button.

## Animating

You've now had enough preparation to begin learning how to animate Sprites. Director is quite good with 2-D animation — as it should be. After all, Macromedia has been in this arena for a long time. The company has worked hard to combine elements of traditional animation with the necessary digital components, creating a blend between the two worlds that tries to ease the transition for traditional animators trying to go digital.

### Keyframes and Tweening

Keyframes are single frames of a Sprite that can hold information. If you look at a multiple-frame Sprite in the Score, you will notice that the first and last frames have either a circle or a rectangle in them, whereas all the rest of the frames simply have a line that runs through them connecting them with their first and last frames. These are keyframes. To select a keyframe, click on the circle (or the rectangle) at the end of the Sprite. To select the whole Sprite, make certain that you click on any frame of the Sprite that does not contain a keyframe.

Keyframes hold information. They can store information on what size a Sprite should be, where it should be located, and at which angle it should be rotated when it arrives at a particular frame. You must give Sprites a defined position at a specific keyframe in order to create an animation sequence. This is done by highlighting a keyframe in the Score and then dragging the Sprite to its new location on the Stage. If you want to modify its size, highlight the keyframe and then resize the box that contains the Sprite on the Stage.

By adding several keyframes and adjusting the specifications of the Sprite for each one, you can create animation. Any frames between any two keyframes of a Sprite will automatically be divided equally into the animated steps necessary to make the transition seamless. This is called In-Betweening, or Tweening for short. You determine some keyframes in an animation sequence, and Director automatically fills in the steps in between. A Sprite that is extended has been tweened with no additional keyframe information with the exception of the original information. Director simply copied and pasted the Sprite into every frame you extended it across.

The first and last frames of every Sprite are keyframes. You can add keyframes to any other frame the Sprite crosses by selecting Insert>Keyframe or delete them by selecting Insert>Remove Keyframe. Keyframes are added or removed from the Score wherever the Playback Head crosses the currently selected Sprite.

*To make sure that you are choosing the correct frame numbers, it may help to have the Control Panel open while you are doing this exercise.*

## Keyframes and Tweening

1. We worked a little with keyframes in the last exercise. Now we will continue with the **Animation.DIR** file that you saved earlier in your **Work in Progress** folder.
2. From the Cast palette, drag "Butterfly" down to channel 16 and extend the Sprite over frames 1 through 50.
3. Insert new keyframes into frames 5, 10, 15, and 20 of the "Butterfly" Sprite.
4. Now you will position the keyframes on the Stage. First, highlight the whole Sprite in the Score. Go to the Stage and drag the Sprite on the Stage to where you want it to start when the movie begins.
5. Next, highlight only frame 5 of the Sprite in the Score and go to the Stage. Move the Sprite to where you want it to be when the movie hits frame 5.
6. Repeat step 5 for frame 10, 15, 20, and 50. You will notice that the keyframes appear as larger colored dots along the animation path. If you don't see the animation path, go to View>Sprite Overlay>Show Paths to turn it on.
7. To delete the white around the butterfly, highlight the entire Sprite in the Score and select Background Transparent from the drop-down menu in the Property Inspector (as done previously with the clouds).
8. Rewind and play the movie. You will notice that the butterfly moves around on the Stage. If there are 10 people in your class, there will be 10 different animations, as this is all based on where you placed your Sprites at each keyframe point. If you don't like where some or all of your keyframes are located on the Stage, simply drag the colored dot representing each one to reposition it.

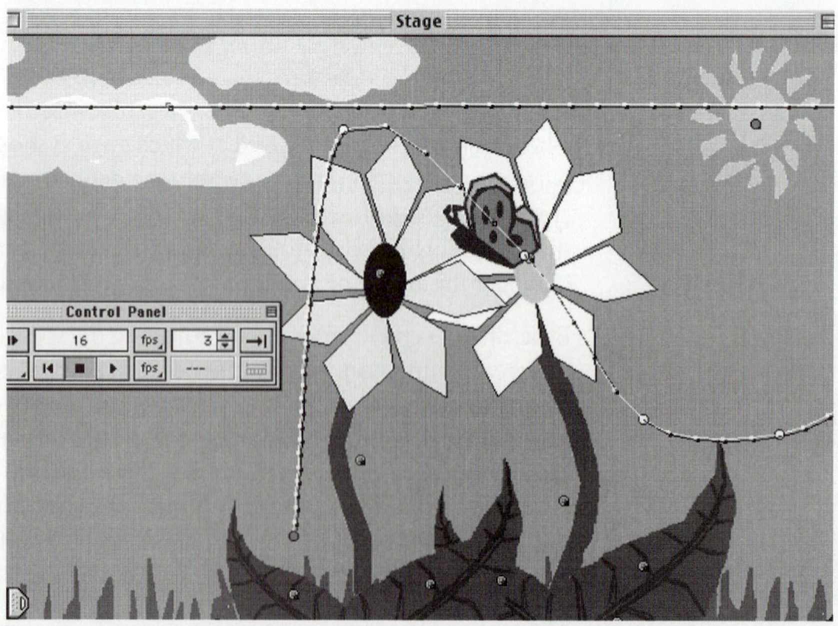


9. Save your changes and keep the movie open for the next exercise.

## Sprite Properties

The properties of each Sprite can be viewed from within the Property Inspector. Such information as width, height, scale, rotate, skew ink effects, and blend percentage is displayed. The box also shows the location of the Sprite on the Stage and allows you to lock a Sprite so that it isn't accidentally moved or edited. To access the Sprite property information, click on the Sprite tab in the Property Inspector while a Sprite is highlighted on the Stage or in the Score.

It is not recommended to scale a Sprite up or down too much, since Sprites require a lot of RAM to handle sizing on the fly as the movie is playing. If you have various Sprites and each one is scaled up and/or down, the movie slows down to a crawl — especially if they are large Sprites, such as backgrounds.

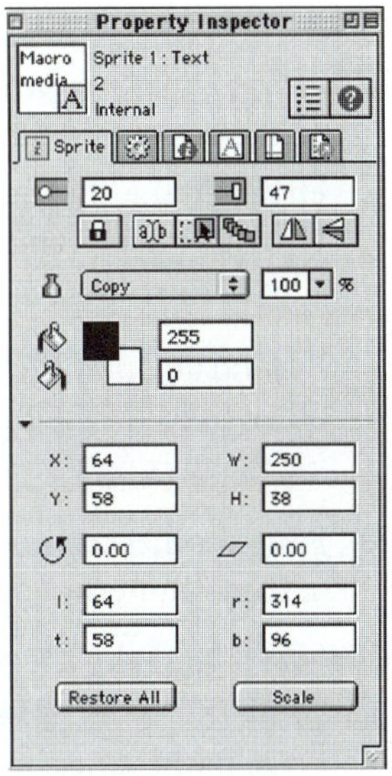


## Animating in Space

Animating in Space allows you to make the same two animations look different. To do this, put a Sprite in the Score and then copy and paste the Sprite into the same frames but into a different channel in the Score. Finally, highlight the entire newly pasted Sprite and move it to a new location on the Stage. Now, when you rewind and play the movie, you will see that two of the same animations are playing at the same time but in different locations. This produces the illusion of two different animations. The farther apart you place them, the more likely they are to appear different.

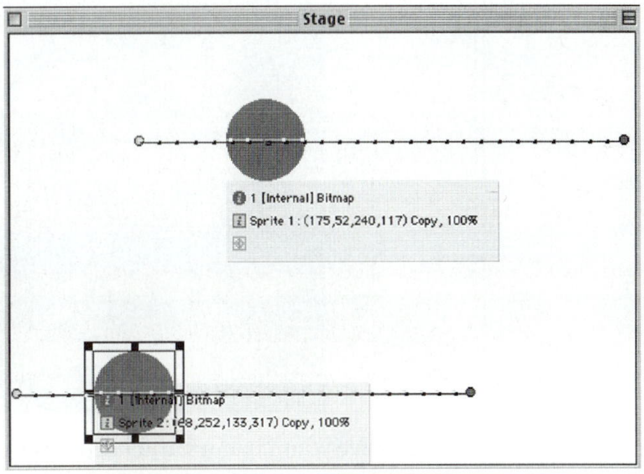

## Animating in Time

Animating in Time involves starting duplicates of the same animation at different times. The process is similar to animating in space except that you paste the second Sprite in the next available channel and in a frame different from the first. Start the new Sprite a few frames later than the first one. This delays the start of the second animation.

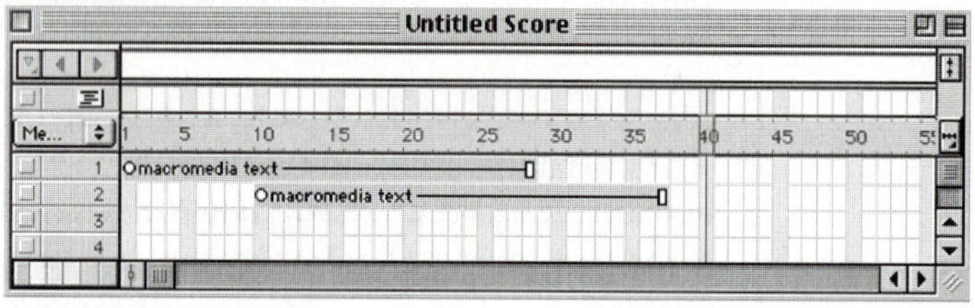

### *Animating in Space and Time*

1. Highlight the "Butterfly" Sprite you placed in channel 16 and copy it. Highlight frame 10 of channel 17 and then paste the copy in frame 10 of channel 17. Drag the right edge of the copied Sprite back toward the left and stop it at frame 50, like all the rest.
2. Rewind and play the movie. Notice that by starting one animation later than the other, they look slightly different. This is an example of animating in time — staggering the starting times of identical animations.
3. Paste another copy of "Butterfly" in channel 18, frame 1 of your Score. You don't need to copy "Butterfly" again because it is still in your clipboard.
4. Highlight the newly pasted Sprite in the Score. This time, go to the Stage and drag the "Butterfly" to a completely different location. Make certain that it is not too close to either of the other butterflies' paths.
5. Rewind and play the movie. This time the new animation looks very different. Though it starts and ends at the same time as the first one, you moved its animation path so that it moves around on another part of the page. This is animating in space.

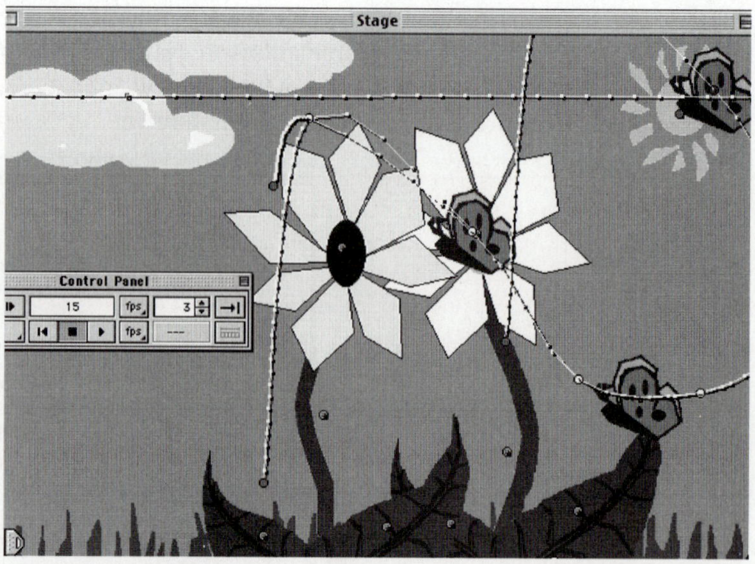


6. Save your changes and keep this movie open for the next exercise.

## Real-Time Recording

Real-Time Recording is simply the recording of an animation as you drag it around the Stage in real time. The first thing you need is a Sprite in the Score to work with. Make certain that it covers at least 30 or 40 frames — you will understand why in the next exercise.

Real-time recording can be turned on by selecting Control>Real-Time Recording. The tempo needs to be kept slow because the Playback Head needs to move across the Score slowly enough to animate the object on the Stage before reaching the end of the Sprite. A tempo of 5 fps or so (set in the Control Panel) will usually work well.

Rewind the Playback Head, go to the Stage, and then drag the Sprite around the Stage in the path that you want the animation to follow. As soon as the Sprite on the Stage is touched, the Playback Head starts moving across the frames. When the Playback Head reaches the end of the Sprite in the Score, you should stop moving your Sprite.

Once this is complete, you can rewind the movie and then play it to see the animation. You can also just look at the animation path on the Stage and drag the Playback Head back and forth to see it frame by frame or at the speed you desire. The animation path will be made up of dozens of keyframes, all of which can be edited.

### *Trying out Real-Time Recording*

1. From the Cast palette, drag a copy of "Ladybug" to channel 19, frames 1-50. Highlight the "Ladybug" Sprite in the Score and drag it to location on the Stage where you want the ladybug to start flying.
2. While your whole Sprite is still highlighted in the Score, you may want to choose Background Transparent from the drop-down menu in the Property Inspector to get rid of the white around your object, making its outline more accurate.
3. With the "Ladybug" Sprite still highlighted in the Score, drag your Playback Head back to frame 1 or click the Rewind button in the Control Panel. Make certain that your tempo is set to 4 or 5 fps in the Control Panel.
4. Turn on real-time recording by selecting Control>Real-Time Recording. You will notice two things: first, there will be a red-and-white striped box around your Sprite on the Stage; second, there will be a small red dot next to the number of the channel that contains the Sprite you are about to animate, indicating that you have activated real-time recording.
5. As soon as you drag your Sprite on the Stage, the recording begins and the Playback Head starts moving across the frames in your Score. Drag the Sprite around the Stage and create your animation path. While you are dragging it around, Director is recording the placement of your Sprite as the Playback Head rolls through each frame. When the Playback Head reaches the end of your "Ladybug" Sprite, at frame 50 in the Score, stop dragging. Director will continue making new frames as long as you keep dragging the Sprite.

*Remember that if you get into trouble, you can always close the file without saving. Then reopen the file and start over.*

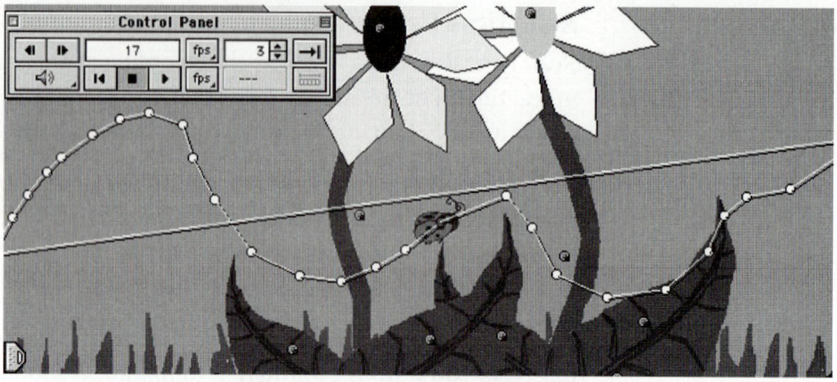


6. Rewind and play the movie. If you don't like the animation, either do it over by deleting the Sprite in your Score and starting again or go to the Stage and reposition the keyframes you are unhappy with.

7. Close the movie and quit the application without saving.

### Reversing an Animation

Reversing an Animation is a quick, easy way to make a copy of a single Sprite animation look different from the original. To try this out, you would highlight your animation and then select Modify>Reverse Sequence. The animation sequence would be reversed frame by frame, resulting in a look that is very different than the original.

A combination of animation techniques will create an even better result. Utilizing these techniques will increase your animation output without exerting much additional time or effort on a project.

***Complete Project B: Redi-Base***

# CHAPTER 4

# TRANSITIONS AND INK EFFECTS

## CHAPTER OBJECTIVE:

To understand transitions and ink effects and how to properly apply them in your project. In Chapter 4, you will:

- Learn about transitions.
- Work with the Transition channel.
- Work with the Transition dialog box.
- Gain an understanding of when to use transitions and which ones to use.
- Learn about ink effects and where can they be found.
- Learn about Paint ink effects.
- Learn about Sprite ink effects.

## PROJECTS TO BE COMPLETED:

- Magic Carpet Tours (Project A)
- Redi-Base (Project B)
- Digital Portfolio (Project C)
- Emily's Photo Album (Project D)
- ABC's (Project E)

# Transitions and Ink Effects

Everyone has probably watched a TV show in which the camera switched from one scene to another using some kind of cool effect to make the transition. The proper use of transitions in a Director movie and how to create them will be discussed in this chapter.

Ink Effects are another way to embellish a movie. They can be applied to individual Sprites using the Property Inspector or to original Cast Members using the Paint window. The ink effects you can apply to individual Sprites will alter how Sprites interact with other Sprites. The effects you can apply in the Paint window will alter how two objects interact in the Paint window while you are creating a Cast Member.

## Transitions

Dissolves, wipes, and fades are three of the most commonly used transitions in traditional filmmaking. Transitions are used to reveal new objects or to make objects disappear from the Stage. A dissolve gradually deletes the pixels of objects on the Stage to allow new objects to show through, providing smooth transitions from one frame to the next.

There are aesthetic issues to consider when choosing a transition. Transitions have been used in television production for 30-some years. As "Charlie's Angels" reruns appear dated, so, too, will your production if you do not choose your transitions wisely.

Keep your subject matter in mind when picking transitions. A checkerboard transition is not appropriate for a professional business meeting, but it may be perfect for a children's interactive CD.

### The Transition Channel

In the Special Channels section of the Score, there is a channel with an icon that looks like a black bow tie. This is the Transition channel. If special channels are not visible, click on the Hide/Show button, shown below.

Transitions should always be placed in the Transition channel of the frame that you are transitioning to. If you have a red box in frame 1 that will dissolve into a purple diamond in frame 2, you would put your transition in the Transition channel of frame 2.

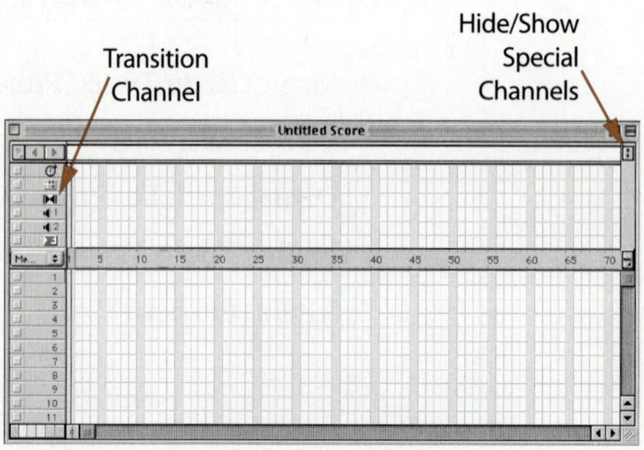

## The Transition Dialog Box

The Transition dialog box provides a variety of categories and transition selections. Double-clicking in the Transition channel of the frame that you want the transition to be placed in will make the Frame Properties: Transition dialog box appear.

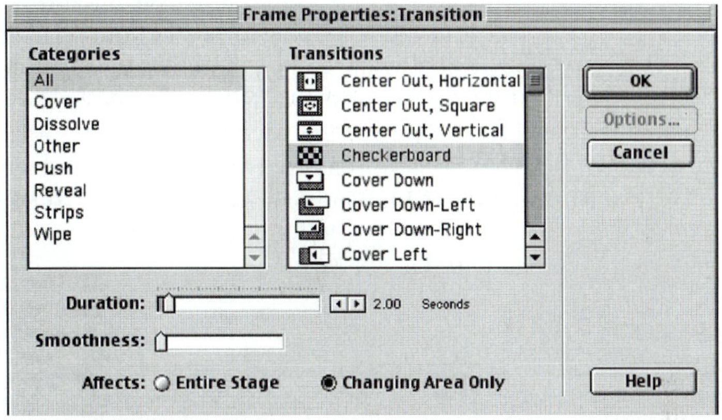


Here, you select the transition of choice and adjust the duration and smoothness. The Duration slider indicates the length of the transition, and the Smoothness slider sets your transition from choppy and obvious to so smooth that you barely realize it is happening. The Affects option allows you to select whether you want the entire Stage or just the objects on the Stage to transition to the next frame.

After you have chosen a transition, look at your Cast. You will notice that Director has created a Cast Member out of your transition. If you need this transition again at a later date, you can simply pull it out of the Cast and into the Transition channel, rather than repeating the steps above.

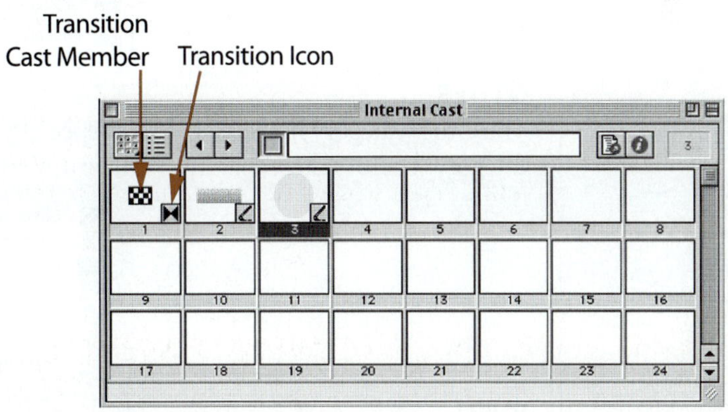

## Types of Transitions

The transitions appear on the right side of the Transition dialog box. There are many types to choose from, and they're broken into categories, listed on the left side of the dialog box. If a category is not selected, the default is automatically set to All, which provides a complete list to choose from. This list appears on the right side of the palette. If you know which category you're looking for, make your selection in advance to display a shorter list of available transitions in order to make your category selection process more efficient. Listed below with a brief description of each are the various categories.

### COVER

Cover transitions act like a blanket to cover up old objects with new ones. Covers can come in from the top, bottom, right, or left.

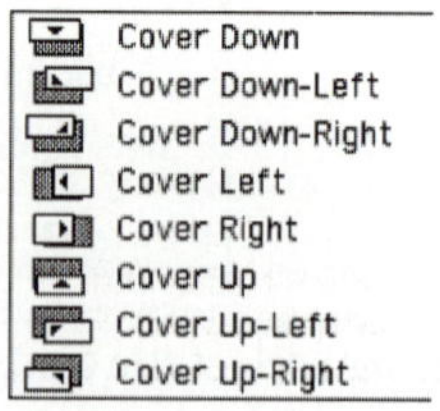


### DISSOLVE

Dissolve transitions dissolve the current objects while allowing the new objects to show through from underneath. You can dissolve at various speeds and with different shapes, such as pixels, bits, squares, or rectangles.

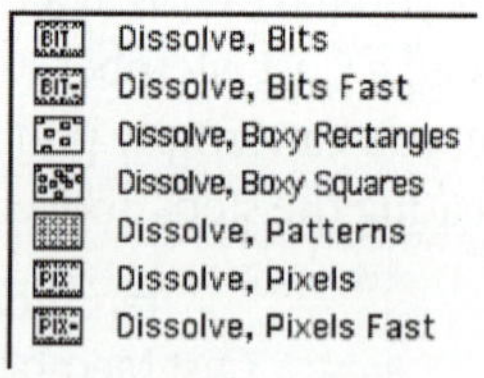


### OTHER

The Other category houses a group of specialty transitions that don't fit into any other category. These include the Checkerboard, Vertical Blinds, and Venetian Blinds.

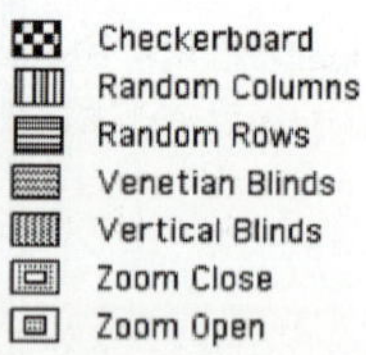


### PUSH

Push transitions make the new frame of objects push the old one off the Stage. These can come across the Stage from the top, bottom, left, or right.

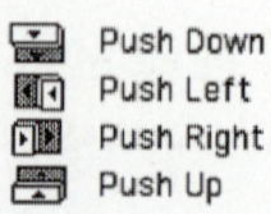

### REVEAL

Reveal transitions are the opposite of Cover transitions — the blanket that is over the old objects is removed to reveal the new objects.

- Reveal Down
- Reveal Down-Left
- Reveal Down-Right
- Reveal Left
- Reveal Right
- Reveal Up
- Reveal Up-Left
- Reveal Up-Right

### STRIPS

Strip transitions slide across the Stage and build on top of one another to cover it. They can start and build from any side of the Stage.

- Strips on Bottom, Build L...
- Strips on Bottom, Build R...
- Strips on Left, Build Down
- Strips on Left, Build Up
- Strips on Right, Build Down
- Strips on Right, Build Up
- Strips on Top, Build Left
- Strips on Top, Build Right

### WIPE

Wipe transitions wipe away the old objects and leave behind the new. They can wipe from the center out and from the edges in, as well as from the right, left, top, and bottom.

- Center Out, Horizont
- Center Out, Square
- Center Out, Vertical
- Edges In, Horizontal
- Edges In, Square
- Edges In, Vertical
- Wipe Down
- Wipe Left

## *Using Transitions*

1. To preview the finished file before you begin this exercise select the **SF-Director>Finished Exercises>FinCedar.DIR** file.
2. From the **SF-Director** folder, select the **Cedarmtn.DIR** file.
3. Save the new movie as "Transition.DIR" in your **Work in Progress** folder.
4. Click on the Movie tab in the Property Inspector. Click on the square to the right of the Paint Bucket icon and change the Stage color to black. While you are still in the Movie tab, make certain the Stage size is set to 640 x 480 pixels.
5. Select Window>Control Panel and verify that the Loop option is turned off. Set the frames per second to 5.

6. Place the following Cast Members in channel 1:

| | |
|---|---|
| Cedarmtn | Frames 1-15 |
| Hiking | Frames 16-30 |
| Camping | Frames 31-45 |
| Canoe | Frames 46-60 |
| Snowboard | Frames 61-75 |
| Picnic | Frames 76-90 |
| Biking | Frames 91-105 |
| Resting | Frames 106-120 |
| Backpack | Frames 121- 135 |
| End | Frames 136-150. |

7. In frame 16, double-click in the Transition channel to bring up the Transition dialog box. Highlight Cover from the list on the left and Cover Down-Right from the Transitions list. Make certain that the duration is set to 2 seconds. Set the Affects option to Changing Area Only and click OK.
8. In the Transition channel of frame 31, set the category to Dissolve and then select Dissolve Bits with the same settings as step 7. Continue to place the following transitions in the following frames:

| | | |
|---|---|---|
| Frame: 46 | Category: Wipe | Type: Center-Out Horizontal |
| Frame: 61 | Category: Push | Type: Push-Left |
| Frame: 76 | Category: Reveal | Type: Reveal-Dowl |
| Frame: 91 | Category: Strips | Type: Strips on Top, Build Left |
| Frame: 106 | Category: Wipe | Type: Edges in, Vertical |
| Frame: 121 | Category: Other | Type: Vertical Blinds |
| Frame: 136 | Category: Other | Type: Random-Rows |

9. From the Control Panel, rewind and play your movie to view a sampling of the transitions Director has to offer. Some of these transitions are fun to work with but will rarely be used in actual production.

*If you are familiar with Adobe Photoshop, ink effects are similar to blending modes.*

# Ink Effects

Ink Effects may be assigned to an object or tool. These effects change the appearance of the object or tool when it comes in contact with other colors. Applying a particular ink effect to the top color of any two colors that overlap will provide a new result.

Ink effects may be used to create special effects as well as to solve everyday production problems. For instance, when used on a paint graphic, the Matte ink effect (on the Sprite tab in the Property Inspector) will remove the white box around the graphic.

You will find the Ink Effects list in both the Paint window and the Property Inspector. There are many to choose from; however, the first five in the list tend to be the most popular and useful.

## Paint Ink Effects

Paint ink effects may be accessed from the Paint window. While creating Cast Members, you can add Smudges, Smears, Gradients, and Blends to your Cast Member.

To apply a Paint ink effect, select a painting tool and then select your ink effect from the menu at the bottom of the Paint window. For an effect to work, there must be paint on your canvas. Apply the second color, and they will blend together to create the desired effect.

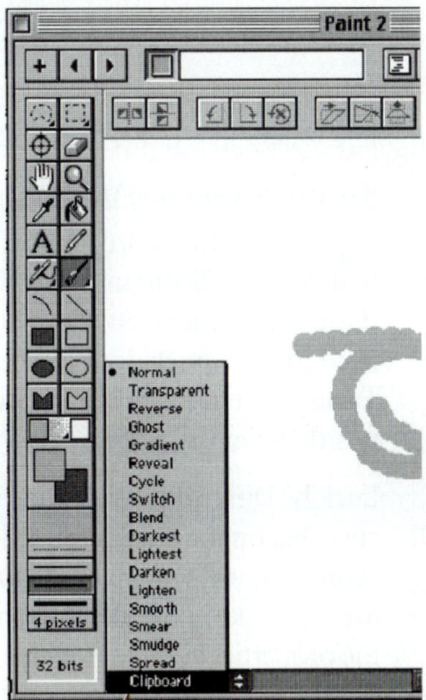


Paint Ink Effects

Some ink effects work better with patterns and some with solid colors. Some even require that you be on a certain tool or tools for them to work properly. If an effect is grayed out on the drop-down menu, you may have selected an incorrect color mode or tool for the effect to work properly.

## Sprite Ink Effects

Sprite ink effects can be added to individual Sprites, so the original Cast Member will not be affected. These ink effects will change the way Sprites interact with each other on the Stage.

To apply an ink effect to a Sprite, highlight the Sprite in the Score and then select the desired effect from the drop-down menu on the Sprite tab in the Property Inspector.

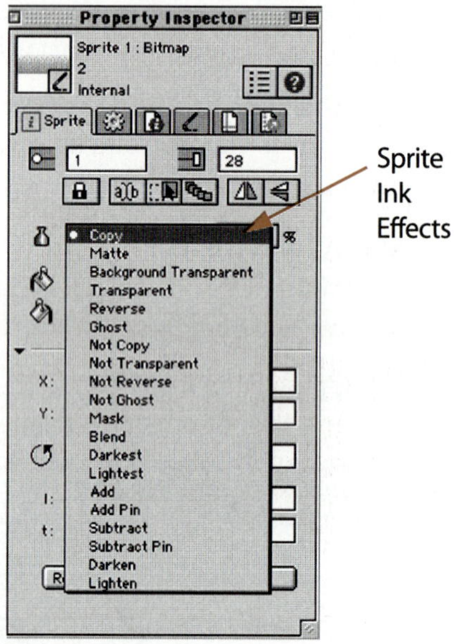


## Sprite Properties Visible in the Score

Typically, in the Score, Sprites are shown with either their name or number on them so that you can distinguish one from the next. This is helpful, but there is a lot of other information that would sometimes be useful to see all at once. For instance, you might need to do a quick double-check to see if all of your Text Sprites were set to Background Transparent, certain blends were set to 50%, and certain Sprites were located in specific positions on the Stage.

Luckily, Director provides an alternative way to check for something like this besides checking on the Sprites individually in the Property Inspector. Looking at the left side of the Score, you will see a drop-down menu with various options. The menu typically defaults to Member, like in the example shown below. Setting it to Extended will allow you to see all the properties available via this method.

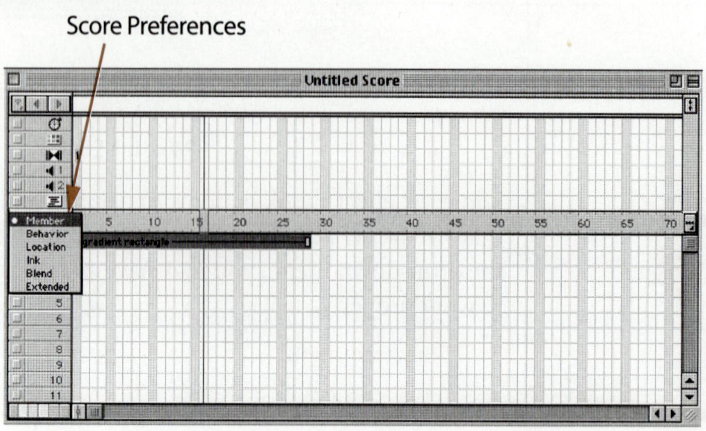

To verify that you have every option available under Extended, you will want to check the Score preferences, located under File>Preferences>Score. Select the options you would like to see displayed on the Sprite in the Score. As long as you have Sprites in your Score and it is set to Extended, you will see the channels get taller to make room for the additional information.

If you only want to check your blends or your inks, you can select Blend or Ink from the drop-down menu, and just that information will be shown. Below is an example of the Extended option.

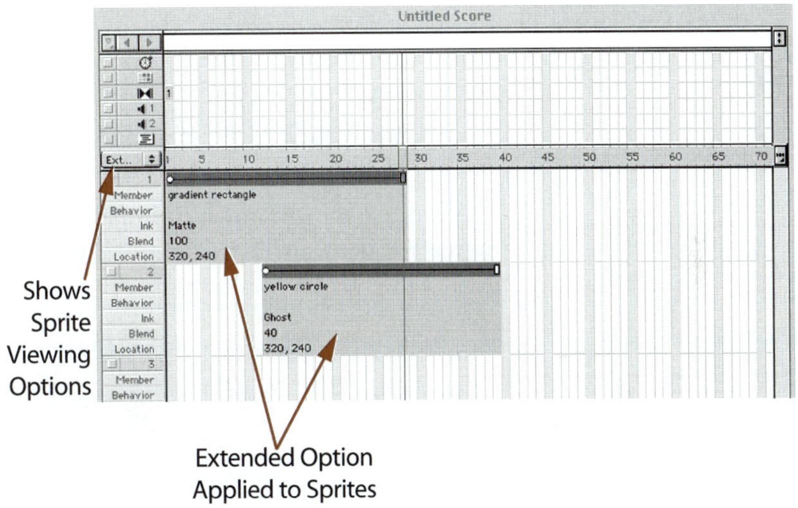

## *Using Ink Effects*

1. From your **SF-Director** folder, open the **InkEff.DIR** file. If you wish to see the finished project at any time, feel free to open up the finished version, **FinInk.DIR** in the **Finished Exercises** folder.
2. Select File>Save As and rename the file "Inks.DIR". Save this file in your **Work in Progress** folder.
3. Play the movie through once to see how it looks. This way you will recognize the changes we make later.
4. The word "Magical" in the title was created using a Paint ink effect from the Paint window. To try this yourself, open the Paint window and set the Paintbrush ink effect to Cycle. Make certain that your foreground color is set to Black and your background color is set to White. This tells the color cycle where to stop and start. The colors black and white are at opposite ends of the 256-color Color palette, so you're telling the ink effect to cycle through all of the colors.
5. Click on your Paintbrush and try to paint the word "Magical". When you feel comfortable with your outcome, continue with the next step.
6. Now we are going to add some Sprite ink effects to several of the Sprites in the Score. First, highlight the Sprite in channel 1 in the Score (the clouds) and choose Not Copy from the list of Sprite ink effects.

7. Continue to apply the following ink effects to the list of Sprites.

| | |
|---|---|
| Channel 6-Sun | Apply: Not Reverse |
| Channel 16-Butterfly | Apply: Ghost |
| Channel 17-Butterfly | Apply: Darken |
| Channel 18-Butterfly | Apply: Add |
| Channel 19-Ladybug | Apply: Darkest |

8. Go to the Score and click on the drop-down menu on the left side. Choose Ink and watch what happens to the Sprites in your Score. All the Inks you applied in the step above are now labeled on each Sprite. Choose Extended from the drop-down menu — take a look at the info listed on each Sprite. When you are finished, set the menu back to Member.
9. Rewind and play the movie. Compare it with the original. Remember, some of these effects will come in handy and some are just for special effects.
10. Save and quit the application.

# CHAPTER 5

# INTERACTIVITY, NAVIGATION, AND BUTTONS

## CHAPTER OBJECTIVE:

To learn about main menus and their usefulness, as well as how to create buttons to add interactivity for the user. To use markers to help navigate through a complex Score. In Chapter 5, you will:

- Learn what a main menu is.
- Create a main menu.
- Work with the Script channel.
- Pause a movie on a specific frame.
- Learn how to create interactive buttons.
- Become familiar with creating Check boxes and Radio buttons.
- Turn Cast Members into buttons.
- Create a Quit button.
- Learn about markers.
- Learn how to navigate using markers.

## PROJECTS TO BE COMPLETED:

- Magic Carpet Tours (Project A)
- Redi-Base (Project B)
- **Digital Portfolio (Project C)**
- Emily's Photo Album (Project D)
- ABC's (Project E)

# Interactivity, Navigation, and Buttons

Before beginning any multimedia project, it is best to have created a flow chart and plenty of sketches. However, there comes a point when you must put those aside and try to make your piece do what you said you wanted it to do on paper — not always an easy task.

Typically, to meet this goal, you must add buttons and interactivity to your movie. Many Director users will want to create cool-looking buttons in some other application, such as Photoshop, Illustrator, or Freehand, and then import them as Cast Members. Whether you create them inside Director or in another graphics program, you will now need to start delving into the wonderful world of Lingo, a scripting language, to make your buttons work.

This chapter takes a look at some of the steps necessary to turn Director movies into interactive experiences.

## Basic Interactivity

Have you ever been to a music store where there is a computer listing various music selections that you can research or sample? You are able to interact with the computer's software, clicking here and there to choose what you would like to see or hear.

The screen that lists all of your options is called the Main menu. It's typically the first list of options you come to if you are using an interactive piece of multimedia. However, if your movie is intended only to be viewed, not interacted with, there may be no need for a Main menu.

Since a Main menu is typically the first area you will have access to in an interactive piece, this is where we will start. First, to familiarize yourself with how a Main menu works, you will view a partially completed example below. Later in the chapter you will learn how to complete it and make it work.

### *Looking at a Main menu*

Note: Make sure to load your ATC fonts before beginning this exercise.

1. If you would like to view the finished version of this exercise before you begin, first open the **FinESAD.DIR** file located in the **Finished Exercises** folder. To begin this exercise, open the **ESADeco.DIR** file located in the **SF-Director** folder.
2. Choose File>Save As and name this file "Art.DIR". Save the file in your **Work in Progress** folder.
3. Play the movie. You will see it move through a series of screens and transitions (dissolves) and end with a map of New York City. The map looks like a grid with some colored squares on it. This is the Main menu for this movie. Notice that some of the buttons are missing. There are only gray boxes marking the spots where the buttons should be.
4. Keep this file open for the next exercise.

## Using a Frame Script to Pause a Movie

When first creating a Main menu page, you will notice that after clicking Play to start the movie, the Playback Head starts on the Sprite containing the Main menu but keeps rolling right over your Sprites, making it impossible to select anything.

This problem can be handled in a few different ways. For now, we will discuss two solutions. Both require the use of the Script channel, which can be found in your Score just above the frame numbers in the Special Channels section.

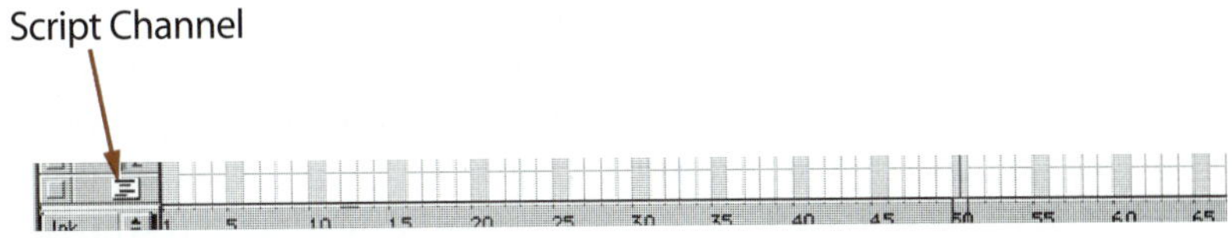


As with the Transition channel, you double-click on the Script channel of the frame that you want your script to be placed in. The double-click opens the Behavior Script window. It will already have the cursor in the correct place. In the example shown below, we entered the word *pause* and then closed the window.

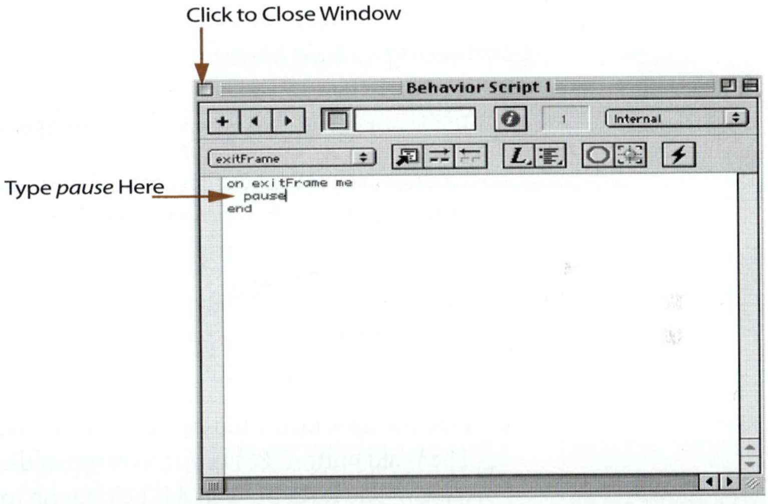

*If **on exitFrame** is not showing in the Behavior Script window, click on the L button and look under E for exitFrame. The command will automatically be inserted into the window when you choose it.*

A Pause command stops a movie in its tracks until another script tells it to continue. Using a Pause can cause a problem: if you have music playing and an animated loop running on the frame, it will stop both, whether you want both stopped or not. To work around this problem, you can use the second option, a *go to the frame* script, to make the Playback Head repeat just the current frame over and over again.

Either of the actions above will create a Frame script, which is an example of the Director scripting language, Lingo. Notice in the image above that there is some text in the dialog box that reads *on exitFrame* and *end.* These are known as handlers. They notify Director to pay attention to the instruction that has been entered. We have simply instructed Director to pause when it is ready to leave this frame, follow this command, and after it has done so, leave this frame.

## Creating a Main Menu

Be aware of how many and what kind of options you want users to have access to on the Main menu. For instance, rather than displaying 52 states on a Main menu, provide regional options such as Northeast, Mid-Atlantic, and Pacific Northwest to narrow down the viewer's choices.

As a general rule, it is a good idea to keep your Main menu options to six or fewer for ease of use. Because of the limited number of options you should have in a menu, most of the time you will find it easier to begin with more general categories and break them down as you go. As stated above, one might start off with just dividing the United States into quadrants: Northeast, Southeast, Northwest, Southwest. If a user were looking for Florida, he or she would choose Southeast. Then, on the next screen the category may be broken down again. For instance, states that start with A-F, G-M, N-R, and S-Z. The user would click on the first option because Florida starts with an "F." From the list of states displayed, he or she would select Florida.

Now we will finish putting together a partially completed Main menu.

### *Completing a Main Menu*

1. If it is not already open, open the **Art.DIR** file in your **Work in Progress** folder.
2. Double-click on the Script channel of frame 200 in the Score and type *go to the frame* in the script and then close the window. This places the command in the Script channel so that the channel stays still long enough for you to work on it and for the end users to click on it.
3. Play the movie and you will see that it stops on frame 200. If you click on any of the buttons on the menu, the movie continues to play.
4. Find the missing buttons in the Cast and place them where they belong on the Stage. The Wald button (86) belongs on top of the gray square next to "The Waldorf Astoria Hotel." The Rock button (84) belongs on top of the gray square under "Rockefeller Center," and the Daily button (88) belongs on top of the gray square under the "The Daily News Building." There is room for each button in the Score next to the corresponding building's text Sprite.

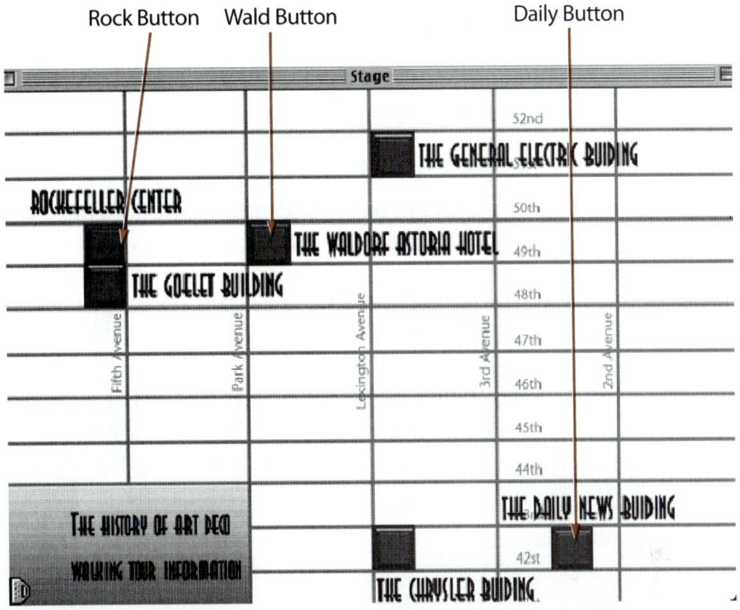


5. Extend all of these Sprites to the same length as the rest of the Sprites in the Main menu, from frame 181-200.

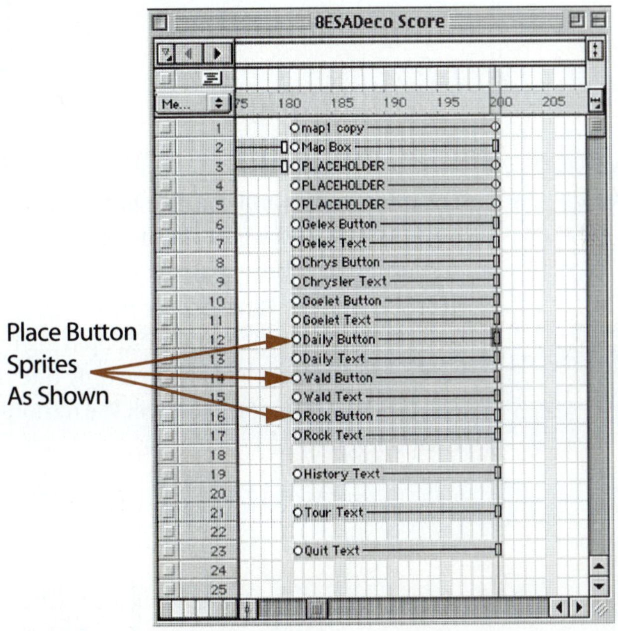

*Please note that graphics will not react with the Highlight When Clicked action until they contain a script making them into buttons. So do not be alarmed if you try it and they don't work right away.*

6. All the other finished buttons on the map become highlighted when they are clicked. To make our new buttons react in the same manner, select them one at a time in the Cast and click on the Bitmap tab in the Property Inspector. Next, check the Highlight When Clicked option.

7. Save your movie and keep it open for the next exercise.

## Interactive Buttons

A few button shapes are provided by Director and can be found in the Tool palette. Additionally, any graphic Cast Member can be assigned a script to make it perform like a button.

### Creating Buttons with the Tool Palette

Buttons can be created right from the Tool palette using any of the Button options provided. By selecting the Button option and dragging it onto the Stage, you will create a smooth-cornered rectangular button. You will have the opportunity to name the button and specify its width. The button's height is determined by the point size of the text within the button.

To change the background color of the rectangular button, double-click on the button on the Stage and choose a background color from the Tool palette.

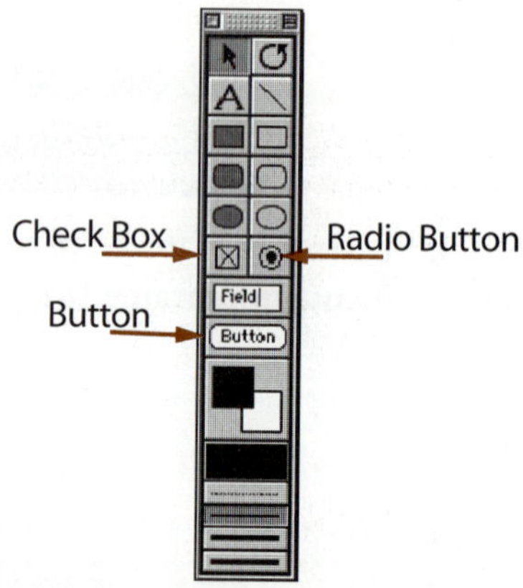


For use in forms and charts, Director also provides ready-made Check boxes and Radio buttons. For Radio buttons, there is even a prescripted behavior listed in the Control section of the Library palette that will allow you to select only one Radio button from a group at any one time. So, for instance, if you have a payment form and you want a person to have to check whether they are paying by Visa, Mastercard, Discover Card, or check, this script will allow them to choose only one method. This is a way of controlling a user's reaction to a question. You will learn more about how to apply and work with Behaviors in Chapter 9.

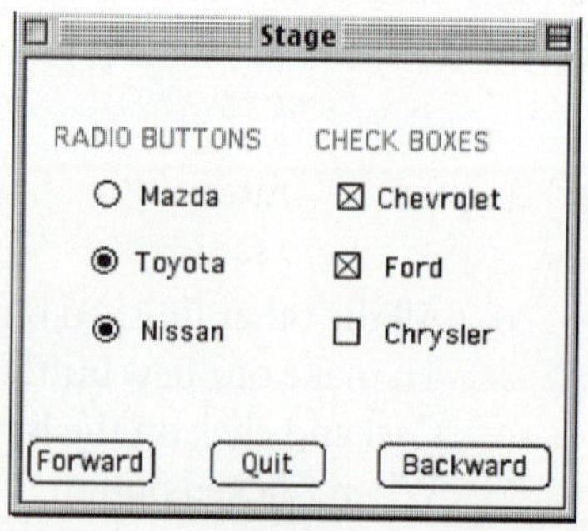


Scripts may be added to buttons by clicking the Cast Member Script button in the Cast and inserting the instructions between the *on mouseUp* and *end mouseUp* handlers.

## Turning Cast Members into Buttons

A Cast Member can be assigned a script to make it perform like a button. This can be done by highlighting the appropriate Cast Member and clicking on the Script button in the upper-right corner of the Cast. Once the Lingo script necessary to direct the button is entered, the Cast Member will have a miniature icon of the Lingo script visible on the left side of the Cast slot.

Cast Member #1
Has a Script As
Shown By This Icon

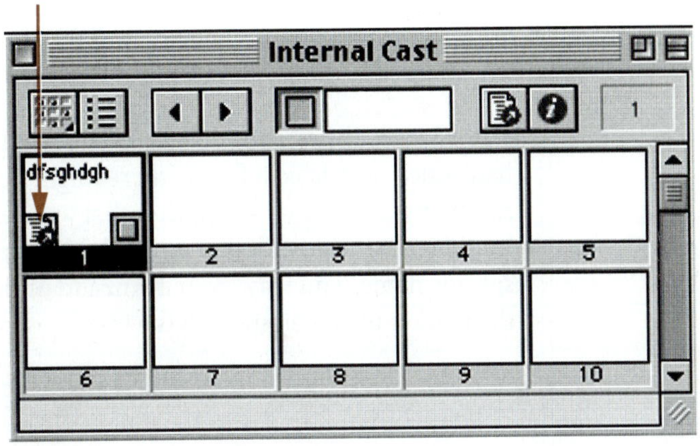

### *Making the Menu Buttons Work*

1. With the same file open, scroll along the Score to frame 500 where the "Waldorf Astoria" Sprites begin. Go to the Cast, highlight the Wald Button and open its Lingo Script window by clicking on the Script button in the upper-right corner of the Cast. Type *go to frame 500.* Don't move the cursor. When you are done, close the box. Now play your movie (click Play on the Control Panel) and try your button. If it works — it should jump to Frame 500 when clicked — move on; if it doesn't, retrace your steps and try it again.
2. Locate the "Rockefeller Center" Sprites in your Score. These begin at frame 220. Go to the Cast and highlight the Rock Button. Open the script and type *go to frame 220.* Now close the script.
3. The last button is for the "Daily News Building" Sprites, which begin on frame 752. Using the same procedure, open the script, type *go to frame 752,* and then close the script.
4. Save your changes. Play the movie and click on your new buttons. Keep this movie open for the next exercise.

## Markers

Markers provide another way of traveling throughout a Score. It is easy enough to locate a particular frame, but as your movies become more complex, you'll find it hard to keep track of exactly what is happening where. This is why Director provides an unlimited supply of markers. Using them is an excellent way of both labeling points of interest and navigating within your Score. Markers work much like tabs in a word processing or page-layout program. There's an area across the top of your Score where you can create as many markers as necessary.

### Lingo and Markers

You can edit, relocate, and delete markers at any time. You can also add or delete frames before or after a marker, and the marker will move along with the frame it is attached to.

In the previous exercise you learned how to use a script to go to a particular frame. If you had added or deleted a frame, there might be some confusion about the correct frame number you desire — the Sprites that were once in frame 135 may now be in frame 134, leading to possible scripting errors. Instead, place a marker at frame 135 and give it a specific name. This way, even if you add or delete a frame, your script still works because the marker moves along with the frame.

Marker names must be placed within quotes in a script, as they are recognized by Lingo as proper names.

### Creating Markers

There is a white strip above the Special Channels section of the Score. To create a marker, you click in this strip directly above the frame you want to mark. A triangle and a cursor appear, allowing you to name the marker. You can then move this marker by sliding the triangle to the left or right. You can delete the marker by dragging the triangle straight down toward the Visual channels.

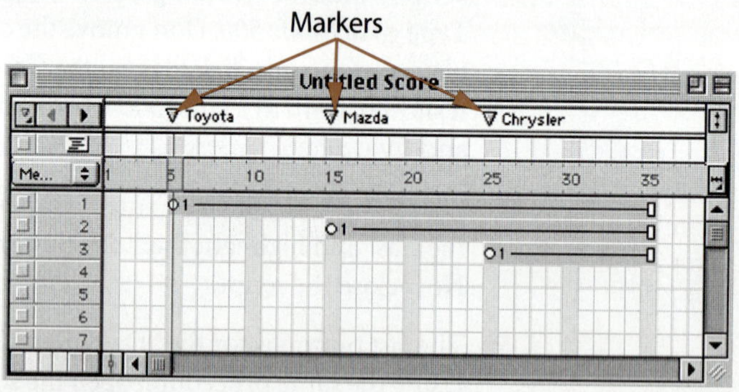


### Navigating to Markers

Customized markers are good for clarity and Lingo scripting, but they also serve another purpose — navigation. Using the Markers window, you can automatically move to any marked frame. Creating markers as you work is similar to creating a roadmap throughout your project. In the Markers window, which is accessed from the Window menu, you can highlight the marker you wish to jump to, and that frame will show up on the Stage.

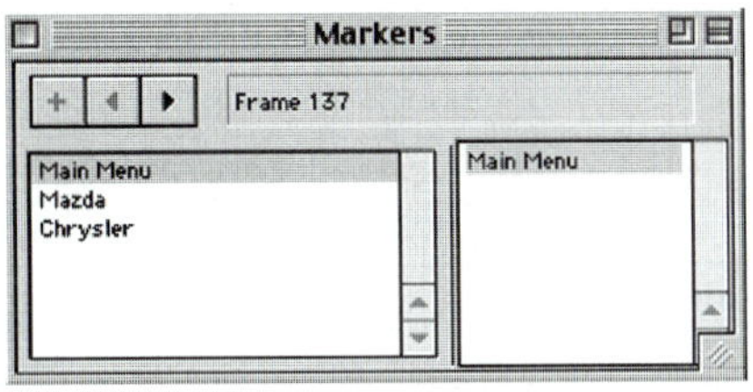


You can also navigate to various markers in your Score by using the Marker Menu button, the one farthest to the left on the Marker bar. Highlight the marker you wish to go to and it will automatically jump the Score to that point.

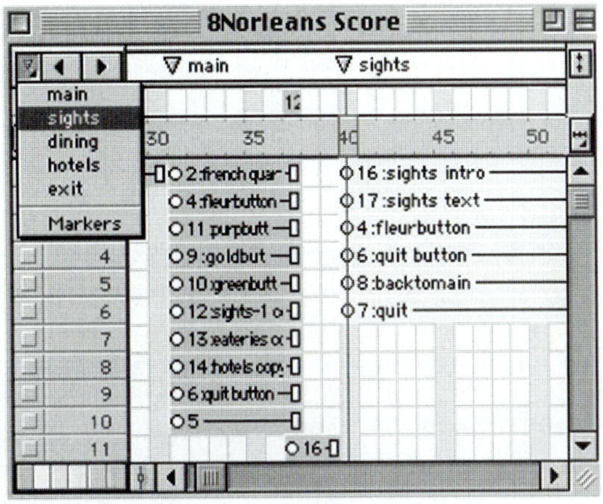


## *Adding Markers and Navigating*

1. With **Art.DIR** still open, you are going to add a couple of markers to the Score.
2. Locate frame 808 on the Score and click the Marker bar. Name this new marker "History".
3. Now move to frame 836 and create a new marker called "Tour Info". These two markers identify where the information will begin.

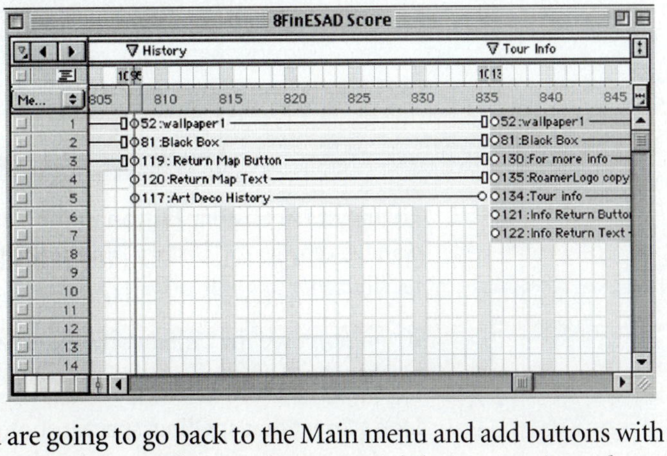


Now you are going to go back to the Main menu and add buttons with scripts that will take you to these markers so that you won't have to navigate through the frames.

4. Move your Playback Head back to the Main menu (frame 200). Go to your Cast and locate the History Button. Place the button on the Stage to the left of "The History of Art Deco." Locate the Tour Button and place it on the Stage next to "Tour Information." Locate the Quit Button and place it on the stage to the left of "Quit."

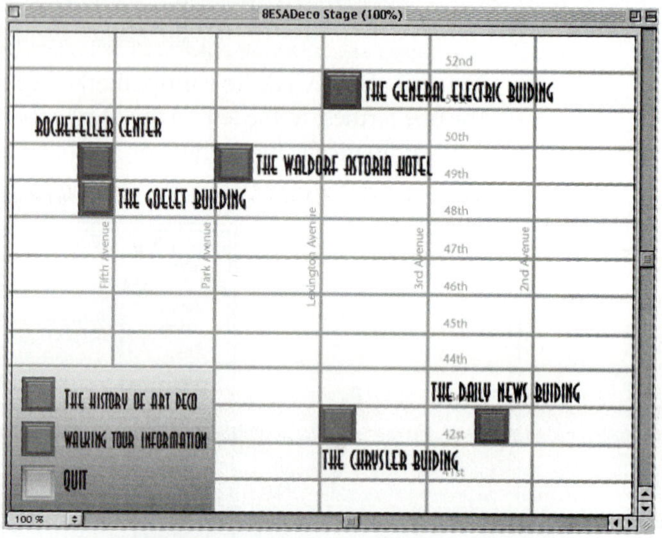


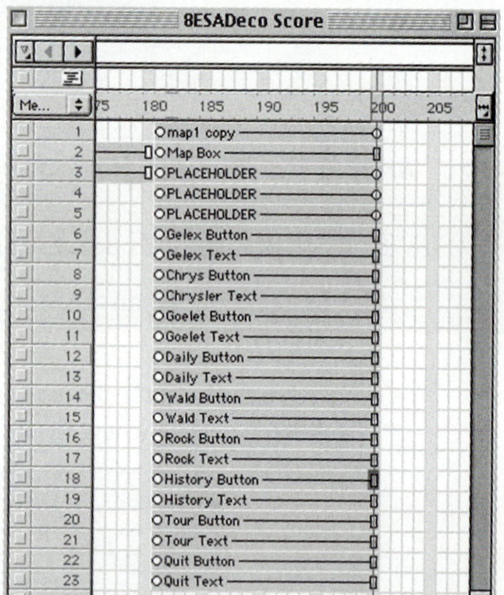

*If **on mouseUp** is not showing in the Script window for step 5, click on the "L" button and look under mo-mov for mouseUp. The command will automatically be inserted into the window when you choose it.*

5. Highlight the History Button in the Cast and click the Script button. This time you want to type *go to "History"* in the script. The Tour button needs a script that says *go to "Tour Info"*.

   If you don't see the *on mouseUp* handler in the Script window, refer to the hint in the sidebar.

   Don't forget that spelling, spaces, quotes and case are all items that must be accurate in a Lingo script for it to work. Work carefully.

6. The Quit button needs a script that says *quit.*

7. Select Window>Markers to display the Marker palette. Click on the different markers you created and watch your Score and Stage. The Playback Head automatically jumps to each position. As you can see, markers are like customized shortcuts.

8. Rewind and play your movie. It should look and act just like the final version (FinESAD.DIR) provided in the Finished Exercises folder.

## ***Complete Project C: Digital Portfolio***

## Notes:

# CHAPTER 6

# ADDING SOUND AND VIDEO

## CHAPTER OBJECTIVE:

To learn about capturing and importing sound and video for use in Director projects. To gain an understanding of how to place sounds and video clips in the Score and make them play in your Director project. In Chapter 6, you will:

- Learn about capturing sounds.
- Learn about accepted sound file formats and how to import sound files.
- Examine sound properties in the Property Inspector.
- Learn about Sound channels.
- Practice importing and playing sounds.
- Learn about capturing video.
- Learn about accepted video file formats and how to import video files.
- Explore the QuickTime palette.
- View video properties in the Property Inspector.
- Learn where to place a video clip in the Score and how to play it.
- Learn about MIAW (Movie in a Window).
- Gain an understanding of copyright issues.

## PROJECTS TO BE COMPLETED:

- Magic Carpet Tours (Project A)
- Redi-Base (Project B)
- Digital Portfolio (Project C)
- Emily's Photo Album (Project D)
- ABC's (Project E)

# Adding Sound and Video

Until now we have been working only with graphics, but to make Director movies a bit more professional, sound and video can be added. These elements will give your projects depth and complexity and will also help create certain moods for your viewers.

One must be careful when matching sounds to animations, graphics, and videos. For only when this match is appropriate will you have created something that is more than the sum of its parts, something so great that a user gets pulled into it inexplicably and cannot let go.

*If you want to try capturing sounds using Director, proceed through the following steps: Start playing your music well before the place you want to start recording. About 20 seconds before you want to start recording, go into Director and select Insert>Media Elements>Sound. When the music hits the spot you were looking for, click Record. When you are finished, click Stop. It will automatically put your sound clip in the Cast. Catching the right spot in your music may take a few tries. To play the sound clip in your Director movie, drag a copy of it from the Cast to one of the Sound channels in the Special Channel section of the Score. This will be discussed in more detail in the Sound channels section of this chapter.*

## Sound

CD-quality sounds can be imported into Director from a variety of external software applications, some of which are mentioned below. Director itself also can capture sounds, but only on the Macintosh platform, and although these sounds won't be digital quality, they are typically fine for the average user.

When capturing audio in general, keep sound clips short so that they don't occupy too much memory and make your movie slow down to a crawl. There are a variety of compression methods that may be used, but as with graphic-compression methods, there's always a trade-off when you use them. Even though a compressed file will be smaller, this reduction might be achieved at the expense of either sound quality or access speed.

A technology that has proven to be good at maintaining quality when compressing sounds is Shockwave Audio, also put out by Macromedia. This technology supports streaming audio, meaning that a sound will start playing as soon as the first part of it has been loaded and that the rest of the sound will continue to be loaded as the sound is played. The sound plays smoothly yet doesn't clog up your computer's memory. Shockwave files can be created in most sound applications, such as those bundled in with Director 8.0 Shockwave Studio (Sound Forge XP, Windows; Peak LE, Macintosh).

### Recording Sound

Director can record sounds from any medium an Apple computer can play, such as CDs and DVDs. Simply cue up your CD or DVD using whatever program you would normally use on your machine to play them.

If you are running Windows 98 or NT, you must use a sound software application to capture sounds, as Director doesn't support audio for Windows 98/NT. Director's Multimedia Studio comes with fairly capable audio programs: Peak LE (light edition) for Macintosh and Sound Forge XP (streamlined version) for Windows. Another popular sound-capture application is Adobe Premiere, which can capture audio or video and be used to edit them.

The exercises in this book will start from the point of importing sounds, not capturing them, since the procedure for capturing differs depending on the software and platform you are using.

## Importing Sounds

Sounds can be linked or embedded. When sounds are linked, whether by default or on purpose, don't forget to keep a copy of the sound in the same folder as your project. It is best to embed only small sound files, such as beeps or chirps, to keep your movie file small. Director will link large files automatically, but if the program has embedded a file that you believe is too large for embedding, just delete it out of your Cast and import it again. This time, however, choose the Link to External File option from the Media drop-down menu.

Director can import various types of sound files:

- AIFF files
- WAV files
- Sun AU files
- Shockwave Audio files
- MP3 files
- IMA files, compressed
- System 7 sounds (Macintosh only)

Multimedia sound commonly offers two bit-depth modes: 8 bit or 16 bit. At 8 bits a sound sample has 256 possible values; at 16 bits the values have 65,536 possible steps. Although the 16-bit option is twice the size, it is well worth the space. Using 16 bit will provide the best results for the least amount of trouble — especially over the Internet. Be certain to set the sampling rate between 44.1KHz and 11.025KHz for adequate playback quality.

### Sound channels

There are two Sound channels in Director. You can have any two sounds playing at the same time; for instance, you might have mellow background music playing while birds chirp.

These Sound channels are special channels located above the numbered frames in the Special Channels section of the Score. They are identified by an icon displaying a loudspeaker, shown below.

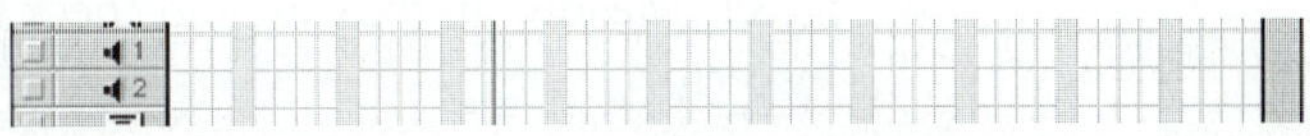

Placing sounds in the Sound channels is no different than creating any other Sprite. The sound is dragged down from the Cast to one of the channels. The Sprite may be extended across as many frames as are necessary to play the full sound.

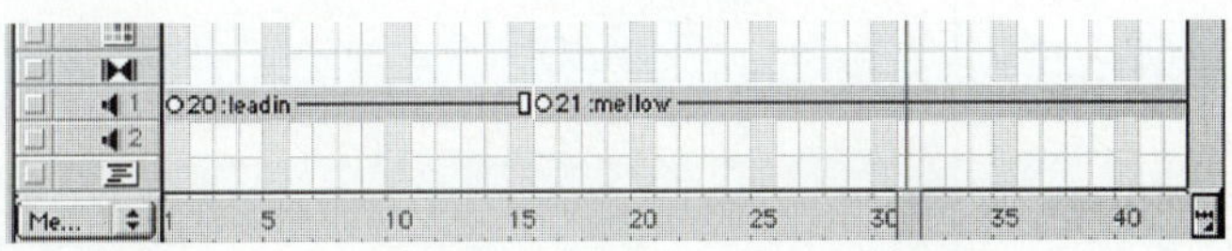

## Sound Properties

To preview sounds before placing them in a Score, access their sound properties through the Property Inspector. The Sound Cast Member Properties tab contains a Play button, which causes the sound to play, and a Loop check box. If this box is checked, the sound will play repeatedly as long as the Playback Head remains on the Sprite in the Score.

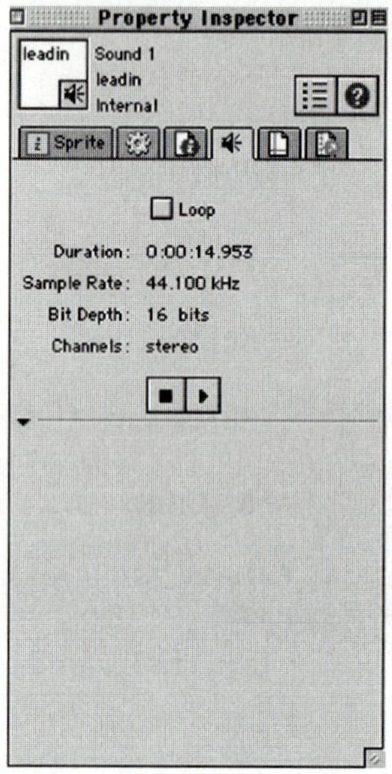

### *Importing and playing sounds*

Be sure to turn your speakers on before you begin.

1. If you wish to view the finished version of this movie, select the **FinSnds.DIR** file from the **Finished Exercises** folder. To begin the exercise, open the **Sounds.DIR** file from your **SF-Director** folder.
2. Select File>Save As and save the movie as "Newsound.DIR" in your **Work In Progress** Folder.
3. Select File>Import and import the sounds **Mellow.AIFF** and **Leadin.AIFF.**
4. Select "Mellow" in the Cast and check the Loop box on the Sound tab of the Property Inspector.
5. Open the Score and place "Leadin" in Sound channel 1, frames 1-15.
6. Double-click on the Tempo channel in frame 15 and set the Wait option to 4 seconds. Click OK.

7. Place "Mellow" in Sound channel 1, frame 16. To extend the Sprite out to frame 150, type "150" in the box in the Property Inspector that has the image of the tail end of a Sprite next to it and then press Enter.

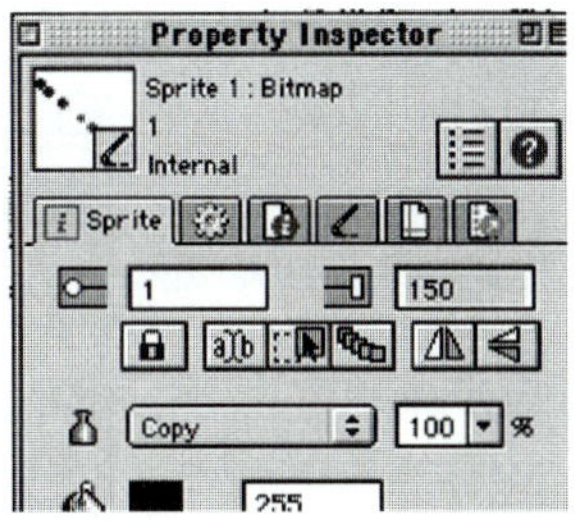


8. Open the Control Panel and set the frame rate to 5 fps if it isn't already set at that rate. The Loop option should be turned off.

9. Rewind and play the movie using the Control Panel.

Your music may sound a bit choppy the first time you play it because it is not streaming. Director is trying to quickly put the whole sound file in RAM, but it sometimes can't keep up, causing the music to skip. Playing the music a second time should clear things up because the sound file will already have been loaded into RAM. Run your movie from your hard drive, not a removable disk. The transfer rate on most removable media will slow down the playback.

## Video

There are several programs that allow you to capture and edit video. The most popular cross-platform one available as of this book's publishing is Adobe Premiere.

For the Macintosh platform, there is a low-cost solution available consisting of a combination of two Apple products: Apple VideoPlayer for capturing video and MoviePlayer for editing and converting video.

### Importing Video

Video is imported the same way as sound. Because they are usually large, digital video files are automatically imported as linked Cast Members. Since such files will be linked, you should always place the file in the same folder as your Director movie before importing to save the time and trouble of having to update links later.

Director supports QuickTime or AVI digital video formats. QuickTime must be installed on any computer playing or creating a movie containing QuickTime video. On the Macintosh platform, Director automatically converts any AVI video to QuickTime as it is being played.

## Exchanging Linked Video Files

What if you import a video file and find out later that it's not the one you wanted? Director has provided a handy little button in the Property Inspector for replacing the file with the correct one. The button is the one shown in the following graphic with the three dots on it.

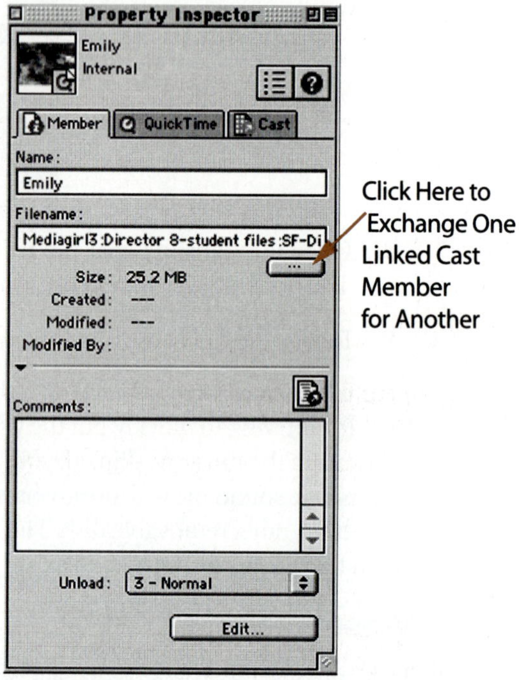


When clicked, the button will bring up a dialog box that allows you to browse for and select the correct video, as shown below.

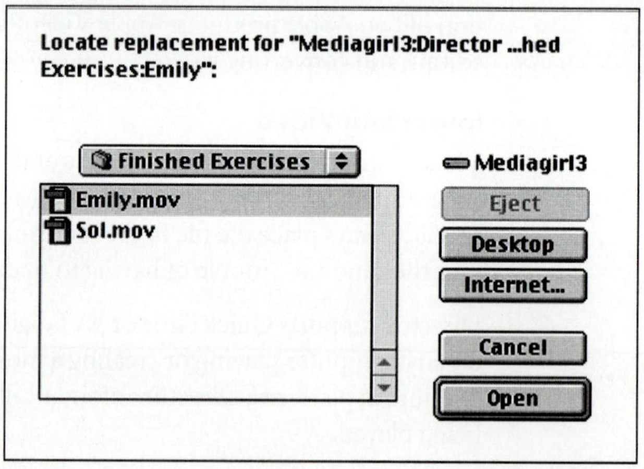

## QuickTime Window

When a video Cast Member is double-clicked, you will see a QuickTime window similar to the one in the following image pop up. You can preview the movie by clicking on the Play button, in the bottom-left corner.

## Video Properties

Video properties can be found in the Property Inspector under the QuickTime tab. This area will allow you to choose whether to allow scaling or cropping of the video as well as whether to show the video, play its sound, stream it, loop it, preload it, or show the Controller, which features Play and Rewind buttons.

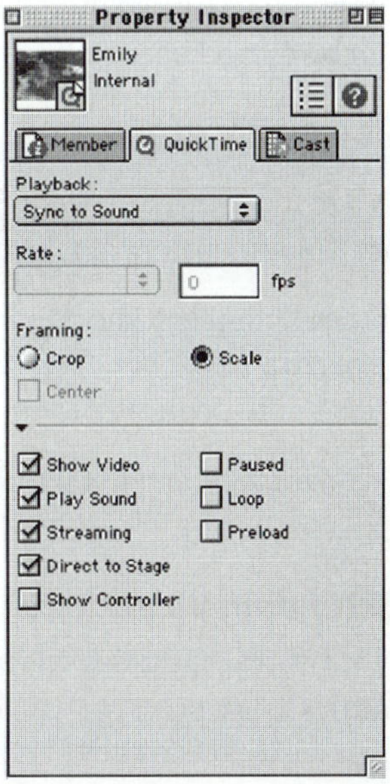

### Placing Video in the Score

Unlike sound, video does not have its own special channel. Video is considered a visual item and, therefore, is placed in a Visual channel like any other graphic.

There is one important fact about video that it is necessary to understand before designing your movie: Unless you turn off the Direct To Stage option on the QuickTime tab of the Property Inspector for each video, your videos will act like separate layers that float above everything else on the Stage, and you will not be able to put any graphics on top of them.

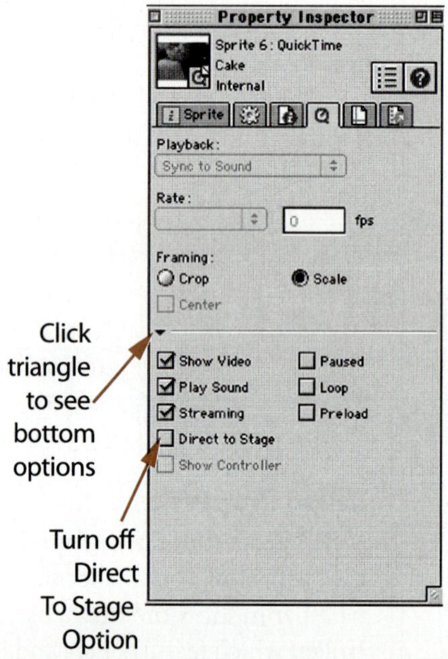


After you've turned off the Direct To Stage, video will behave like any other graphic sand can be moved back or brought forward by changing its location in the channels.

## Playing Video

When it comes to playing video, there are several issues to consider. The size of the video clip (in dimension), the size of the file, and the speed of the viewer's machine are just a few.

As a rule, smaller, shorter video clips are better. Be selective and tell your story with the fewest frames. If you have several small clips that you want to use, combine them together with a video-editing program or place them one after the other to play in sequence.

We are now going to take a look at a few different ways to play and control a video clip in Director.

### Extending Video Across Many Frames

One way to play a video is by placing the video in the Score and extending it across as many frames as are necessary to play your clip in its entirety. This method is *not* recommended for a clip that is more than two or three seconds long. A two- or three-second clip at 30 fps will occupy 60 to 90 frames. A one-minute clip will occupy 1,800 frames — far too many to work with.

### Playing Video Using Tempo Channel

A video can take up only one frame and still play just fine. There are two ways to do this. The first involves using a Tempo channel. First, place a video in the Score and make it cover only one frame. Double-click on the Tempo channel and click on the Wait for Cue Point radio button. From the Channel drop-down menu, choose the name of your movie, and from the Cue Point drop-down menu, choose End.

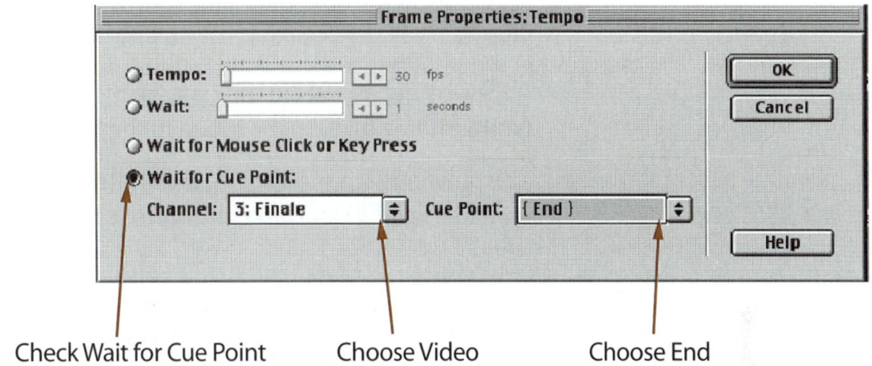


Director will play the video clip until it ends and then continue moving through the rest of the frames in your movie.

### Playing Video Using Lingo

The second way to play video across one frame requires a *go to the frame* Frame script. Drag a copy of the video into a single frame of the Score and put the Frame script in the Script channel of the same frame. This will tell Director to play the frame over and over again.

However, you will need to add buttons to this frame so that your viewers can move on to the next part of your presentation once the video clip has finished playing; otherwise, Director would play this frame indefinitely.

### Playing Video Using Buttons

There are times when it is necessary to create buttons to start and stop a video rather than allowing the Playback Head to take control.

You might need buttons on a menu that contain a *go to frame* script to take you to the exact frame that starts the video.

You may also want to have Play and Stop buttons on the frames that contain the video clip. This allows the viewer to stop it at will during its playback. The script for a Play button is *continue*. The script for a Stop button is *pause*.

### *Importing and Playing Video*

1. To preview a finished version of this movie, open the **FinAmthe.DIR** file located in the **Finished Exercises** folder. To begin this exercise, open the **Amtheat.DIR** file in the **SF-Director** folder.

2. Select File>Save As and save the movie as "Theatre.DIR" in your **Work in Progress** folder.

3. If they are not already in the Cast, import the QuickTime video clips **Sol.MOV** and **Emily.MOV,** which can be found in the **SF-Director** folder.

4. This amateur film project is half completed. All the pieces are here, but the video clips need to be placed and all of the buttons need to have scripts attached in order to work.

   The film has a menu called "Coming Attractions," located in channel 6, frames 57-82. The goal is to allow your viewers to pick their film of choice. Double-click on the Script channel of frame 82 and type *pause*. Then close the Script window.

5. Place the Sol movie in channel 9, frame 85. In this movie you will play the video in one frame using the *go to the frame* Frame script. In the Script channel of frame 85, type *go to the frame*. Move the Playback Head to frame 85 and play the movie to make sure that it works.

6. The Emily video clip should be placed in channel 9, frames 83-84. To allow this clip to play in its entirety, we will use the Tempo channel. In the Tempo channel of frame 84, choose the Wait for Mouse Click or Key Press option and then close the window. This will hold the movie on the current frame (allowing Emily to continue to play) until the Stage is clicked.

7. Now let's add some functionality to the buttons. Drag your Playback Head back to the Coming Attractions screen. You will see two buttons, one for the Little Girl Easter (Emily) and one for the Sol's Life (Sol) video clips. We want the Playback Head to go to the frame where the Emily video starts (frame 83) when we click the Little Girl Easter button. Go to the Cast and highlight the Little Girl Easter button. Click on the Script button in the upper-right corner of the Cast. Type *go to frame 83* and then close the window.

8. Now add a *go to frame* script to the Sol's Life button. The Sol video clip starts in frame 85.

9. Drag your Playback Head to frame 83. You will see two buttons at the bottom of the screen, Attractions and The End. These two buttons need scripts to make them work. The Attractions button needs to take you back to where the Coming Attractions screen pauses, frame 82. The Cast Member script for the Attractions button should read *go to frame 82.*

10. The last button is the End button. Drag your Playback Head past the videos and you will see that the rest of the Sprites in the Score show the screen pulling up and the curtains closing. The button should go to the beginning of this section, frame 87. The Cast Member script for the End button should read *go to frame 87.*

11. Set the tempo in the Control Panel to 15.
12. Rewind and play your movie. Close the movie and quit the application when you're finished.

## Movie in a Window (MIAW)

If you want to have more than one video clip playing at a time, some Lingo scripting is required. In Director you have the option of using a Movie in a Window. With a MIAW, one video clip remains open at all times while others are being opened and closed. MIAWs are typically used as floating Tool palettes or custom dialog boxes that can be used for almost anything. Each window can be completely interactive, which means you can click buttons in the window and the movie will respond.

Using MIAWs is tricky because the scripting can sometimes interfere with your movie scripting, causing a big mess. Some scripts will work only for the movie the Lingo script resides in, but others will command any movie currently open. Because of the above-mentioned reasons, it is important to recognize which script elements movies share and which they do not when creating MIAWs. This is all done with the use of extensive and advanced Lingo commands. The commands, combined with the fact that MIAWs can be very temperamental and that MIAWs tend not to be widely used in everyday productions, was a deciding factor in determining that the creation and use of MIAWs will not be addressed this book. Refer to the Macromedia Director 8.0 manual that came with your software for further information if you wish to attempt to create one.

## Copyright Laws

Copyright laws concerning digital files are very complex. With the advent of the Internet and the ability to access images and copy with a click of the mouse, there are clearly a lot of gray areas still being defined.

The only way to be completely safe from any possible repercussions is to create all the sound and video, as well as the graphics, you want to use in your movies yourself. If that is not possible because of lack of expertise or lack of materials and equipment, there are other options available.

For images, there are many companies that sell low- and high-resolution stock images. These images can be purchased in bulk on CD-ROM or one at a time over the Internet. Many of the images used in this book were purchased from PhotoDisc, a stock-photography company in Seattle, WA.

Stock music is also available. The music used in many of the exercises in this book was purchased from The Music Bakery, a provider of royalty-free music and sounds located in Dallas, TX.

## Notes:

# CHAPTER 7

# PAINT TOOLS AND VECTOR-BASED GRAPHICS

## CHAPTER OBJECTIVE:

To learn about additional tools in the Paint window and how to use them.
To practice using Onion Skinning within the Paint window.
To use the Vector Shape window's tools. In Chapter 7, you will:

- Learn about rulers.
- Use the Registration Point tool.
- Learn about and practice using a few advanced paint tools.
- Learn about and practice using Onion Skinning.
- Explore the tools in the Vector Shape window.
- Practice using the Pen tool.
- Practice using other tools in the Vector Shape window.

## PROJECTS TO BE COMPLETED:

- Magic Carpet Tours (Project A)
- Redi-Base (Project B)
- Digital Portfolio (Project C)
- **Emily's Photo Album (Project D)**
- ABC's (Project E)

# Paint Tools and Vector-Based Graphics

Since Macromedia introduced the Vector Shape window in Director 7, two types of graphics have been available to work with: vector and bitmap. The decision of which format to use for which application is a simple one and one that will be familiar to those of you who have worked with other illustration and photo-manipulation programs, such as Illustrator, FreeHand, and Photoshop.

The bitmap format is ideal when working with complex images because it allows you to control your image on a pixel-by-pixel basis. Bitmaps store information about each pixel, making these files occupy more RAM and disk space than vector graphics.

The vector format is best for simple graphics that do not require great detail. Vector graphics can be resized without distortion, and they require less RAM and disk space and therefore will download faster from the Web and be more efficient. In situations where either bitmap or vector graphics will work, vector is the obvious choice if for no other reason than keeping the files small.

## Paint Window Tools

Although Director's Paint window does not have the number of tools that high-end graphics applications like Corel Painter and Adobe Photoshop do, it does offer some powerful ones. Some of its tools allow you to align and measure graphics, and others allow you to modify graphics after they have been created. We will be exploring some of these tools in this chapter.

## Rulers

Rulers are available in the Paint window only and are typically used to give users an idea of the size of the objects they are creating. The ruler can be set to measure in pixels, inches, or centimeters. Typically, when working in multimedia- or Web-design programs, pixels are used. Director automatically defaults to pixels.

The rulers can be viewed in the Paint window by selecting to View>Rulers. The units can be changed by clicking on the intersection point of the rulers.

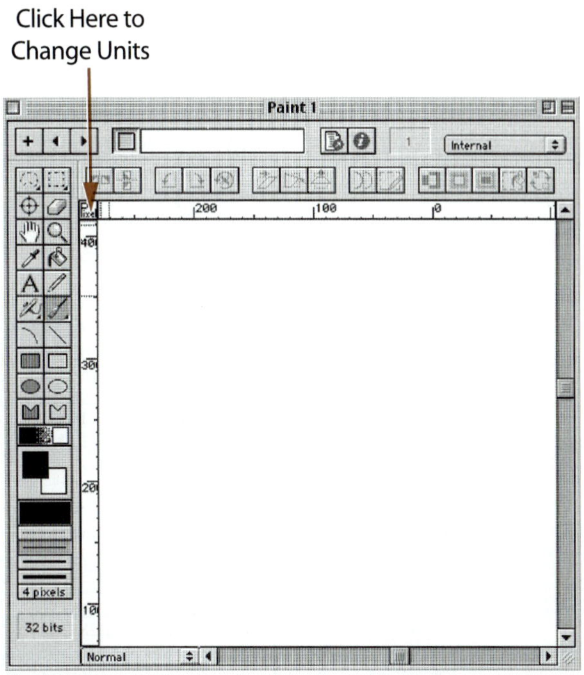


### Registration Point Tool

When you place a Sprite on the Stage by dragging a Cast Member to the Score, the Sprite appears centered on the Stage because Director calculates the center of the Sprite as well as the center of the Stage. In order for Director to do this and other calculations, each Cast Member is given a registration point. In the case of animation, the registration point of your graphic is the one that will touch and follow all the keyframes in a sequence.

With the Registration Point tool, you can set or change the registration point of your graphic to any point within it you desire.

For instance, to create a spinning ball, you should leave the registration point in the center of the ball. However, to make the hands of a clock rotate, you will want to move the registration point to the end of each of the hands so that the hands will rotate from a fixed, central point, creating correctly moving clock hands.

The Registration Point tool is located under the Lasso tool in the Paint window. When it is activated, it displays cross hairs identifying the registration point.

To change the registration point, click where the lines intersect in the Paint window and drag the intersection to a new point. As you can see in the following example, the registration point is exactly in the center of the rectangle.

The Vector Shape window also has a Registration Point tool, and it works the same way.

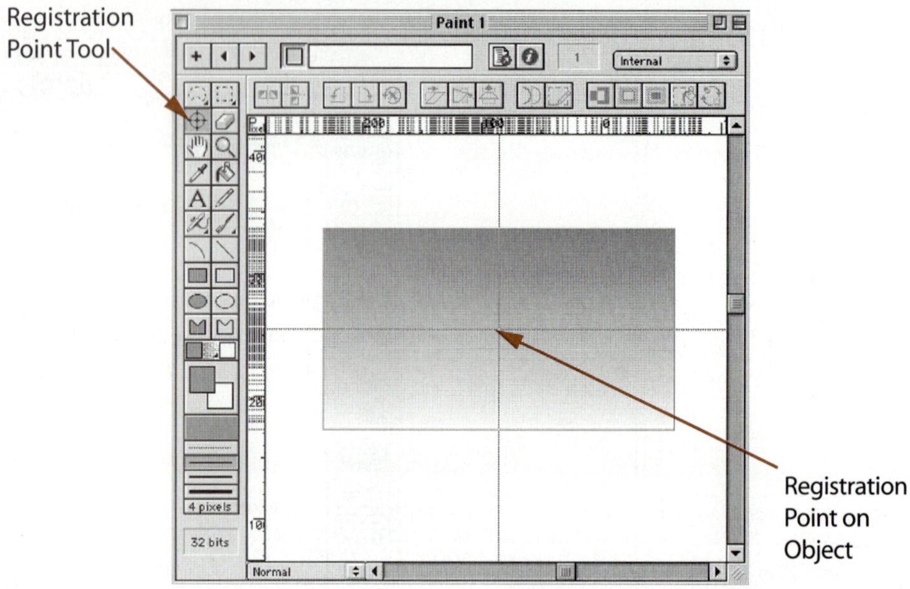


## Rotation Tools

The Paint window offers a set of rotation tools. To access them, or any of the tools across the top of the Paint window, you must first select an entire graphic with the Marquee tool. Be certain that you are using the Marquee tool and not the Lasso tool. The Lasso tool is used to select only a portion of a graphic.

The Rotate Left and Rotate Right tools allow you to rotate your graphic 90 degrees at a time, clockwise or counterclockwise. The Free Rotate tool allows you to rotate from any corner of your graphic.

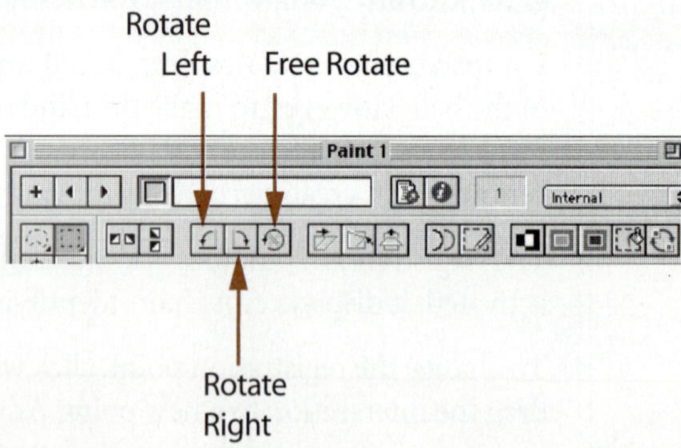


## Skew/Warp/Perspective

The next group of buttons across the top of the Paint window contains the Skew, Warp, and Perspective tools. These tools work the same way as the Free Rotate tool. Click on the tool you wish to use, click on a corner of your graphic, and then beginning dragging. Note that depending on which tool you have selected, the corner points of the selection box surrounding your graphic will change shape.

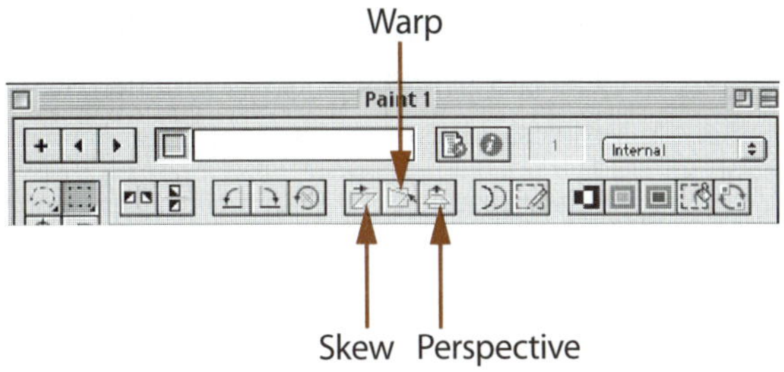


### Smooth/Trace Edges

The Smooth button performs a version of anti-aliasing on the selected items, smoothing the transitions between one color and another. The result is a blur effect. Smoothing can be increasingly applied to your graphic with each click of the button. The Smooth effect works only on 32-bit images. To increase bit depth, go to Modify>Transform Bitmap and change it to 32.

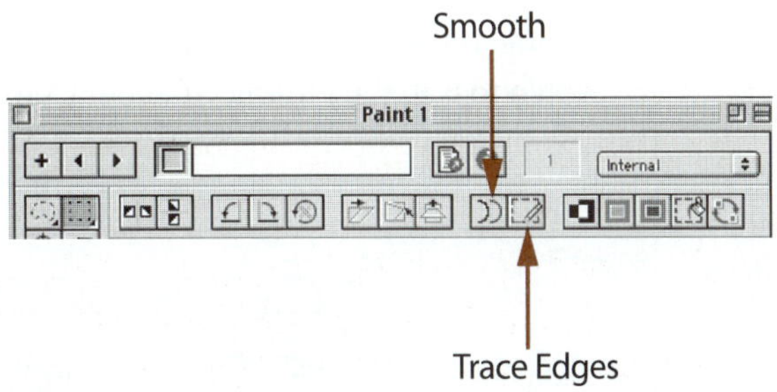


The Trace Edges button produces an outline of the object and deletes the original. If you repeatedly apply the effect, you get consecutive outlines. For example, the four outlines below were created by applying the Trace Edges effect four times.

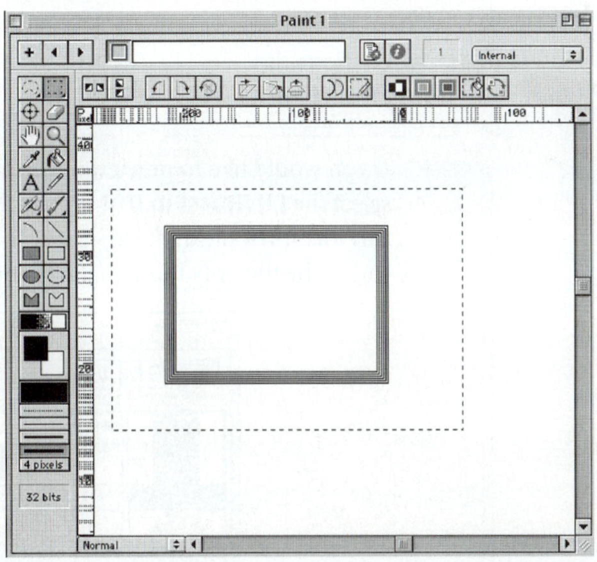

## Invert/Lighten/Darken/Fill/Switch Colors

The last group of buttons contains the Invert, Lighten, Darken, Fill, and Switch Colors effects.

Invert reverses the colors of the graphic you have selected to the color opposite them on the color wheel. Black becomes white, red becomes green, and so on.

Lighten and Darken either increase (darken) or decrease (lighten)the contrast of your image, depending on which tool you choose. The behavior of these effects will vary depending on the bit depth of the graphic you are working with. Both work fine on 32-bit graphics, but they do not work at all on 16-bit graphics.

*When working in 32-bit color, the Switch Colors tool only works on the part of your object that has been selected with the Lasso tool. Both the Lasso and the Marquee tool work for other bit depths.*

Fill will fill the selected area with your current foreground color. This effect works similarly to the Paint Bucket.

Switch Colors substitutes a single color in the selected area with another color. All the other colors will remain unaffected. You must, however, be certain that the current color of the graphic is the color located in your Beginning Gradient Color box and the one you wish to switch to is in the Ending Gradient Color box.

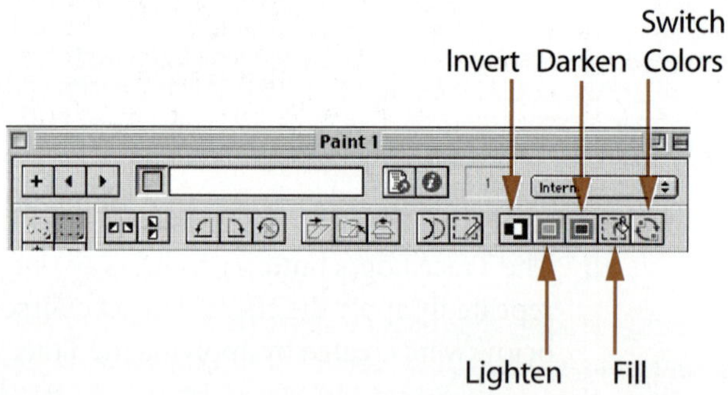

### *Using Paint Tools*

1. If you would like to preview a completed version of this exercise file before you begin, select the **CH7HatsFin.DIR** file from the **Finished Exercises** folder. Open the **Ch7hats.DIR** file in the **SF-Director** folder. When you first open the file, the Cast should be the only thing that has anything placed in it.

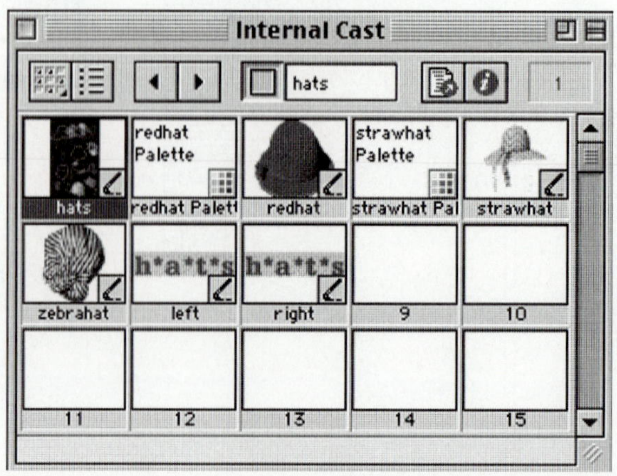

2. Click on the Stage and then go to the Movie tab in the Property Inspector. Once there, change the background color to black.

3. Drag a copy of "Hats" from the Cast to channel 1, frame 1 of the Score. Extend it to frame 30. Because you dragged the Cast Member directly to the Score, it will be centered on the Stage.

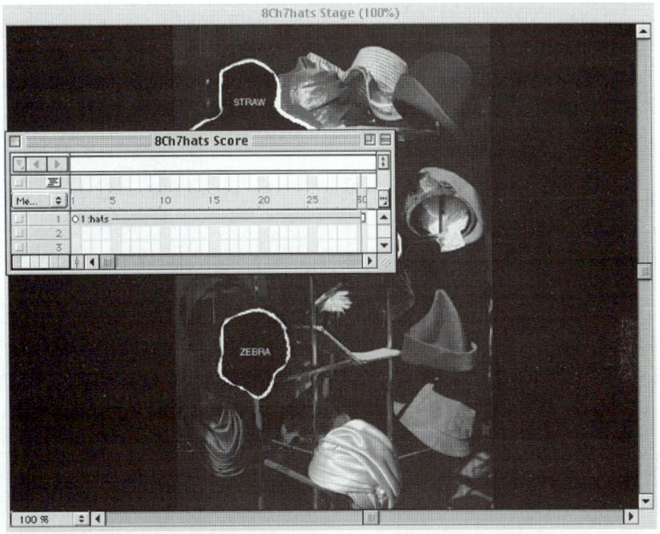


4. Double-click on the Cast Member named "Left" (7) in the Cast so that it opens up in the Paint window. Use the Rectangular Marquee tool (make certain it is set to Shrink) to select the graphic. Click once on the Rotate Left tool so that the graphic rotates to the left 90 degrees.

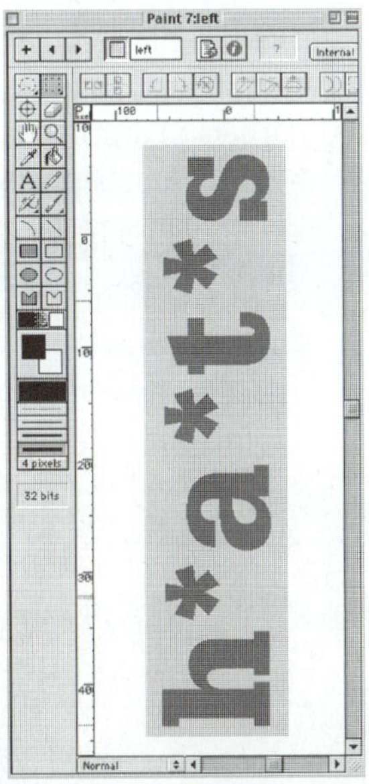

5. Click the Next Cast Member button, (the one with the right arrow on it in the upper-left corner of the Paint window) to display the Cast Member named "Right". Again, select the graphic with the Rectangular Marquee tool. Now click once on the Rotate Right tool to rotate the graphic 90 degrees to the right. Close the Paint window.
6. Place Cast Members "Right" and "Left" on the Stage as shown below. Next, move their Sprites into channels 2 and 3, frames 1-30 of the Score.

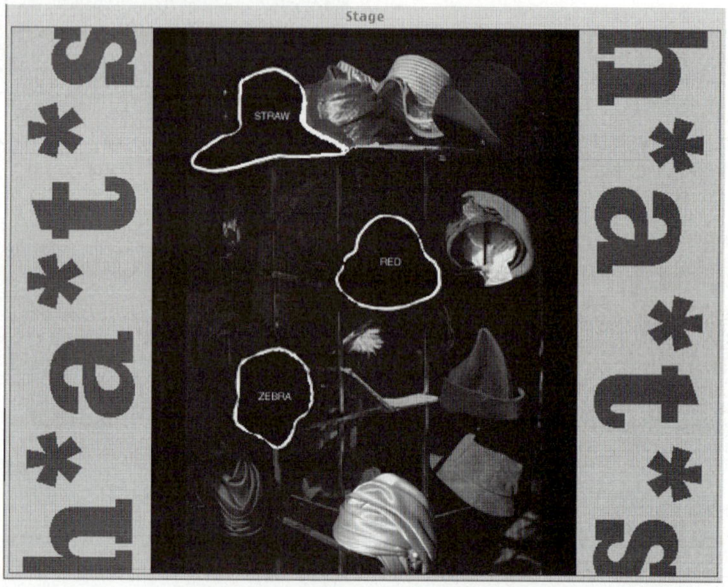

*In step 7, you can't choose Background Transparent or all the white stripes would become transparent.*

7. Drag the "Zebrahat" from the Cast into channel 4, frames 1-30. Highlight the "Zebrahat" Sprite in the Score and select Matte from the Sprite ink effects list.
8. Double-click on the "Redhat" in the Cast to display it in the Paint window. Use the Rectangular Marquee tool to select the graphic. Click the Skew button and drag the corners to distort the hat. Notice that it may or may not change the color and texture — this often happens with indexed color images (256 colors). Be certain that your skewed hat stays larger than the original so that it covers the spot marked "RED" on the hat image. Close the Paint window.
9. Drag the "Redhat" from the Cast and put it in channel 5, frames 1-30 of the Score. Select Matte from the Sprite ink effects list.

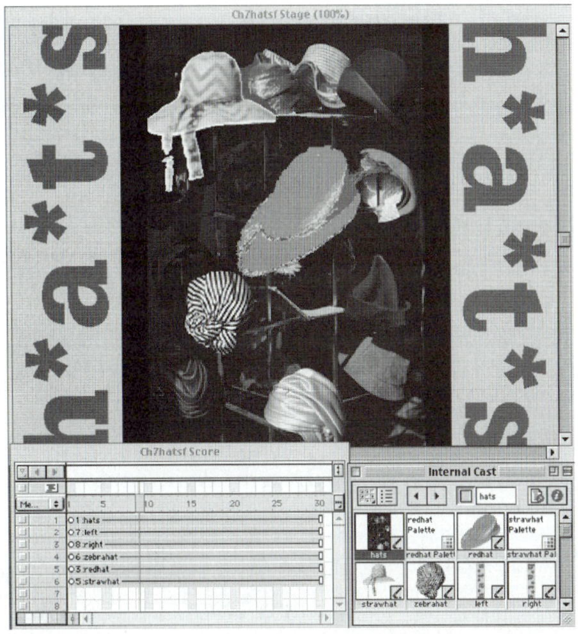

10. Double-click on the "Strawhat" to display it in the Paint window. Select it with the Rectangular Marquee tool. Click the Smooth button once to smooth the whole image. Now close the Paint window and drag the Cast Member into channel 6, frames 1-30 of the Score. Select Matte from the Sprite ink effects list.

11. Double-click on the "Hats" Cast Member to display it in the Paint window. Using the Lasso tool, select the pea green hat (looks like Peter Pan's hat). Click the Darken button a couple of times to darken the hat to a chocolate-brown color. Close the Paint window when finished.

12. This exercise is complete. Quit Director without saving.

## Onion Skinning

Onion Skinning is a term used by animators working with traditional 2-D animation. They would work with see-through paper (tracing paper) to quickly create overlays to reference the last position of a character or a scene while they painted the new one. This allowed them to make certain that the new image was the correct size and in the correct position.

Director has an Onion Skin palette, which can be accessed from the View menu. The Onion Skin palette is available only while you are working in the Paint window. You must have at least one Cast Member for the Onion Skin feature to work.

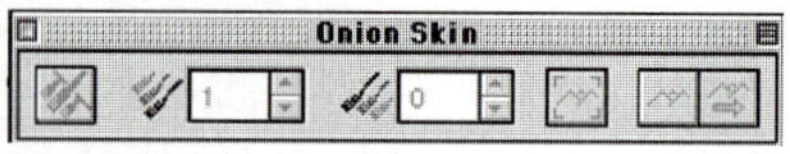


To use the Onion Skin feature:

- Open the Paint window and click the "+" in the top-left corner to go to the next empty Cast slot.
- Create an object in the Paint window and then click the "+" to go to the next empty Cast slot.
- Open the Onion Skin palette by selecting View>Onion Skin.
- Turn on onion skinning by clicking the first button on the left side of the palette.
- Set the number in the first white box in the palette to 1. This means that you can now see one previous Cast Member in your Paint window. Although it is grayed out, and you cannot access it, you will be able to see it and use it as a reference.

You can change the number in the first white box to the number of previous Cast Members you wish to use as references.

You can change the number in the second white box to the number of following Cast Members you wish to use as references.

The remaining three buttons on the Onion Skin palette are Set Background, which is used to select a certain Cast Member for use as a background; Show Background, which is used to reference just the background you selected, no matter where it is in the Cast; and Track Background, which basically pulls the background Cast Member along and always keeps it in the previous Cast window as you make each new Cast Member.

In the following example, we created a square. Next, the circle was created to sit on top of the square using Onion Skin set to 1 previous Cast Member. This way the square was referenced for position. Finally, the rectangle outline was created to encompass both the square and the circle with Onion Skin set to 2 previous Cast Members.

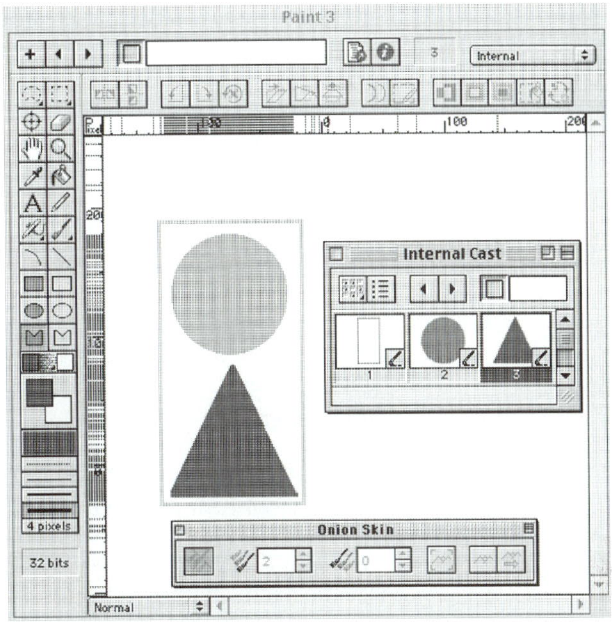



## *Working with the Onion Skin Feature*

1. If you would like to preview a completed version of this exercise file before you begin, select the **CH7OnFin.DIR** file from the **Finished Exercises** folder. Open the **Ch7onion.DIR** file in the **SF-Director** folder.

2. For this exercise, you need to create a new hat to fit the empty hat-shaped space shown in the previous image. Select View>Onion Skin to access the Onion Skin palette.

3. Select Window>Cast to open your Cast. Click on the empty slot of Cast Member 2. Next, select Window>Paint to display the Paint window. This opens the Paint window on Cast Member 2.

4. Click the first button on the left side of the Onion Skin palette to turn the Onion Skin feature on.

5. Set the first white box to 1 and the second to 0. The hat image should have faded slightly in your Paint window. You can now paint anywhere on top of the image without altering it.

6. Using your paint tools, paint on top of the white hat area, using it for reference. Create a hat of your own that will fit in the area. When finished, close the Paint window.

7. Place the hat in channel 7, frames 1-30 of the Score.

8. Select save the movie as "Hatfun.DIR" in your **Work in Progress** folder. Keep this movie open for the next exercise.

## Vector Shape Window

As stated previously Director includes a way to create vector shapes. These shapes consist of a series of points with connecting lines. They are clean, smooth shapes that are best used for simple objects. They can be resized without distortion. Geometric in nature, vector shapes are created and displayed using mathematical formulas. The Vector Shape window may be accessed by selecting Window>Vector Shape.

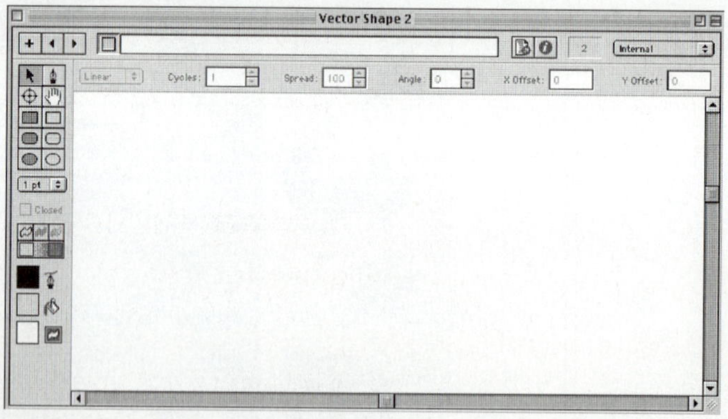


### Vector Shape Tools

The Vector Shape window offers tools similar to those in the Paint window. It has Rectangle, Ellipse, and Rounded Edge Rectangle tools. These shapes have points (and handles that come off the points) on them. By dragging the different points in or out, you can create an infinite number of new shapes.

In the following example, the filled circle has four points. Each point has a set of handles protruding from it that determines the angle and the length of the curve. Rather than using predetermined vector shapes, these points and curves can also be created with the Pen tool.

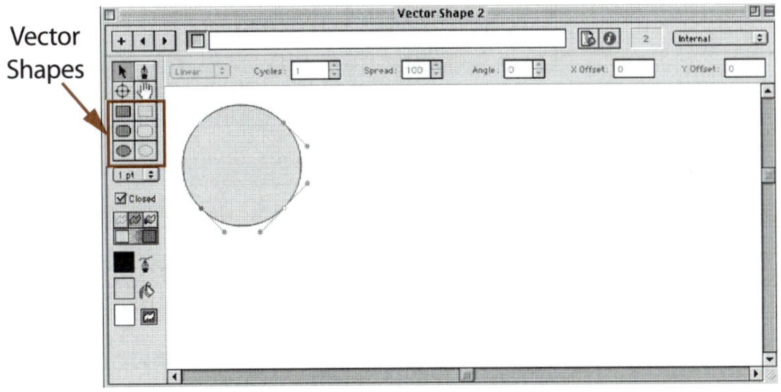


## Pen Tool

The Pen tool in Director is similar to the Pen tool found in Photoshop, Illustrator, PageMaker, QuarkXPress, and FreeHand.

The Pen tool can create lines and curves between points. Once the Pen tool is accessed, you can click in each area that you want to place a point. For curves, click and then drag. When you drag, you create handles that determine how the line will curve through your point. Extending the handles determines the length of the curve; rotating the handles determines the angle of the curve. If you plan to add color to your shape, be sure to close the shape entirely by clicking back on its first point.

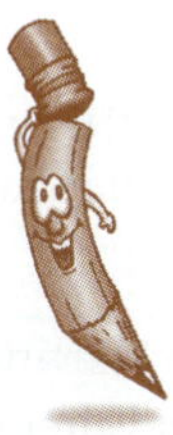

*If there are not any handles extended on any of the pen points in an object, just select the Arrow tool and Option/Alt-drag each pen point twice to extend both sides of the handles for each point.*

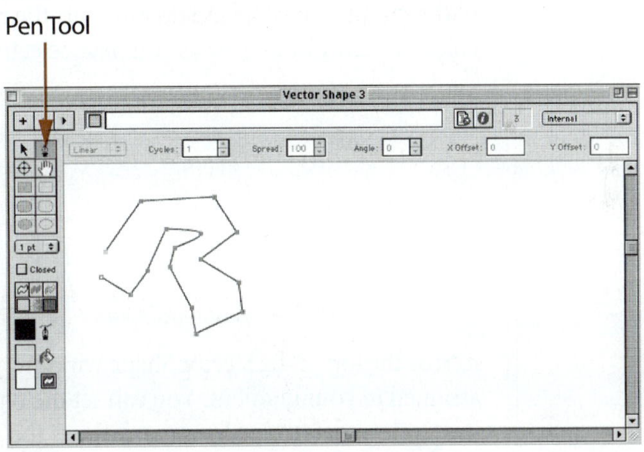


To achieve soft corners in curved shapes, drag each point out to approximately 1/2" to display the handles. If you select the Arrow tool, you can then click on the end of the handles to manipulate them.

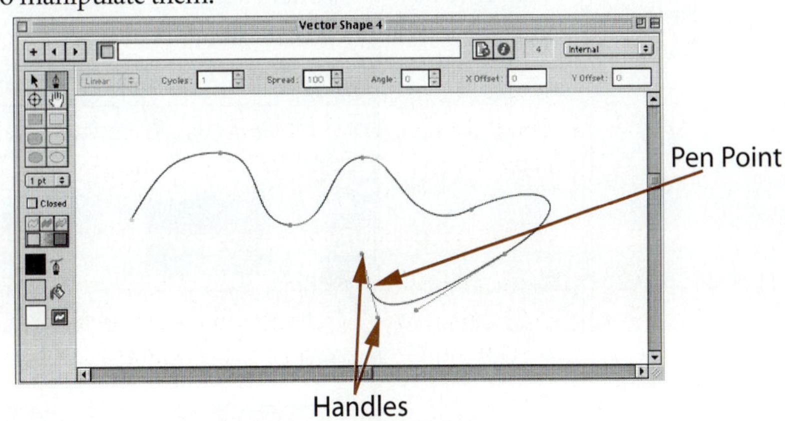

## Stroke/Fill/Background

Once you have created a closed vector shape, you can fill it with solid colors or gradients.

To use Stroke, Fill, and Background, just click on the button of choice and the Color palette appears. Select a color — that's all there is to it.

Stroke changes the color of the outside line of your object. You can change the thickness of this line as well. It is set to default to 1 pt. but can be changed by selecting an alternate line weight from the drop-down menu under the vector shapes.

Fill Color uses the color you choose to fill your shape. Background provides a background color around your shape.

## Gradients

Gradients can be created within vector shapes. The top row of the Gradient box, from left to right, offers you No Fill, Solid, or Gradient. So, to create a gradient, first you must create a shape and then click on the third option, Gradient.

There are two options available for gradient colors. The Foreground sets the starting color of the gradient and the Destination sets the ending color. You can choose and alter the colors at any time as long as you have selected Gradient from the Fill Type options.

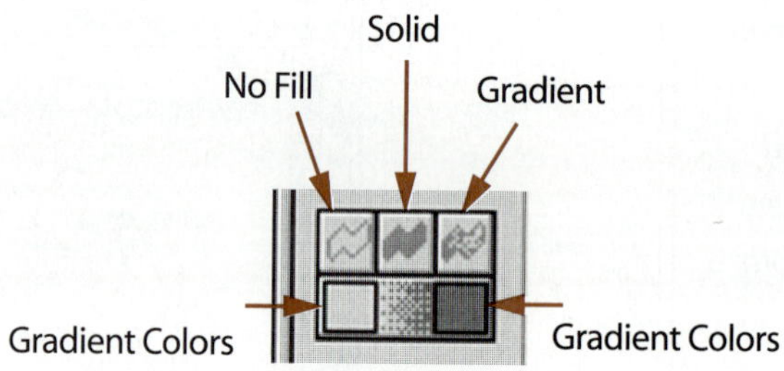


Across the top of the Vector Shape window, there are additional options that can be assigned to your gradient. You can set the type of gradient to Linear or Radial. You can set the Cycle to determine how many times the gradient will repeat inside the object. You can set the Spread to affect how sharp or smooth the transition between colors will be, and you can set the Angle at which the gradient will be based on.

The "X" Offset (horizontal) and "Y" Offset (vertical) offset the gradient within your shape by a specified amount of pixels.

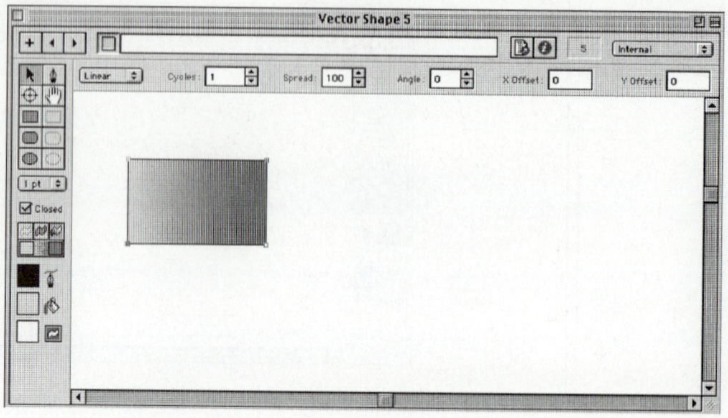

## *Creating Vector Shapes*

1. If it is not already open, open the **Hatfun.DIR** file in your **Work in Progress** folder. Select Window>Cast to display the Cast window. Click on Cast slot 10.
2. Select Window>Vector Shapes to display the Vector Shape window.
3. With the Pen tool, try to create the starlike symbol seen on the Stage between the letters in the word "hats" (see the shape below). Click to place each point. When you get back to the beginning, click on the starting point again to close the shape. Make the shape roughly between 1 and 2" in diameter.

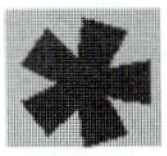

4. Click the button that looks like a lightning bolt in the row above the gradient colors. This is the Solid tool, which allows you to fill your shape with a solid color.
5. Click on the color swatch next to the Paint Can button and choose a color. This is the Fill Color button. The center of the star will be filled with the color you select.
6. Click on the color swatch next to the button above the Paint Can and choose another color, the same color, or white. This is the Stroke color button. The outline of the shape will take on the color you select.
7. Name the shape "Star" in the Text box at the top of the Vector Shape window. Then press Return/Enter.

8. Drag a copy of "Star" down to the Score and place it in channel 8, frames 2-5. Now, place it randomly on the Stage. If it is too big, reduce its size by double-clicking on the Cast Member, which will bring you back into the Vector Shape window, where you can adjust each of the points to make it smaller.

Bring another copy of "Star" down and place it in channel 8, frames 7-10. Now place it randomly on the Stage. Place additional copies of the star randomly on the Stage in channel 8, frames 12-15, 17-20, 22-25, and 27-30. Channel 8 in your Score should now match channel 8 in the image that follows.

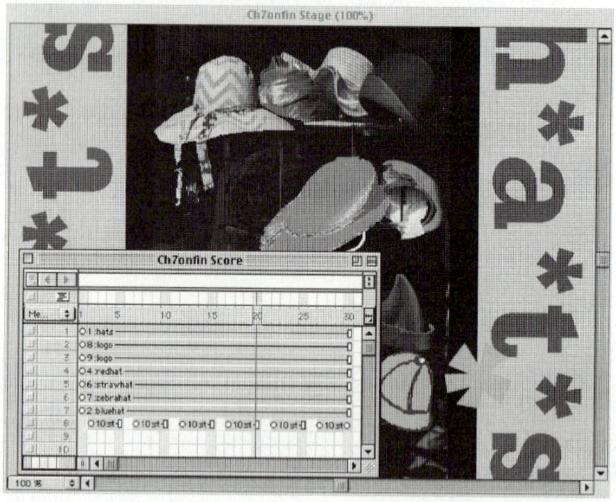


9. Add the Matte Sprite ink effect to all the star Sprites in the Score.
10. Rewind and play your production. If you would like to practice more with the Pen tool, continue on with the remaining steps of this exercise.
11. Open the Vector Shape window again and select the Pen tool.
12. Make a soft-edged shape like a cloud. Drag each point out a bit to get the handles. The length and angle of these handles determines the length and angle of your curve.
13. To adjust your handles, select the Arrow tool and then select and adjust each anchor point and handle individually.
14. Fill your image using the Fill Color tool.

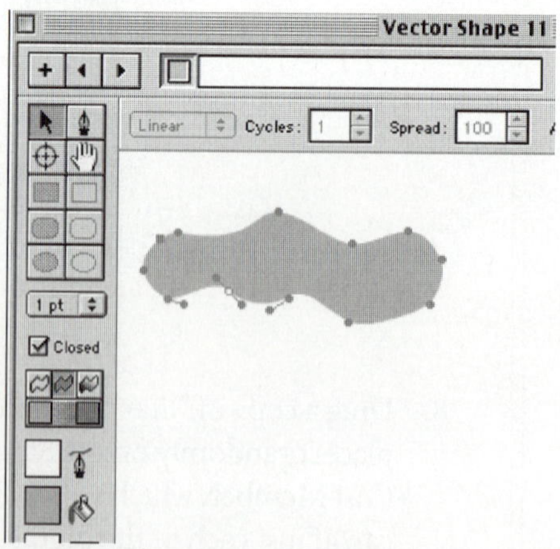


15. Quit the application without saving when finished.

**_Complete Project D: Emily's Photo Album_**

# Project Assignment #1

## Assignment

The Copper Creek Mall is a new shopping venue opening in your area. Your design firm has been selected to produce a multimedia presentation that will be displayed on large screens located at the mall's main entrances. If the client approves the work, you will also produce an interactive map of the various floors showcasing individual stores.

Remember that this is a self-playing loop, so the movie has to have a clear beginning and end yet be interesting in small pieces as well.

## Applying Your Skills

Be sure to:

- Use all the images currently located in the Cast provided in your Student Files folder.
- Use tasteful transitions to move from one section to the next.
- Use the sounds provided in the Cast.
- Create at least six animations — the more the better.
- Come up with a mascot for the mall, create it, and use it in the animations.
- Use the name Copper Creek Mall and create a vector graphic that can be used throughout the project.
- Create several bitmap images, either as backgrounds or as Cast members. Apply several different ink effects to the graphics you create.
- Use a command tempo from the channel to separate the end of the loop from the start frame.
- Use the Text window to create the copy for the project.
- Use the Paint window to create any headlines.

## Specifications

The total play time of the piece should be more than 30 seconds but less than 60 seconds.

Add a Wait for 10 Seconds command in the Tempo channel of the last frame so that the movie doesn't replay constantly. In the Script channel of the last frame, put a *go to frame 1* script so that after the 10 seconds are up, the movie will go back to the first frame and play over.

## Components

We have supplied a Cast in a file named "Project1.DIR" which can be found on the student CD. Use the sounds and Cast Members from this file as the basis for your project.

Alternatively, you can collect your own images and/or create your own sounds. If you choose to use the materials we have provided, they can be found in the `Director` folder on your student CD-ROM.

## Publisher's Comments

The difficult part of creating a loop project like this is grabbing people's attention so that everyone will spend the few seconds it takes to watch it. Consider text growing or dissolving into a solid background, and make certain that you time the sounds properly to create the correct feel and tempo for the loop.

Remember that malls are places where parents take their kids, who can be very demanding when they want to see something. Consider playing to the children to gain initial attention for your project. Adults, on the other hand, need something that will catch their interest and hold it for the length of the presentation.

# Review #1

## Chapters 1 Through 7:

In Chapters 1 through 7, you learned how to set up a new Director movie. You practiced animating Sprites by working with Keyframes and Tweening. You learned how to apply Ink Effects and Transitions to your Director movies. You injected Interactivity through various means and created Markers to help keep track of the interactivity. You learned the benefits of having a Main Menu in your projects. You learned how to add sound and video to a Director movie and how to control both. After the first half of this course, you should:

- Understand and be able to navigate through Director's interface, especially the four primary windows needed to create a Director movie.
- Know how to create a new Director movie and adjust various settings to your liking using the Property Inspector. You should understand how to create your own Cast Members using the Paint and Text windows.
- Be familiar with placing Sprites on the Stage and in the Score and understand the basic use of Sprite Overlays, grids, guides, tweaking, and aligning. You should be aware of the options available in the Sprite Preferences dialog box. You should be able to produce basic animation using keyframes and tweening.
- Understand the various transitions and ink effects, as well as the appropriate use of both.
- Understand the usefulness of a Main menu and how to create buttons to add interactivity for the viewer. You should know how to create and work with markers in order to easily navigate through a complex Score.
- Be comfortable with importing sound and video for use in Director projects. You should know how to place sounds and video clips in the Score and make them play in your Director project. You should understand basic copyright issues regarding sound and video.
- Be familiar with the more advanced tools in the Paint window and know how to use them. You should know how and when to utilize the Onion Skinning feature within the Paint window. You also should be able to use Director's Vector Shape window to create basic vector graphics.

# CHAPTER 8

# MASKS AND ALPHA CHANNELS

## CHAPTER OBJECTIVE:

To understand and practice the concept of creating masks for use as alpha channels. In Chapter 8, you will:

- Learn about alpha channels.
- Learn about masks.
- Create masks for use as alpha channels.
- Use masks to create vignettes.
- Explore real-world applications for masks.

## PROJECTS TO BE COMPLETED:

- Magic Carpet Tours (Project A)
- Redi-Base (Project B)
- Digital Portfolio (Project C)
- Emily's Photo Album (Project D)
- ABC's (Project E)

# Masks and Alpha Channels

Director offers a special Sprite ink effect called Mask. Mask allows you to simulate Alpha Channels. If you are at all familiar with Photoshop or FreeHand, you have probably worked with channels before and may have created an alpha channel or two.

Alpha channels store additional information for each pixel of an image. Alpha channels can be made up of any pattern of grayscale pixels that you wish to interact with a graphic. This pattern of pixels is called the mask. This new Director feature offers you the ability to improve graphics and create some spectacular effects.

You can work with alpha channels to fade out images, make objects appear out of a haze, merge images (similar to morphing), vignette images, make images appear within type, and even create glassy or watery effects.

To do this, a black/white, or grayscale, gradient image — the mask — is created (in the Paint window) in the shape of the object that you want to keep or to hide. The image that you want it to affect is put in the Cast slot before it. After you drag the image to the Stage or Score, you can turn on the masking feature by choosing Mask from the Sprite ink effects list in the Property Inspector. The image should interact with the mask you made, creating something new.

In this chapter, you will be completing one big project that utilizes two different uses of masking several times so that you can practice it as you read along. You will be creating an animated advertisement for a fictitious magazine called OutDoor Life. This advertisement could be a running advertisement on a Web page or on a promotional CD.

## Using Type to Create Masks

You can effectively put images into type by creating a type mask. This technique naturally works best if the type is large enough to contain enough of an image so that it can be recognized. Running video or images inside of 9 pt. type would hardly be useful. On the other hand, a 200 pt. bold or ultra typeface could potentially display a considerable amount of image.

In the following exercise, you will explore the use of type masks.

### *Masking Images into Type*

Note: This project will probably be easier if you work with your Cast in thumbnail form. Also, remember to open your ATC fonts before proceeding.

1. If you wish to view the final piece before starting, feel free to open the **Mask.dir** file from the **Finished Exercises** folder within the **SF-Director** folder. When you are ready, open the **Startmask.dir** file in your **SF-Director** folder.
2. The first thing you are going to do is mask some images into type. Highlight the empty Cast slot to the right of the "Canoe" Cast Member. Open the Paint window so that we can create a mask in the next step.

*If you don't like the placement of the image within the type outline, go back into the Paint window of the mask (the word "OUT") and select the Registration Point tool so that the registration point (intersection) shows up in the window. Drag the intersection point in the direction of your liking and then go back to the Stage to see how your tweaking worked out. Keep tweaking it until you like it.*

3. In the Paint Window, double-click on the Type tool and choose ATC Monsoon, 200 pt., and black type. Click OK. Type "OUT" in the Paint window. Name the Cast Member "Out Mask." Double-click on the Registration Point tool before leaving the Paint window to make sure the type is centered on its registration point.

4. Drag a copy of the "Canoe" Cast Member to the Score and place it in channel 2, frames 1-87. Center it on the upper third of the Stage (see below). Now, while the Sprite is still highlighted, go to the Property Inspector and choose Mask from the Ink Effect drop-down menu. You should see something like the image shown below.

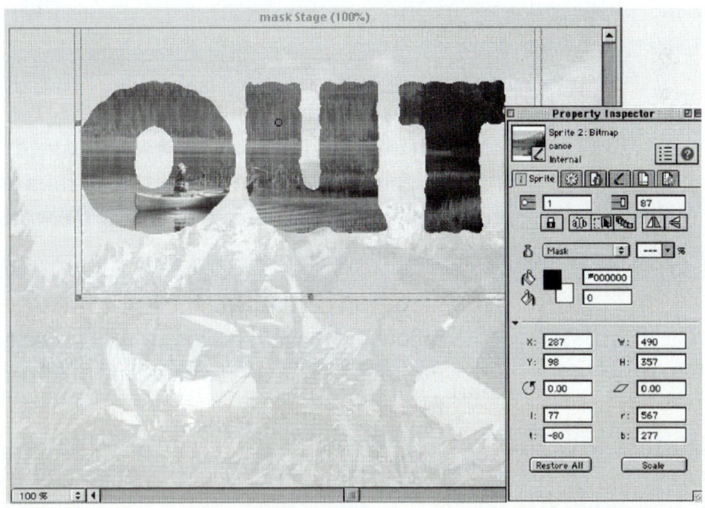


5. Insert a keyframe in frame 34 of the "Canoe" Sprite. Now highlight the first keyframe of the Sprite and set the blend percentage in the Property Inspector to 0%. Highlight the second keyframe (frame 34) and set the blend percentage to 100%. Now the child will fade into the background as the word "OUT" fades into full color.

6. In this step, you will turn the word "DOOR" into a mask and use the camping image to fill it. Highlight the empty Cast slot to the right of the "Camping" Cast Member and go back into the Paint window. Set the Text tool to black 150 pt. ATC Monsoon. Click OK and type "DOOR" in the Paint window. Reset the registration point by double-clicking on the Registration Point tool.

7. Drag a copy of the "Camping" Cast Member to the Score and place it in channel 3, frames 35-87. Center it on the middle third of the Stage (see below) while overlapping the bottom of the word "OUT" just a bit. Now, while the Sprite is still highlighted, go to the Property Inspector and choose Mask from the Ink Effect drop-down menu. You should see something like the image shown below.

8. Insert a keyframe in frame 60 of the "Camping" Sprite. Now highlight the first keyframe of the Sprite and set the blend percentage in the Property Inspector to 0%. Highlight the second keyframe in frame 60 (the new one you just made) and set the blend percentage to 100%. Now the word "DOOR" slowly fades into full color to join the word "OUT."

9. Next, you need to add the word "LIFE" to the Stage and Score as shown in the following image. There is already a Cast Member created for this purpose, "Life Text." Put the "Life Text" Cast Member in channel 4, frames 61-87. Add a keyframe to frames 70 and 73.

10. The goal is to make the word "LIFE" start out the size of a pinhead, get really large, and then shrink back down to an acceptable size. To do this, highlight the first keyframe and shrink down the word to a small dot. Using your Arrow keys, center it back on top of the other keyframe dots on the Stage so that you don't get any vertical or horizontal movement.

    At the first new keyframe (frame 70), make the word "LIFE" larger than life and center it on the keyframe dots on the Stage.

    At the next keyframe (frame 73), make it shrink back down to an acceptable size and center it again where it will stay until the Playback Head reaches the end of the Sprite.

    So far, the top row of your Cast should look like this:

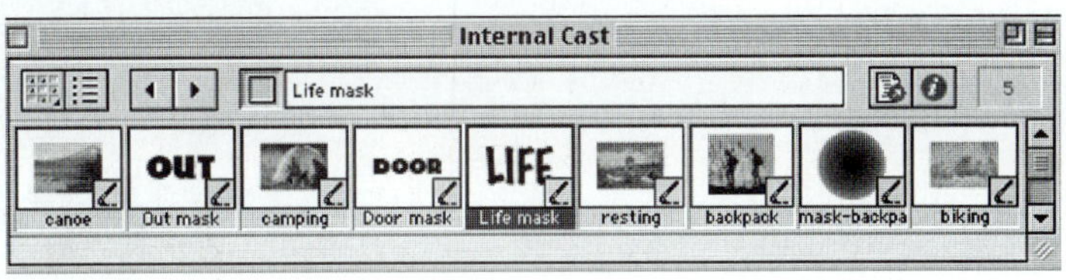

11. Next, add the "Mag Text" Cast Member to the Stage as shown in the following image. It should be placed in channel 5, frames 83-87.

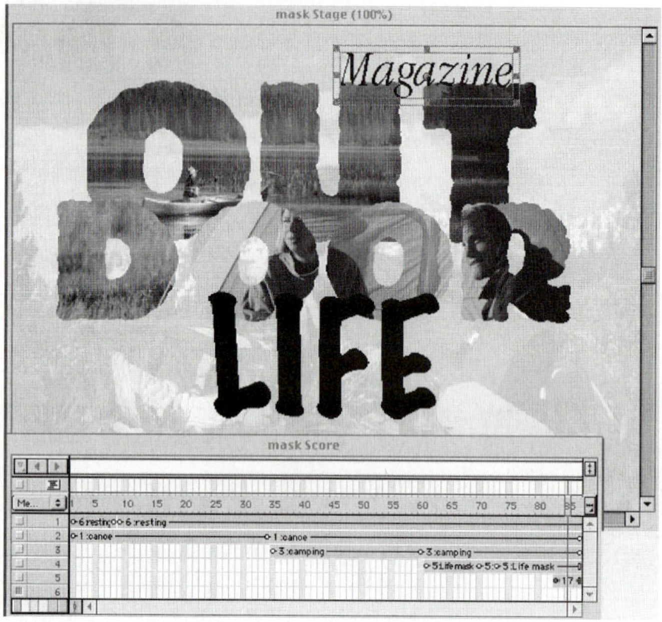


## *Adding Scrolling Text*

1. Drag a copy of the "Website Text" Cast Member into channel 5, frames 1-82. Add a keyframe to frame 9. Move the text to the bottom of the screen as shown in the following image.

2. At the first keyframe, set the blend mode to 10%. At the second keyframe (frame 9) set the blend percentage to 70%. Now the Web site information will slowly appear and get darker but not too dark and overpowering. It will stop at 70%.

3. To make it scroll, we will use something called a Behavior from the Library palette, which will be discussed further in the next chapter. Open the Library palette from the Window menu. Choose Text from the drop-down menu shown in the following image.

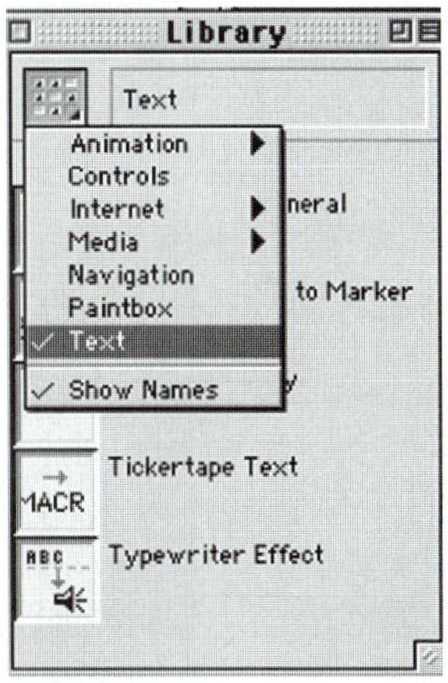


Find the behavior named Tickertape Text. If you can't see it in your window, click on the down arrow at the bottom of the window or drag the bottom-right corner of the window to enlarge it.

4. Drag a copy of the Tickertape Text behavior down to the Score and drop it on top of the "Website Text" Sprite. A Parameters dialog box will pop up. Set the slider to "5" and click OK. Now your text will scroll from right to left until the Playback Head reaches the end of the Sprite.

5. One last thing to do in this section: Double-click on the Tempo channel in frame 87 and choose the Wait for Seconds option and move the slider to 3 seconds. This will make Director wait for an additional three seconds after everything has slid into place before moving on to the next section. This pause gives you a chance to read or admire the screen.

## Gradient Vignette Masks

You can use a black-to-white gradient as a mask. The resultant effect — a solid image that fades in one or more directions is called a vignette. It's sort of like putting a square picture into an oval picture frame. The darker areas of the gradient allow the most image to show through and the whiter areas are where the image fades away.

Starting in the next exercise you'll combine a combination of different gradient masks and images to gain experience working with this popular technique.

### *Using Masks to Create Vignettes*

The first mask we will use has already been created for you so that you have some idea what the rest should look like later. This mask is the one labeled "Mask-Backpack." It is the mask for the backpack image. It is a gradient circle (black in the center, white at the edges). Let's put it together to see what it looks like.

1. Drag a copy of the "Backpack" Cast Member into channel 2, frames 88-107 of the Score. Center it on the Stage. Set the ink effect for the Sprite to Mask and watch what happens on the Stage. If you don't like how the image is centered in the circle, adjust the registration point of the circle. It should look like the following image.

## *Creating Gradient Masks*

Now it is your turn to create the rest of the gradient masks for the hiking, biking, and snowboarding images in the Cast.

1. First, highlight the empty Cast slot to the right of "Hiking." If it is not empty, rearrange your Cast Members so that it is. Go into the Paint window and go to the Gradient Settings dialog box. Choose the settings shown below.

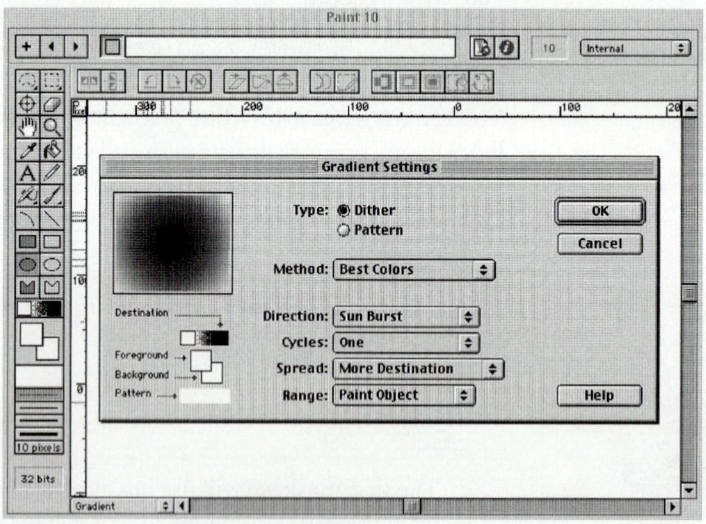


Make certain that your gradient colors are set to white and black, as shown above, or this exercise will not work.

*Remember, the Mask ink effect only works when the mask is immediately to the right of the image it is being applied to.*

2. Select the Filled Ellipse tool and choose Gradient from the Paint ink effects drop-down list at the bottom of the Paint window (shown in the previous image).

3. Go to View>Onion Skin and turn on onion skinning. Set it to 1 preceding Cast Member. Using this Cast Member as a reference, create a tall ellipse over the hikers. This may take a few tries. If you don't like the first one, double-click on the eraser to delete it and start again. It should look something like the following image. (Remember, onion skinning is turned on).

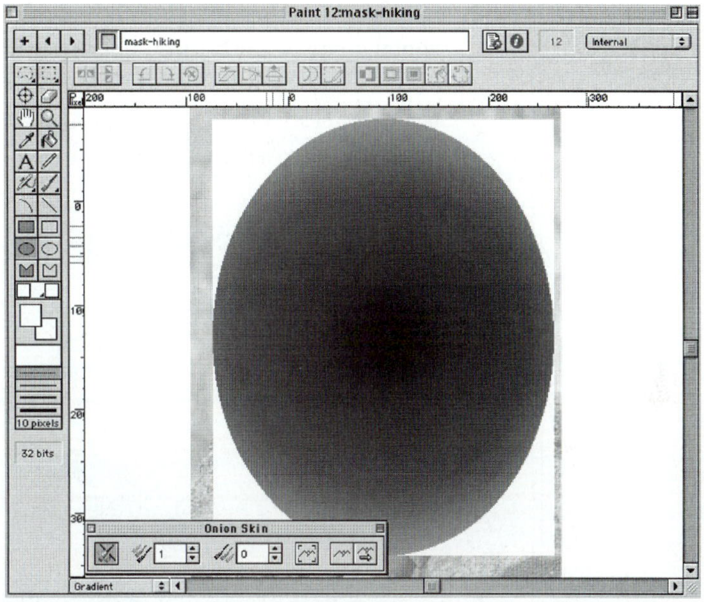


4. You now want to create the same types of gradient masks for the other two images, biking and snowboarding. One at a time, select the Cast slot to the right of each and create an appropriate gradient shape for each one. For instance, both the biking and snowboarding images would probably look good with long, horizontal ellipses.

## Creating Vignettes

Before you put the next vignette in the Score, you need to add a piece of type to the "Backpack" vignette you have already placed in the Score/Stage.

1. First, click on the Guides and Grid tab in the Property Inspector and drag a horizontal guide to the bottom of the page, as shown in the following image. Next, drag a copy of the "Your Text" Cast Member to the Score and place it in channel 3, frames 88-155. On the Stage, place it as shown in the following image, aligning the baseline of the type with the guide. Set the ink effect for this Sprite to Background Transparent.

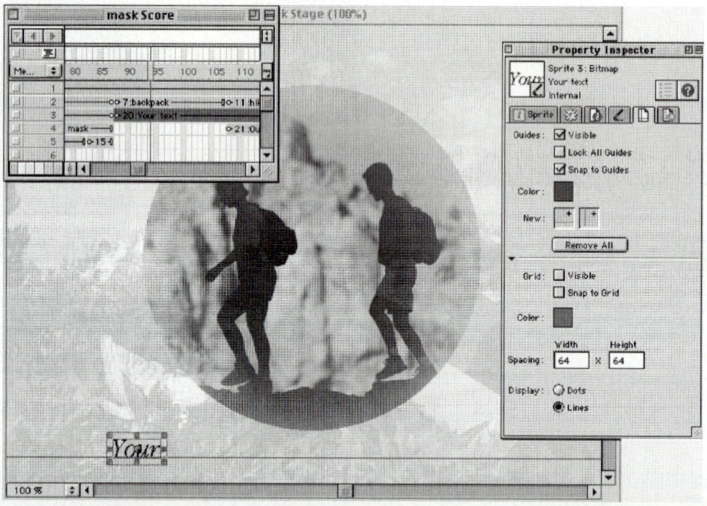


2. To create the next vignette, drag a copy of the "Hiking" Cast Member into channel 2, frames 108-123. By doing so, it should automatically be centered on the Stage. Change the Sprite ink effect to Mask. It should look like this:

3. Add "Outdoor Text" to the Score in channel 4, frames 108-155. Place it as shown in the image above. Set the ink effect for this Sprite to Background Transparent.

4. To create the next vignette, drag a copy of the "Biking" Cast Member into channel 2, frames 124-138. It will automatically be centered on the Stage. Change the Sprite ink effect to Mask. It should look like the one in the following image.

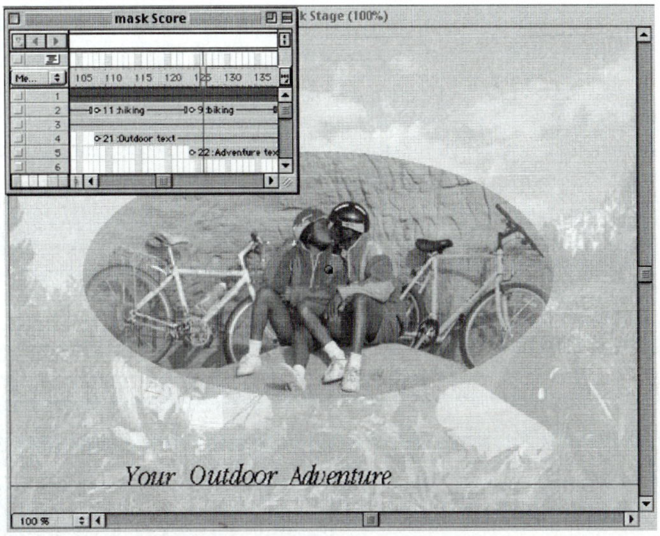


5. Add "Adventure Text" to the Score in channel 5, frames 124-155. Place it as shown in the previous image. Set the ink effect for this Sprite to Background Transparent.

6. To create the last vignette, drag a copy of the "Snowboarding" Cast Member into channel 2, frames 139-155. Change the Sprite ink effect to Mask. It should look like the image that follows.

7. Add "Magazine Text" to the Score in channel 5, frames 139-155. Place it as shown in the previous image. Set the ink effect for this Sprite to Background Transparent.

## *Adjusting the Tempo and Adding Transitions*

1. Double-click on the Tempo channel in frame 107. Choose the Wait for Seconds option and set it to 1 second. Do the same for frames 123 and 138.
2. Double-click on the Transition channel in frame 88 and choose Dissolve, Pixels from the list of available transitions. Leave the settings to their default and click OK. Do the same for frames 108, 124, and 139. This will allow for nice, smooth transitions between sections.

   Your Score with the Tempo channel adjustments and the transitions in the Transition channel should look like this:

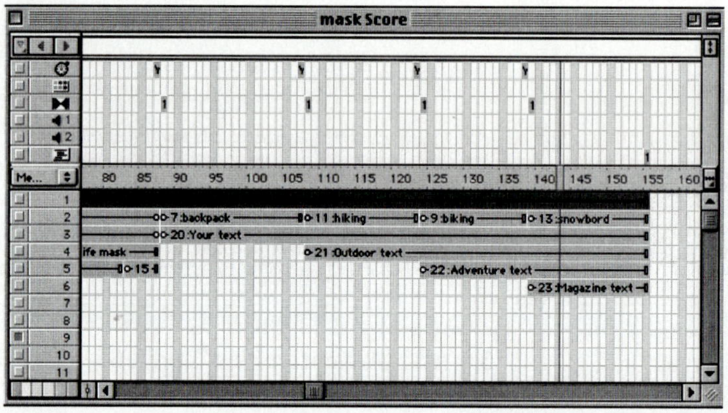


3. Now, rewind and play the advertisement. When it reaches the end, it should automatically go to frame 1 and start over because of the Frame script already inserted in frame 155. If you have any questions, don't forget to look at the finished version. To do this, go to **SF-Director>Finished Exercises>Mask.dir**.

# Chapter 9

# Applying Behaviors

## Chapter Objective:

To learn about the different types of behaviors that can be applied to Sprites using the Library palette. To discuss the different categories of behaviors and the necessity of the Behavior Inspector. In Chapter 9, you will:

- Gain an understanding of behaviors and their uses.
- Learn how to use the Library palette.
- Learn about Automatic and Interactive Animation behaviors.
- Learn about Control behaviors.
- Learn about different types of Internet behaviors.
- Learn about different types of Media behaviors (Flash, QuickTime, and Sound).
- Learn about Navigation behaviors.
- Learn about different Paintbox and Text behaviors.
- Explore the Behavior Inspector and its uses.
- Practice applying behaviors to Sprites.

## Projects to be Completed:

- Magic Carpet Tours (Project A)
- Redi-Base (Project B)
- Digital Portfolio (Project C)
- Emily's Photo Album (Project D)
- ABC's (Project E)

# Applying Behaviors

Behaviors offer a quick and efficient path to making Sprites and frames interactive without venturing into the complex world of Lingo.

A behavior is a script that is attached to a Sprite or frame in the Behavior channel. By dragging a behavior on top of a Sprite or to a Frame Script channel, you can quickly apply special effects and actions that would otherwise require a sequence of Lingo codes. Many behaviors may be attached to a Sprite, but only one may be attached to a frame.

## The Library Palette

The Library palette contains prescripted Lingo behaviors. These behaviors are dragged from the Library palette and dropped onto a Sprite or frame to attach them. You can access the Library palette from the Window menu.

The image below shows what the Library palette looks like when you first access it. Each behavior is identified and defined. If you place your cursor over any of the Behavior buttons, a Tool tip containing a detailed explanation of the button's function appears.

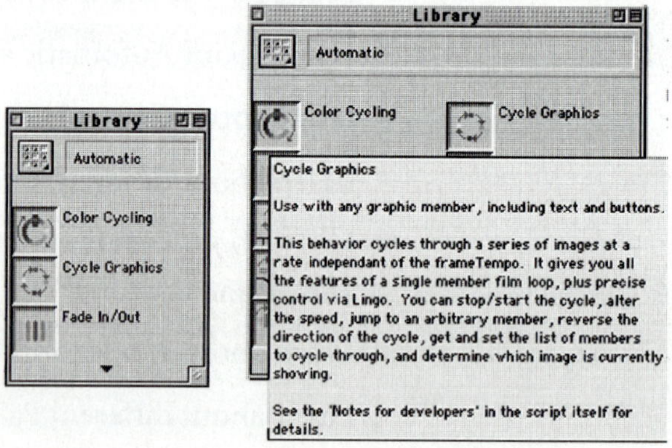


The button in the top-left corner of the Library palette displays a list of libraries to choose from, such as various Internet forms and Animation Behaviors.

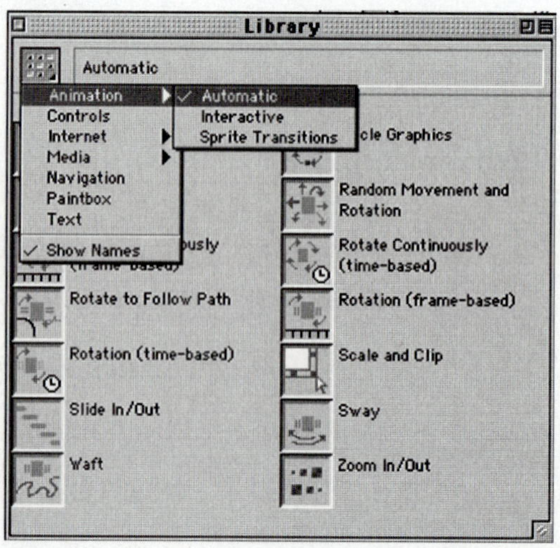

## Animation Behaviors

The Animation category consists of automatic behaviors, interactive behaviors and Sprite transitions. These are all behaviors that relate to animating Sprites or animation in general.

### Automatic Animation Behaviors

The Automatic Animation behaviors include Rotate Continuously, Random Movement and Rotation, Color Cycling, and Wafting.

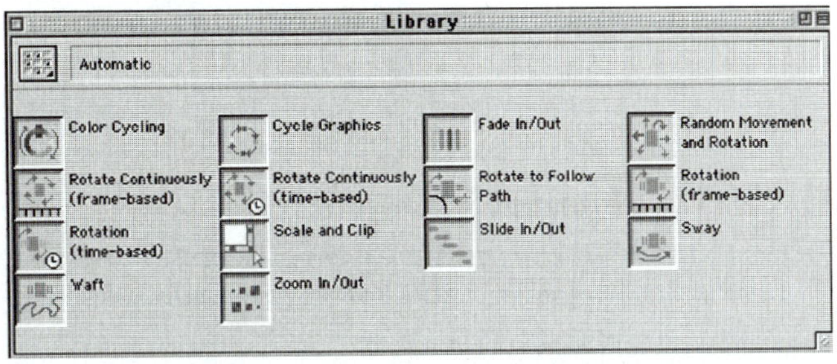


### Interactive Animation Behaviors

The next group is Interactive Animation behaviors. With these options you can create interactive graphics. For example, you can set up a graphic to avoid the mouse — the graphic will stay one step ahead of the pointer, no matter how fast it is chased. If you set a graphic's behavior to Sprite Track Mouse, the graphic will chase the mouse pointer.

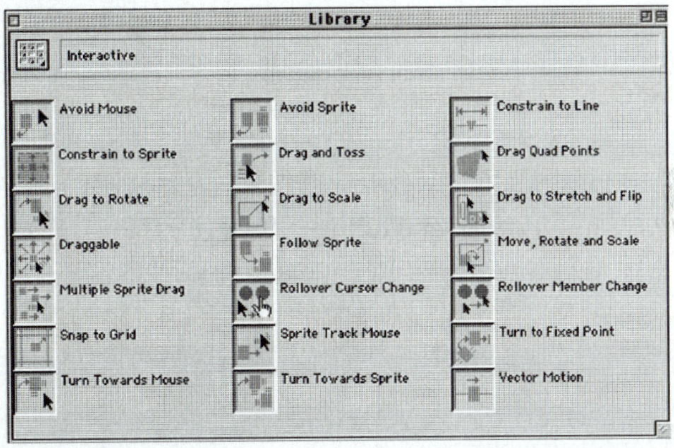


### Sprite Transition Behaviors

The Sprite Transition behaviors are very similar to the transitions you learned about in Chapter 4 except that these affect an individual Sprite only, not the whole frame.

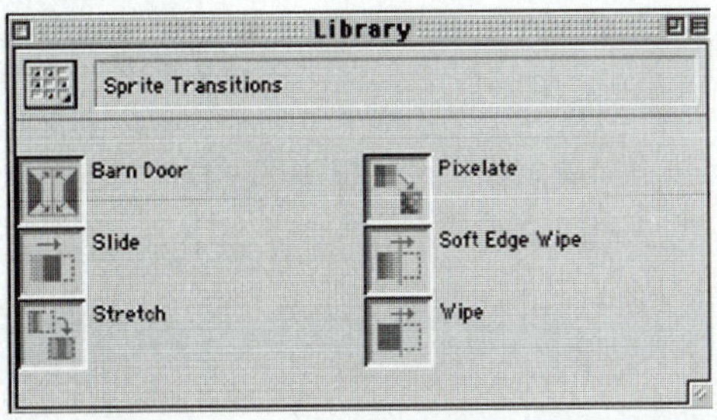

## Controls Behaviors

The Controls section of the Library palette provide behaviors to control your movie and allow you to set buttons to Jump Forward, Jump Back, Jump to Marker, and more.

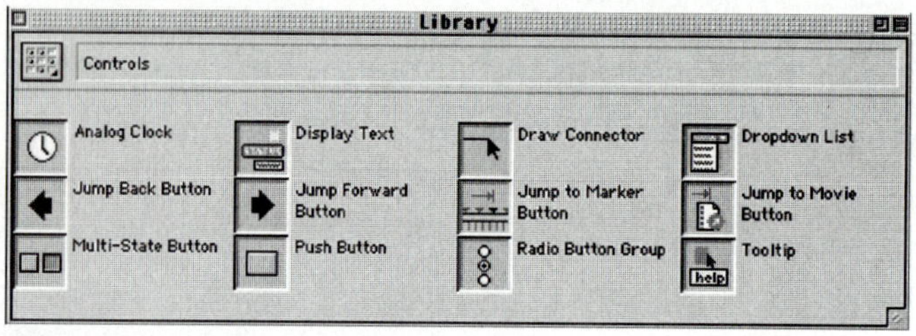


## Internet Behaviors

The Internet Behaviors category consists of forms, multiuser behaviors, and streaming behaviors. These are all behaviors related to publishing your Director piece on the World Wide Web.

### Internet Forms Behaviors

Internet Forms behaviors are fairly advanced features and deal specifically with forms that can be created on the Internet and posted back to a Web server.

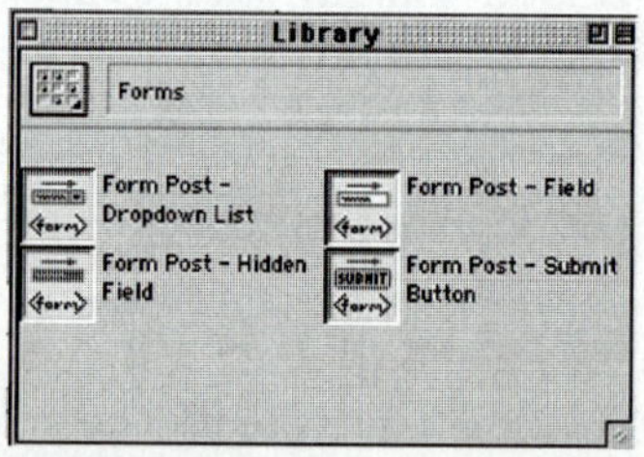


### Internet Multiuser Behaviors

The Internet Multiuser category contains behaviors that can be applied to Sprites so they can, among other things, connect to and disconnect from servers when clicked.

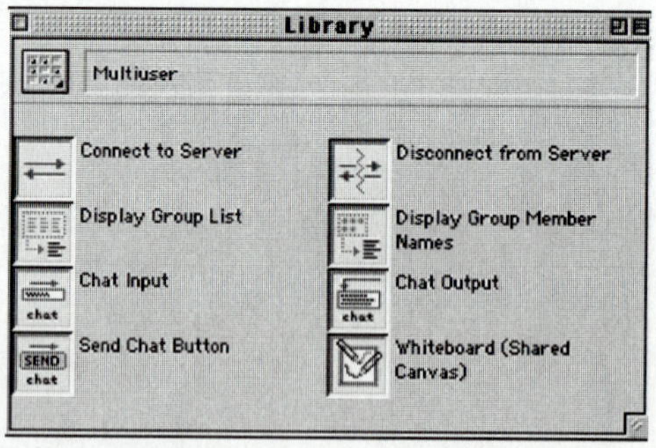

### Internet Streaming Behaviors

Internet Streaming behaviors allow you to stream media over the Internet, continuously feeding small, consecutive amounts of information. This category enables you to place progress bars, jump to other frames, and loop until your media is done playing, to name a few of the options.

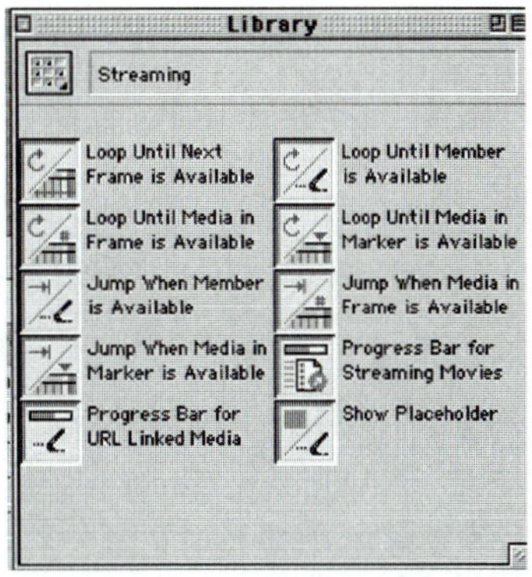


## Media Behaviors

The Media category consists of Flash, QuickTime, and sound behaviors. These behaviors are to be used with Flash files, QuickTime files, or sound files, respectively. They are used to enhance the quality and control of these various third-party file types.

### Media Flash Behaviors

The Media Flash behaviors work only on graphics that have been created using Macromedia's Flash software. Unless you are dealing with Flash graphics, you needn't worry about this category.

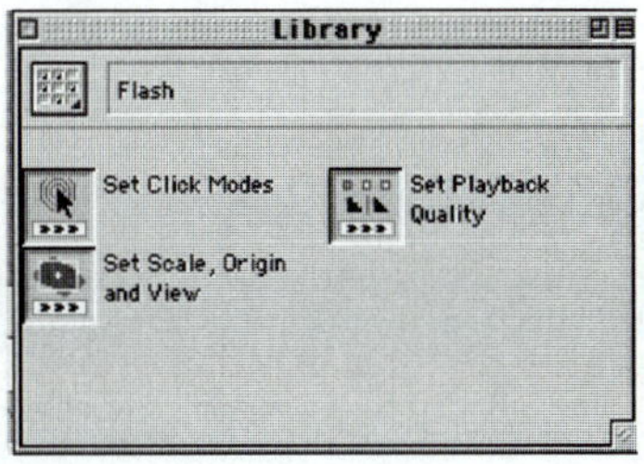


### Media QuickTime Behaviors

Media QuickTime behaviors work only on Apple's QuickTime format. In this category you can choose to show the QuickTime controls and/or slider with any QuickTime video.

### Media Sound Behaviors

Using the Media Sound behaviors, you can play, pause, or stop a sound file, Make your computer beep when you click your mouse on a graphic, or add volume or pan sliders for better control.

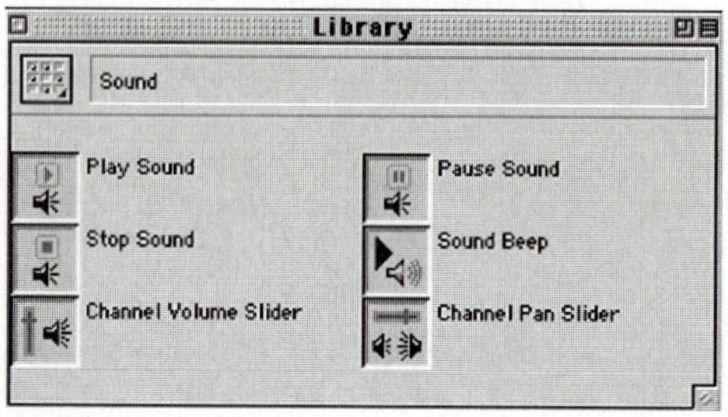


## Navigation Behaviors

The Navigation category contains behaviors that allow you to navigate through the different frames of a Director movie. Some options are Go Previous Button, Go Loop, and Hold on Current Frame.

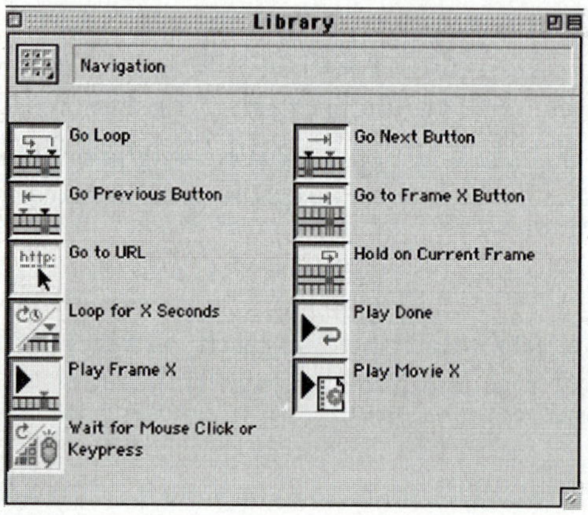


## Text Behaviors

The Text behaviors can be used for many things, from creating hyperlinks for the Internet to adding commas to large numbers so that they are easier to read.

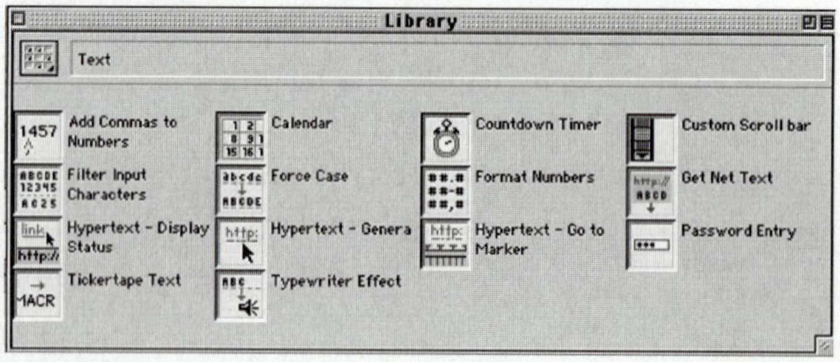

### Paintbox Behaviors

The Paintbox behaviors can be attached to Sprites to make them act like a canvas, meaning that you can use the Paintbrush tool to paint on them, among other things.

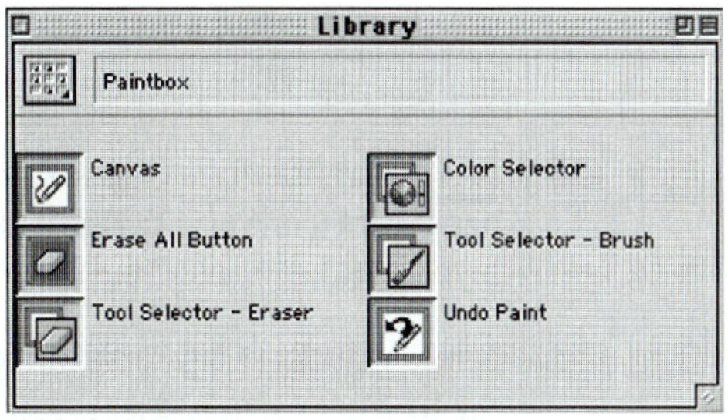


## The Behavior Inspector

The Behavior Inspector is a palette used to create, track, and modify behaviors. Here, you can change the order of multiple behaviors attached to a single Sprite. Switching the order is often necessary since Director follows Lingo or behavior instructions in the order that they were applied to a Sprite. Since each script is most likely attempting to do different things, keeping track of them can quickly get confusing.

The top section of the palette provides a list of the behaviors currently applied to the currently selected Sprite. To add a new behavior, click the "+" button in the top-left corner of the palette.

The middle section of the palette allows you to set the time frame in which a new behavior will be triggered, as well as what action might be applied. The bottom section displays the descriptions of the behaviors that have been used.

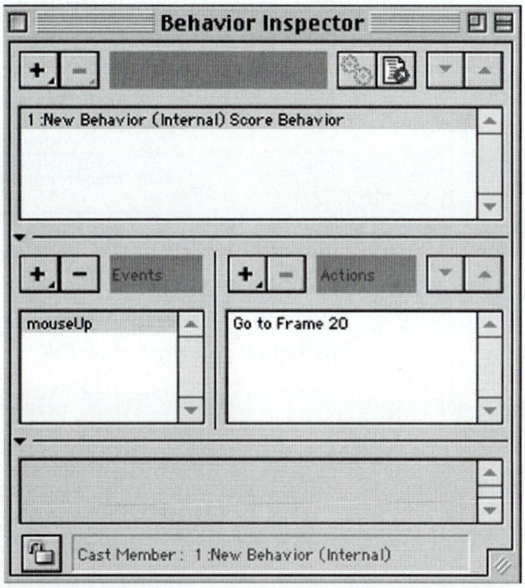

## *Applying behaviors*

1. If you would like to preview a completed version of this exercise file before you begin, select the **CH9BeFin.DIR** file from the **Finished Exercises** folder. To begin the exercise, open the **Ch9behav.DIR** file from the **SF- Director** folder.
2. All the Sprites in this file are already in the Score and on the Stage. You will be adding behaviors to several of them and setting the parameters for their behaviors. To begin, highlight the "Daisy" Sprite in the Score.
3. Select Window>Library to display the Library palette. From the drop-down menu in the top-left corner, select Animation>Interactive. From the list of icons, find the Turn Towards Mouse icon. You are going to set the daisy to turn toward the mouse cursor all the time.
4. Drag a copy of this icon down on top of the "Daisy" Sprite in the Score. The Parameters dialog box appears. Click OK.

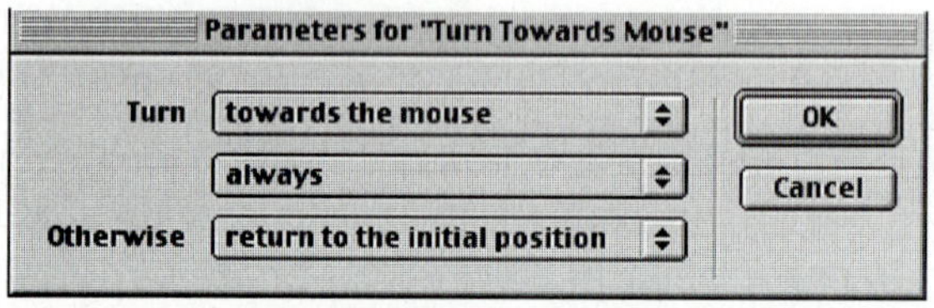


5. Highlight the "Black-eyed Susan" Sprite in your Score. Drag a copy of the same behavior you used down on top of the Sprite. Change the parameters to match the dialog box below and then click OK. By changing the one parameter, you will make the "Black-eyed Susan" Sprite tilt toward the mouse whenever you click on the Stage.

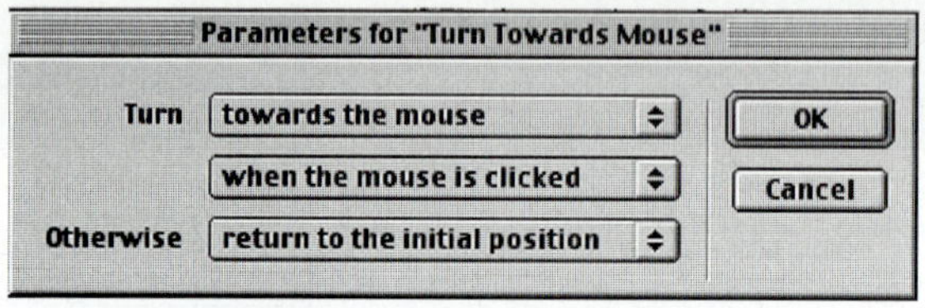


6. Highlight the "Butterfly" Sprite in your Score. Enlarge the Library palette to see all the available behaviors. At the top you will find the Avoid Mouse behavior. Drag a copy of it onto the "Butterfly" Sprite in the Score. Change the parameters to match the dialog box below and then click OK.

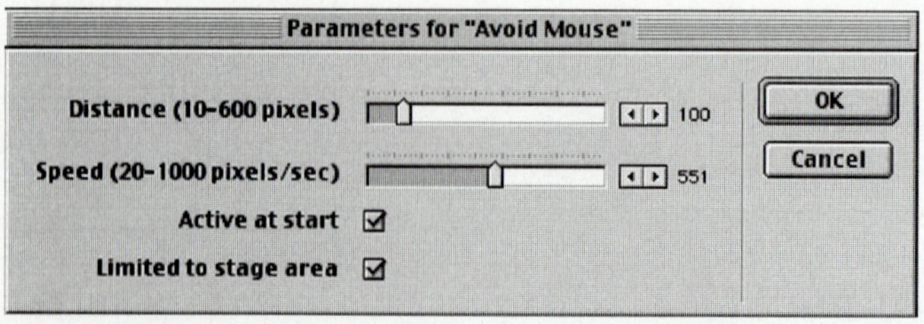


7. Each behavior has been placed in your Cast as a Cast Member. That means that they can be highlighted one at a time and that their scripts may be accessed. To give you an idea of the time you are saving, a small portion of the script that makes up the Avoid Mouse behavior is shown below.

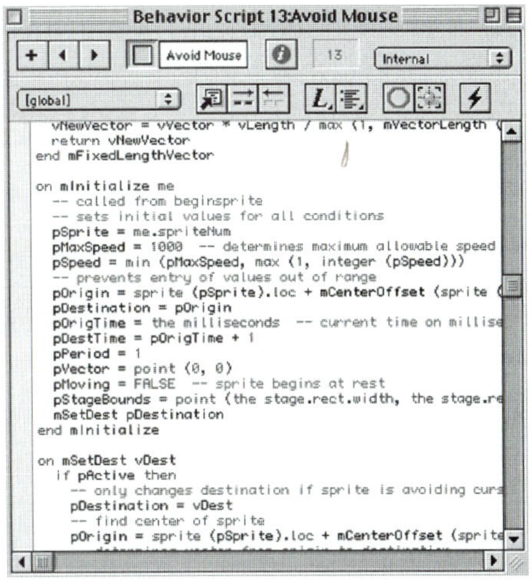


8. The "Ladybug" Sprite will follow the mouse cursor around.Select Animation>Interactive and drag a copy of the Sprite Track Mouse behavior down on top of the Sprite in the Score. Change the parameters to match the dialog box below and then click OK.

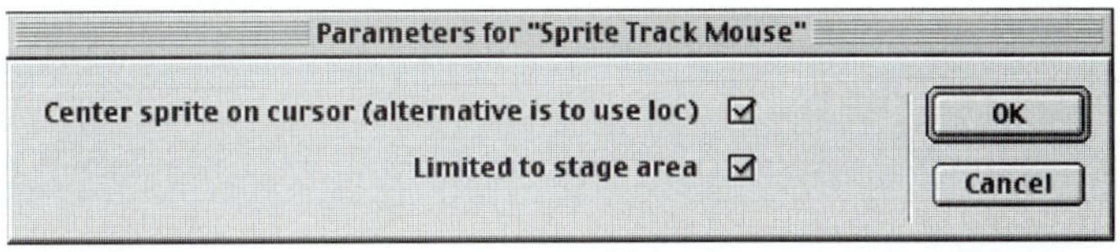


9. The last Sprite we are going to apply a behavior to is the "Leaf". In the Animation>Automatic category in the Library palette, find the Waft behavior. This behavior allows the leaf to gently waft to the ground. Drag a copy of it down on top of the "Leaf" Sprite in your Score. Change the parameters to match the following dialog box and then click OK.

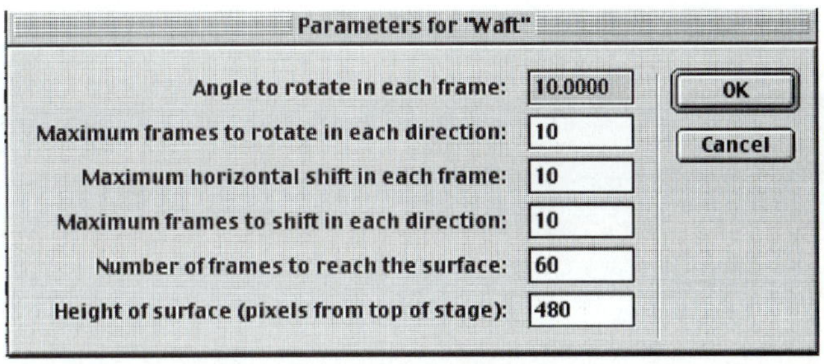


10. The following image displays a copy of the finished Cast. Note that it doesn't matter if the order of your behaviors differs from the order in the Cast.

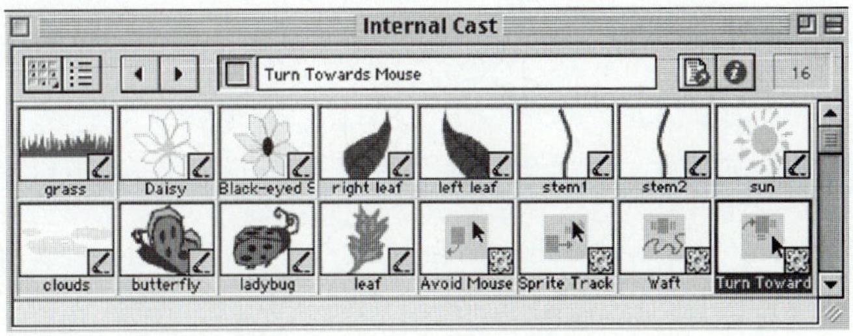

11. Rewind and play your Director movie. Move your mouse around and watch the ladybug follow it. Watch the daisy spin. Try to catch the butterfly — you won't be able to. Watch the leaf waft gently to the ground, and click once in a while to see the black-eyed Susan tilt your way.
12. These are just a few of the many behaviors available in the Library palette. Many more behaviors can be scripted with Lingo.
13. Save the movie if you wish and go to File>New>Movie to close it.

# CHAPTER 10

# MANIPULATING SPRITES

## CHAPTER OBJECTIVE:

To experiment with manipulating Sprites via the Property Inspector. To learn about the properties and settings a Sprite can have. To learn how to use Sprites to create film loops. In Chapter 10, you will:

- Learn about more Sprite properties and settings.
- Learn how to manipulate Sprites using these properties and settings.
- Practice shortcuts to use when moving Sprites around.
- Learn about film loops and how they are made.
- Create a film loop.
- Learn about the Sprite Tweening dialog box and its uses.

## PROJECTS TO BE COMPLETED:

- Magic Carpet Tours (Project A)
- Redi-Base (Project B)
- Digital Portfolio (Project C)
- Emily's Photo Album (Project D)
- ABC's (Project E)

# Manipulating Sprites

Sprites can be manipulated in a multitude of ways. Sprite properties can be found under the Sprite tab in the Property Inspector. These properties range from the length of the Sprite and its placement on the Stage to which ink effects are attached to it and what blend percentage it has.

Each Sprite's properties can be changed to create interesting and unique animations. However, what would you do if you needed to have multiple Sprites uniformly move across the Stage? For instance, say you have a dog, and you have made his feet move, his nose make sniffing motions, and his tail wag by using many different Sprites and now you want him to waltz across the Stage — how would you get all of those pieces to work together accurately?

That can be accomplished by taking every Sprite that makes up the dog and his body motions, putting them in the Score in the correct order, and then turning them all into a single Cast Member called a Film Loop. The film loop can then be placed in the Score as a single Sprite and animated across the screen using keyframes, just like any other Sprite.

When explored and used to their fullest potential, altering Sprite properties and adding film loops can make a huge difference in the impact your movie has.

## Sprite Properties and Settings

A Sprite's properties and variable settings can be found under the Sprite tab in the Property Inspector, shown below. The tab contains all sorts of information about the currently selected Sprite. If there is no Sprite currently selected, there will not be a Sprite tab available in the Property Inspector. The following sections explain the properties and settings a Sprite can have.

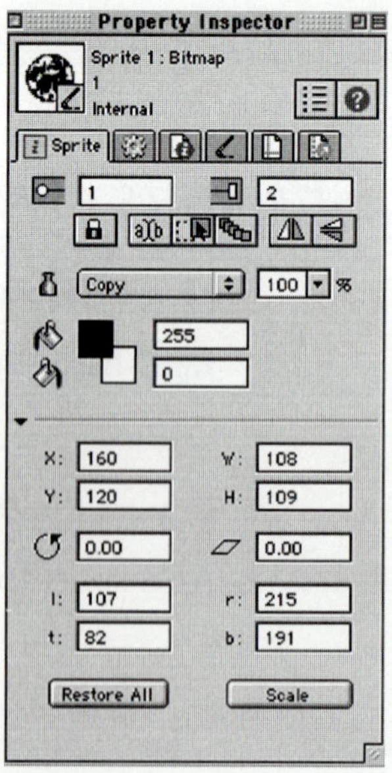

### The Active Sprite

The icon in the top-left corner of the Sprite tab displays the Sprite that is currently active. It also provides some basic information about the Sprite. In the image below, the selected Sprite is a bitmap and is located in the first slot of the Cast. It is also part of the Internal Cast.

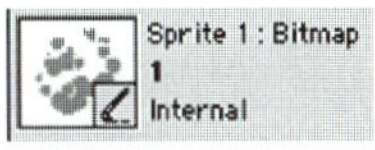


### Start/End Frames

The frame number that a Sprite starts on appears in the left field and the one it ends with appears in the right field. Enter new values in these fields to adjust the length of the Sprite or to move it to different frames within the Score.

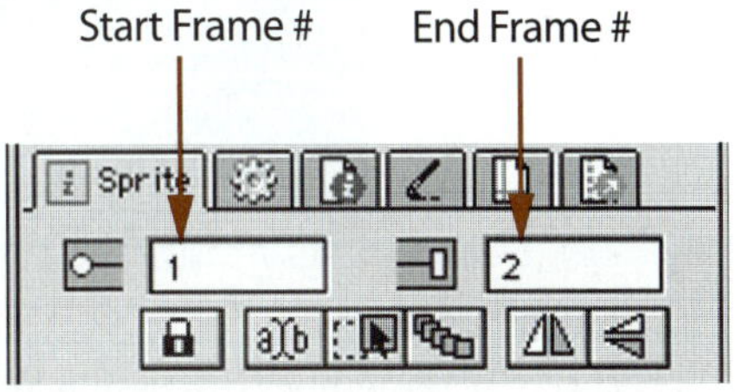


### Editable/Moveable/Trails

The Editable, Movable, and Trails buttons are grouped together in the middle of the row below the Start Frame and End Frame fields.

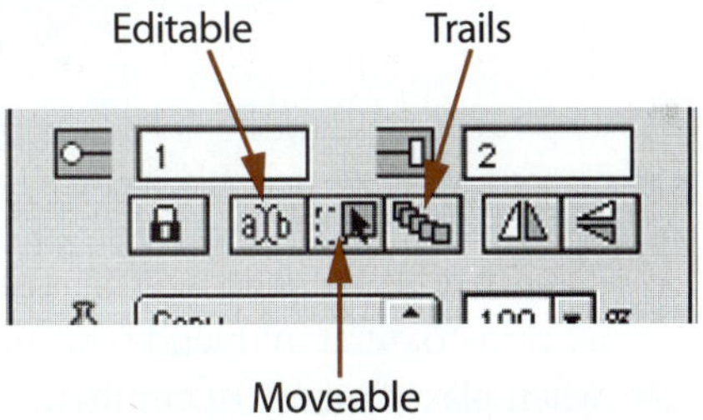


The Editable button, on the left, is used when you want a person to be able to enter information in a Text box or edit some text currently in a box while a Director movie is playing. This feature might be used for an order form or a sign-in book.

The Moveable button is used when you want a viewer to be able to drag a Cast Member around while a movie is playing. An example might be a digital paper doll on which a child must drag and drop pieces of clothing to increase his or her hand-eye coordination.

The Trails button is used when you want to make the selected Sprite remain on the Stage and leave a trail of images along its path as the movie plays. If you highlight a Sprite while animating, click the Trails button, and then turn on Real-Time Recording or use regular keyframes and tweening, the result will be a trail of Sprites behind the original that you are animating.

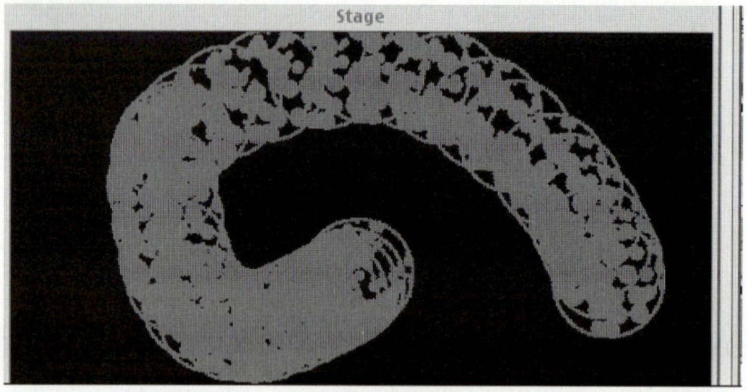


## Ink Effects

You may remember discussing Sprite ink effects in an earlier chapter. The item in the drop-down menu displays the ink effect that has been applied to the selected Sprite.

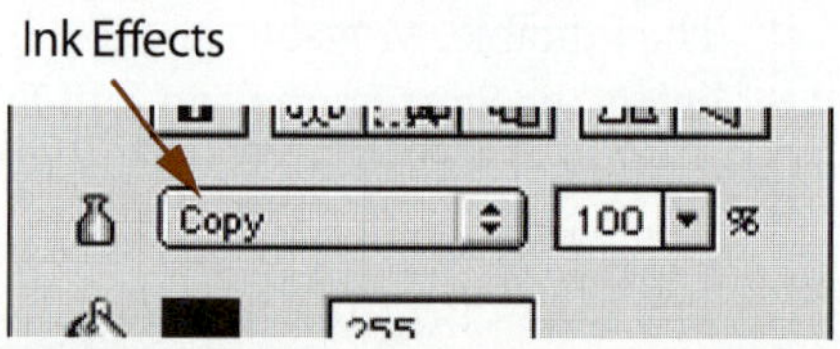


## Blend Percentage

The Blend Percentage setting is to the right of the Sprite ink effects menu. Here, you can set a Sprite to different blend percentages, making the Sprite become more or less transparent when placed on top of another.

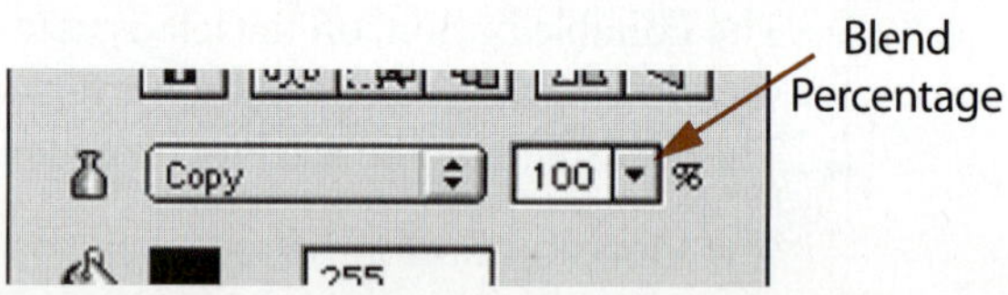


## Foreground/Background Color

By using the Foreground and Background Color swatches, you can change the colors of simple Sprites and backgrounds without going back into the Paint window. Highlight a Sprite in the Score and then click the color swatches to choose new foreground and background colors. This will not work with film loops (which we will discuss later), as they are made up of multiple versions of a Sprite.

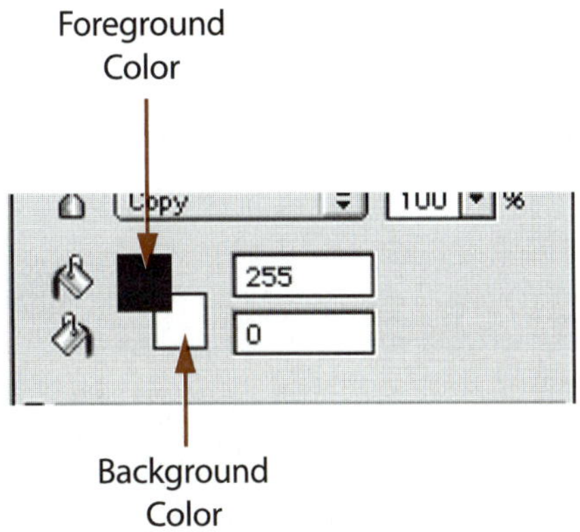


## X/Y Coordinates

The X and Y coordinates of a Sprite (in pixels) are based on the distance from its registration point to either the left side (X) or the top (Y) of the Stage. For instance, below, the Sprite's registration point is at 170 pixels on the X axis and 256 pixels on the Y axis. You can move Sprites around the Stage by changing these numbers and pressing Return/Enter.

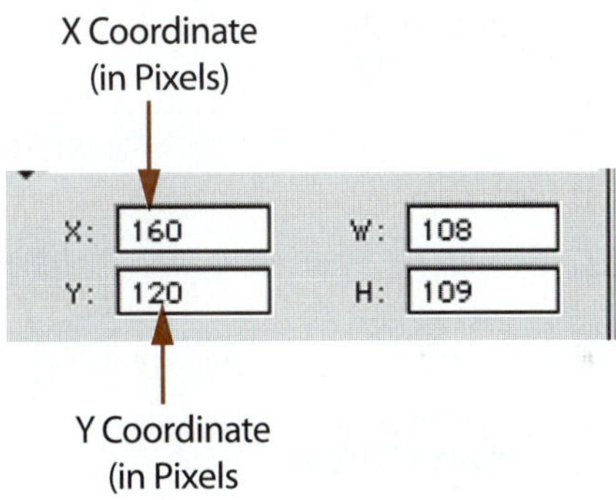


## Width/Height

The Width and Height boxes denote how wide and high a Sprite is in pixels. Here, again, you can change the numbers in these boxes to alter the width and height of a Sprite, but your changes will not affect the original Cast Member.

It is not recommended that you enlarge or reduce Cast Members too much beyond their original size. Major changes in dimension slow down Director dramatically based on the file size of the Cast Member. Going to Modify>Transform Bitmap and then changing the size of the original is the preferred method of altering a graphic's size.

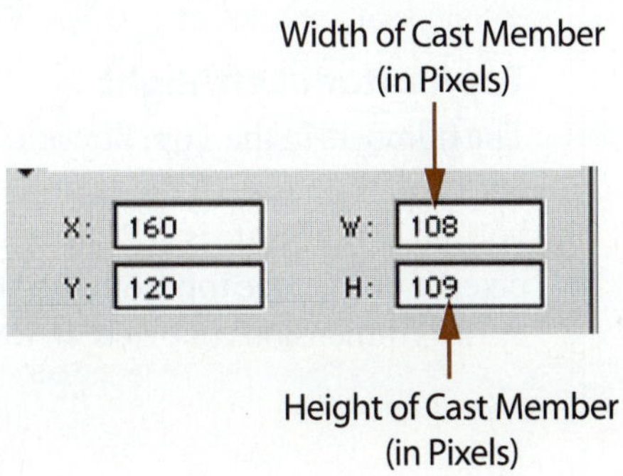

### Flip Horizontal/Vertical

The Flip Horizontal button flips a selected Sprite horizontally, and the Flip Vertical button flips a selected Sprite vertically.

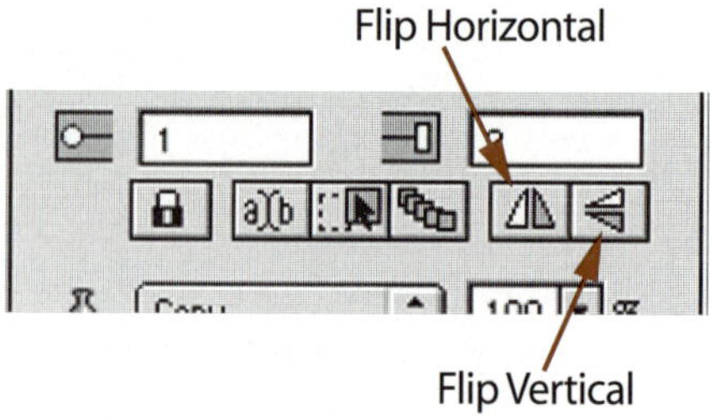


### Lock

The Lock button locks a Sprite temporarily so that no one moves or alters it while creating other pieces or testing your presentation. A locked Sprite cannot be selected and, therefore, is nearly impossible to disrupt in any way.

To lock a Sprite, first highlight it, and then click the Lock button. To unlock the Sprite, you must highlight it in the Score and then click on the Lock button again, making it selectable and editable.

### Rotate/Skew

The Rotate field may be changed to rotate a Sprite. The Skew field is used to set the skew angle of a Sprite. After entering a number in either or both of these fields, press Return/Enter for your changes to take effect. Again, these are only Sprite settings, so the original Cast Member will not be affected.

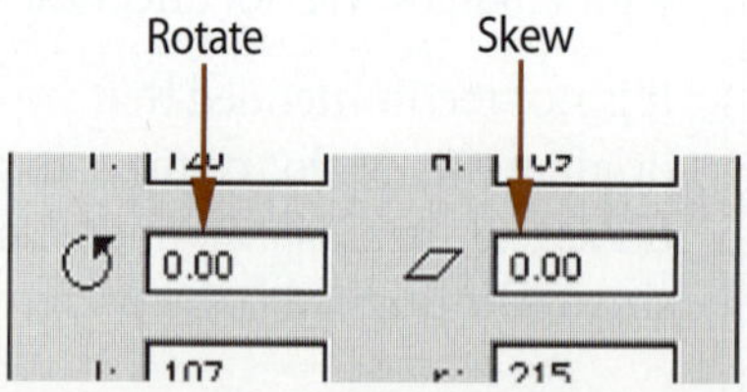


### Top/Bottom/Left/Right

The numbers in the Top, Bottom, Left, and Right fields refer to the specific location of a Sprite on the Stage. In the example below, the top edge of the Sprite is at 131 pixels, the bottom of the Sprite is at 212 pixels, the left edge is at 216 pixels, and the right edge is at 297 pixels. Subtract the top from the bottom and the left from the right to determine your Sprite's dimensions in pixels. In this example they are 81 pixels × 81 pixels.

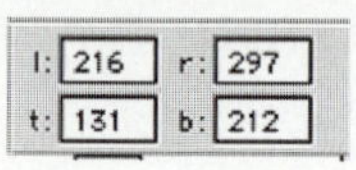

### *Altering Sprite properties*

1. If it is not already open, launch Director.
2. In the Paint window, use one of the shape tools to draw an object.
3. Drag it into channel 1, frame 1 of the Score to create a Sprite. Make certain that the whole Sprite is highlighted.
4. Go to the Sprite tab in the Property Inspector. Type "150" in End Frame field and press Return/Enter to extend the Sprite to frame 150.
5. In the Start Frame field, type "30" and then press Return/Enter. Your Sprite now begins at frame 30 and extends to frame 150.
6. Choose a new color from the Foreground Color swatch. Your object changes to the color you selected.
7. Experiment with the Flip Horizontal and Flip Vertical options. Try clicking on the Registration Point tool (in the Paint window) and moving the registration point to a different spot before flipping to see what happens. To reset the registration point, simply double-click on the Registration Point tool in the Paint window.
8. In the Skew field, type "20" and then press Return/Enter.
9. Holding the Option/Alt key, drag a copy of the Sprite into channel 2, frame 30. It automatically extends out to frame 150 because it is a copy of the first one.
10. Highlight the new Sprite and change its blend percentage to 30%. (To see the effect, which shows up in step 12, make certain that the Sprites are on top of each other on the Stage.)
11. While the Sprite in channel 2 is still highlighted, click on the Moveable button. Now turn on looping by checking the Loop option in the Control Panel.
12. Rewind and play the movie. As it plays drag Sprite 2 around the Stage. You won't be able to budge Sprite 1. Notice how the blend becomes obvious as the Sprite is moved.

## Film Loops

Film loops are useful for animating repetitive motions. You can use film loops to take a repetitive sequence that covers several frames and turn it into a Sprite that can be as small as one frame. A film loop would be useful to make a dog's tail wag or a ball roll.

Once you have created a film loop, you cannot move or rename any of the original Cast Members. It is also impossible to apply ink effects to a film loop. If you want to apply any ink effects, such as Matte or Background Transparent, do it to the individual Sprites before you convert them into a film loop.

There are four basic steps to creating a Film Loop:

- Highlight the Sprites in your Score that you want to include in your film loop.
- Select Insert>Film Loop.
- Name the film loop in the dialog box that appears and click OK. The film loop appears in your Cast as a separate Cast Member.
- Go back to the Score and erase the Sprites you had highlighted to make your loop because you no longer require them. Remember not to delete your original Cast Members by accident!

### *Creating a Film Loop*

1. Select File>New>Movie. In the Paint window, create a ball that is spotted or colored with various shades. We want the ball to spin, appearing as if it is rolling.
2. Take the rectangular Marquee tool (set to shrink), and select the ball.

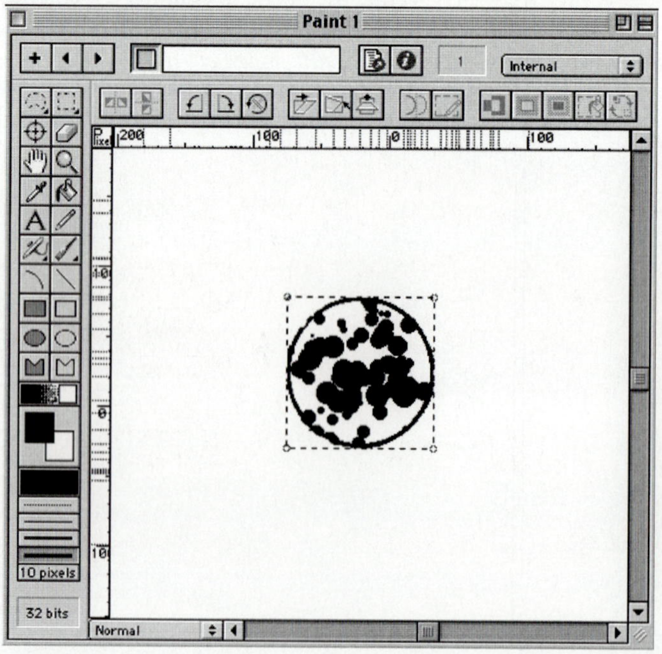

3. Click on the Rotate Right button four times (each click will result in a 1/4 turn). At the end of the fourth click, the ball will be upright again. You have created a full revolution of the ball, which Director has temporarily memorized.

4. From the Menu bar at the top of the screen, select Xtras>Auto Distort. Type "7" in the field and click Begin. Director takes the full revolution (rotation) from its memory and generates seven new Cast Members. Each new Cast Member now shows up in the Cast. Notice that the one full revolution of the ball is now divided into eight steps.

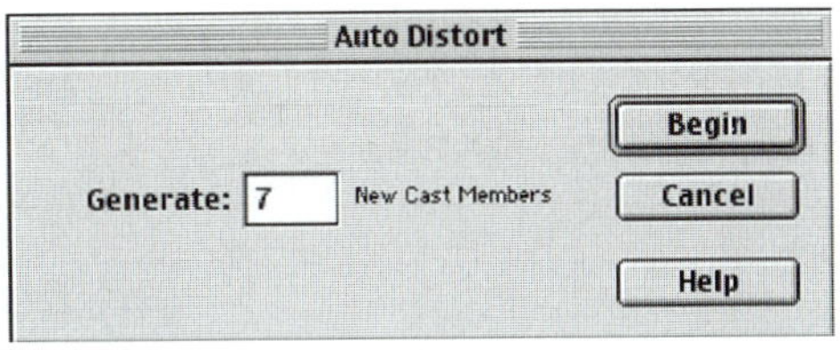


5. Notice that the last Cast Member (8) is identical to the first. Since it is identical, it is not needed. Select it and delete it.

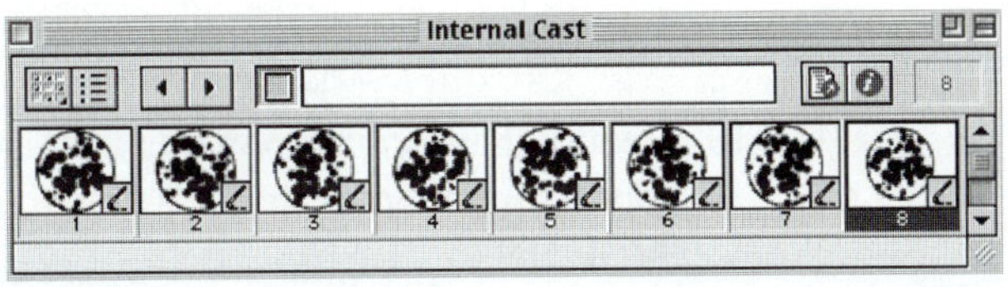


6. Now highlight the first Cast Member and then hold down the Shift key and highlight the seventh Cast Member. This should have selected all seven Cast Members. Next, go to Modify>Cast to Time, and you will notice a new Sprite in your Score. The Sprite contains the seven Cast Members in a row.

7. While the Sprite is still selected, choose Matte or Background Transparent as necessary. Remember, your must add any wanted ink effects to the Sprite before it becomes a film loop — they cannot be added afterward. If you forget, you must throw out the film loop and re-create it.

   If you played the movie right now, you would see the ball spin. However, you are not quite finished. Next, you will turn the Sprite into a single Cast Member.

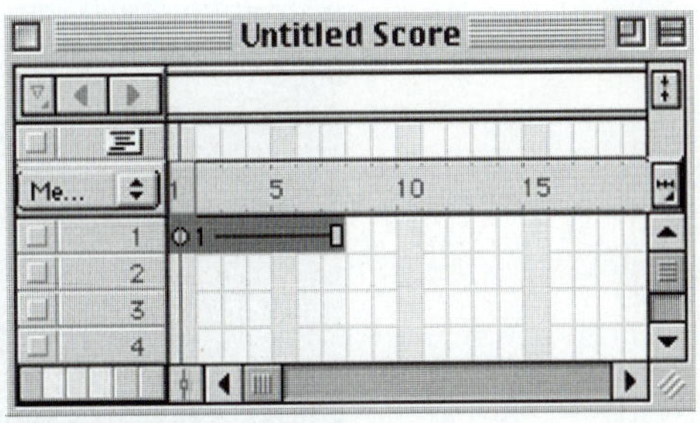

8. While that Spite is still highlighted, select Insert>Film Loop.

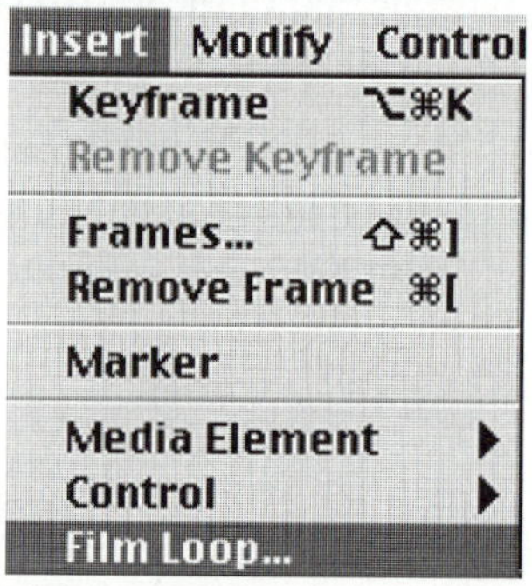


9. Name the film loop "ball" and click OK.

10. Notice that the film loop is in Cast slot 7. Now go back to the Score and delete the Sprites in the Score that you used to make the film loop.

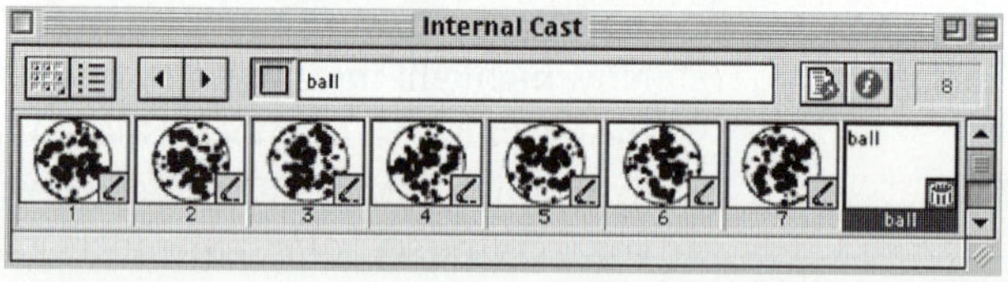


11. Drag a copy of the film loop into channel 1, frame 1 of the Score and make it 30 frames long. Rewind and play the movie. Your ball should spin in the center of the Stage.

12. Insert a few more keyframes and animate the Sprite. The one below has a keyframe every few frames and was twisted into a spiral. This can also be done using real-time recording if you wish.

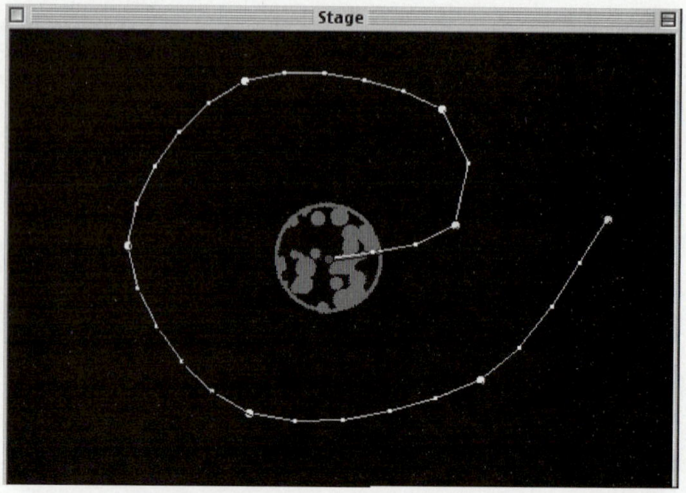

13. To help achieve a soft or hard edge on your keyframes, select Modify>Sprite>Tweening to display the Sprite Tweening dialog box. You can adjust the Curvature slider to sharpen or soften the edges or arcs that your keyframes form.

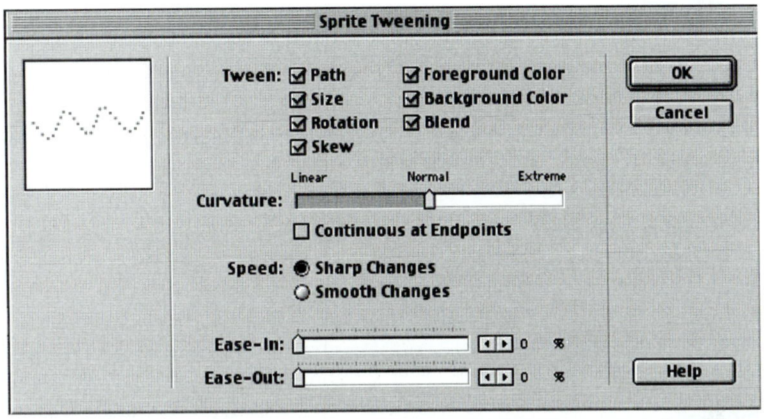


14. The Check boxes at the top provide options that you can turn on or off before you tween an animation. If you turn off Blend, for instance, Director will not tween the blend, even if you highlight your keyframes and change the blends within them. Instead, it would just start with one blend percentage and switch to the next one at the next keyframe.

15. Save and close the file.

## Notes:

# CHAPTER 11

# THE CURSOR

## CHAPTER OBJECTIVE:

To learn why cursors are important and why you should occasionally use more than one in a project. To learn how to change the cursor from its default and how to create custom ones. To learn about animated cursors and how to create and apply them. In Chapter 11, you will:

- Learn about the importance of cursors.
- Learn how to change your current cursor.
- Explore the Cursor Properties Editor.
- Create and apply a custom cursor to a project.
- Learn how to create an animated cursor and apply it to a project.

## PROJECTS TO BE COMPLETED:

- Magic Carpet Tours (Project A)
- Redi-Base (Project B)
- Digital Portfolio (Project C)
- Emily's Photo Album (Project D)
- **ABC's (Project E)**

# The Cursor

Cursors are a great feature for any form of interactive media and are most often used to prompt users to do something. There are various cursors built into the Macintosh and Windows operating systems, but you can design custom cursors and add them to your movies to create your own look.

You can associate specific cursors with individual Sprites to prompt the user to perform a particular action. You can even hide cursors for situations in which you want the user to do nothing.

We often don't realize the power of suggestion a cursor change gives when we are playing a computer game or surfing the Internet. For instance, it might let us know that we can "pick up" an item, click on it, or use it in some other fashion.

When planning and creating an interactive project of any kind, it is a good idea to plan the use of multiple custom cursors, animated cursors, and rollover cursor changes. Cursors can be used to add that extra-professional look.

## Changing the Cursor

There are a few different ways to change the cursor. One option is to use Lingo and script the change. Unless you are making a Shockwave movie, there are quicker and more efficient alternatives.

The Behavior Inspector is another option. A Sprite can be given a specific instruction, such as "while the mouse is in this particular area, use this cursor."

However, the most efficient way to change a cursor is through the Library palette. The Rollover Cursor Change is a prescripted behavior that may be added to a Sprite. The behavior is actually attached to the Sprite, and when the cursor moves inside the bounds of that Sprite, it changes to the cursor specified.

To set the cursor to something other than the arrow, you need to create a background so that it is a Cast Member. When the background Cast Member is dragged to the Score, it becomes a Sprite, and the Rollover Cursor Change behavior can then be attached to it and set to the cursor of choice. This way, the cursor is always gliding over a Sprite (the background) with a Rollover Cursor behavior attached to it; it will never have the chance to default to the arrow.

## The Cursor Properties Editor

The Cursor Properties Editor, located under Insert>Media Elements, offers the ability to select a bitmap Cast Member and tell it to become a Cursor Cast Member. You can make adjustments to the way the cursor displays and behaves.

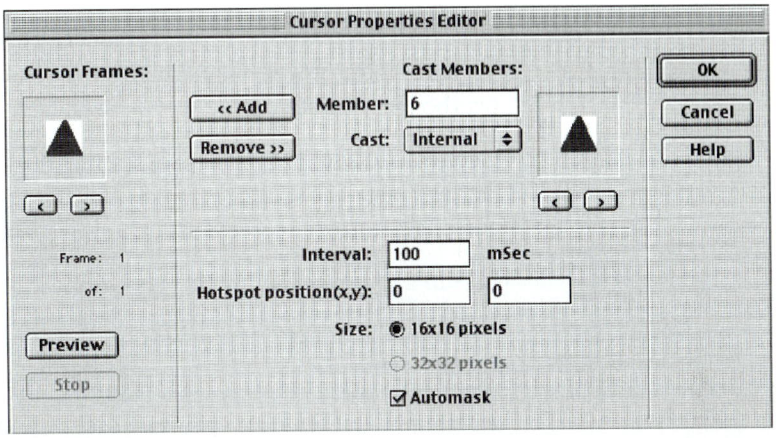


For a Cast Member to display in the Cast Member box on the top-right side of the editor, it must be an 8-bit graphic (also referred to as indexed color or 256 colors). When you make a graphic in the Paint window, it is automatically a 32-bit graphic. To change the bit depth, the graphic must be opened from within the Paint window and then Modify>Transform Bitmap needs to be selected. Here, the setting can be changed to 8-bit.

As you shuffle through the available 8-bit Cast Members, you have the option to click the Add button when you reach the one you want to turn into a cursor. The Automask check box should be checked to make any white around the edges of the graphic transparent.

The resulting cursor size on a Macintosh has to be 16 pixels × 16 pixels, so it defaults to this size (notice that 32 × 32 is grayed out). If you are working with Windows 95/98, the 32 × 32 pixels option might become available. If you are working with Windows NT, you can use either 16 × 16 or 32 × 32 pixels.

The Hotspot position is the precise area of the cursor that you want to become your "activating" area. An example might be a paintbrush — the very tip of the brush would be the hotspot. The hotspot dimensions (in pixels) can't be larger than the size of the graphic. With a 16 × 16 pixel graphic and the brush tip placed in the bottom-left corner, the coordinates would be set to X: 0, Y: 16.

### *Creating and Applying a Custom Cursor*

1. Launch Director if it is not already open. Open the Paint window and make a small filled circle. Name it "Circle."

2. Click the "+" button in the top-left corner of the Paint window to display the next available empty Cast slot. Create a small filled square. Name it "Square."

3. Select Modify>Transform Bitmap and change "Square" to 8-bit. Click Transform. A warning message appears alerting you to the fact that you cannot undo this operation. Click OK.

4. Drag a copy of "Circle" to the Score and place it in channel 1, frames 1-30.

5. Select Insert>Media Element>Cursor. The Cursor Properties Editor appears. Since "Square" is the only 8-bit graphic you've created so far, it displays in the Cast Members box immediately.

6. Click Add to add it to the Cursor Frames box. Make certain that Automask is checked. Set the hotspot coordinates to 8,8, which is the middle of your graphic. Set your cursor size to 16 × 16 pixels and then click OK.

7. In your Cast name the cursor "My Cursor".

8. Highlight the "Circle" Sprite in your Score and open the Library palette.

9. Select Animation>Interactive Category in the Library palette and click the Down arrow until you find the Rollover Cursor Change behavior. Drag a copy of it down on top of the Sprite in the Score.

*If when you run your cursor past the outside edges of the circle (or any other irregular shape) and it still sometimes turns into your custom cursor, highlight your Sprite in the Score and select Matte from your Score Ink Effects drop-down menu. This will remove the white (extra hotspot area) around your irregular shape. Now it should work perfectly.*

10. The Parameters box appears. Choose Cursor Member from the top drop-down menu. Ignore the second menu (it deals with using the built-in cursors that come with Director). Choose "My Cursor" from the bottom drop-down menu and click OK.

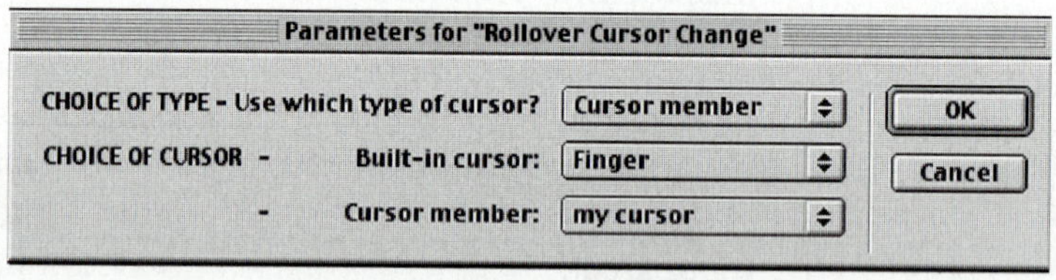


11. Open the Control Panel if it's not already open. Make certain the Loop option is turned on.

12. Rewind and play your movie. Move your cursor around the Stage. Your cursor is an arrow until it goes over the circle, at which point it turns into the square you created.

13. Quit Director without saving.

## Animated Cursors

Now that we know how to turn a Cast Member into a cursor and apply it to a Sprite, animating the cursor won't be too difficult to learn. The following is a list of the steps in the process.

- Create various Cast Members to turn into an animation.
- Convert the graphics into 8-bit.
- Turn each one into a single cursor member by selecting Insert>Media Element>Cursor. Each Cast Member is added, one at a time, until they are all on the Cursor side of the dialog box.

- Preview the animation and modify it until you are happy with the sequence.
- Apply the appropriate behavior — for example, Rollover Cursor Change — to a Sprite the same way as is done with the single cursor.

### Creating an Animated Cursor

1. If you would like to preview a completed version of this exercise file before you begin, open the **FinShape.DIR** file in the **Finished Exercises** folder.

   From the File menu open **Shapes.DIR** in the **SF-Director folder**. Your Stage should look like the example below. This is a mock main menu for a game disk.

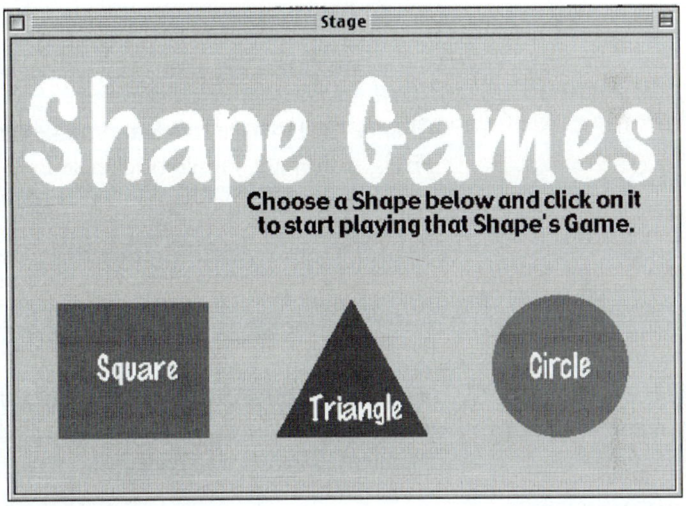


2. From the Paint window, click the "+" button to choose the next empty Cast Member slot. Draw a small yellow square.
3. Click the "+" button again to choose the next empty Cast Member slot. Activate the Onion Skinning option from the View menu and set it to 1 preceding Cast Member. Now you should see a hint of the yellow square. If the Onion Skinning option is not available, click on your Paint window to make sure it's active and then try to access the option again.
4. Create a purple triangle on top of the faint outline of the yellow square. This allows you to make the triangle about the same size as the square.
5. Change the setting in the Onion Skin palette to 2 preceding Cast Members. Now click the "+" sign in the Paint window for the next available slot.
6. Draw a light blue circle on top of the other two shapes.
7. Go to the Cast window and name the new members "Cursor1", "Cursor2", and "Cursor3".
8. Select them one at a time and then choose Modify>Transform Bitmap to convert them each to 8-bit.

9. Select Insert>Media Element>Cursor. Shuffle through the Cast Members until you get to the square (Cursor1) and then click Add to add it to the Cursor Frames window. Now add the triangle (Cursor2) and the circle (Cursor3).

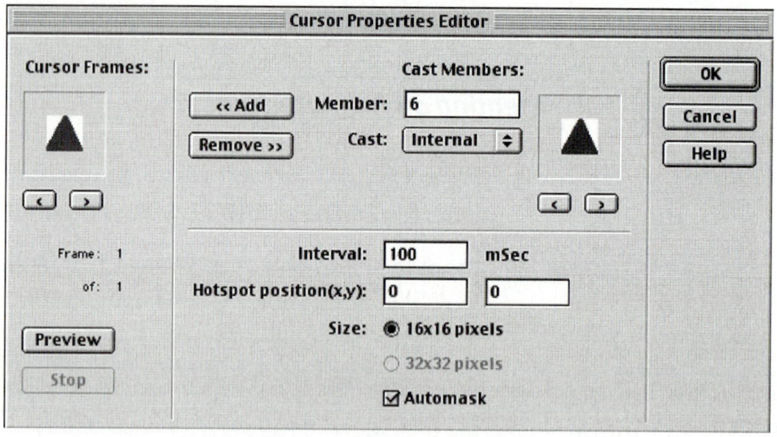


10. Change the Hotspot to 8,8 and make certain that the cursor size is set to 16 × 16 pixels. Automask should be checked.

11. Click the Preview button and your cursor begins to animate. The interval should be set to 100, or whatever number looks best in your opinion. Click Stop and then OK.

12. Now go to the Score and highlight the Sprite named "Square". Then open the Library palette.

13. Select Animation>Interactive in the Library palette and click the Down arrow until you find the Rollover Cursor Change behavior. Drag a copy of it down on top of the "Square" Sprite in the Score.

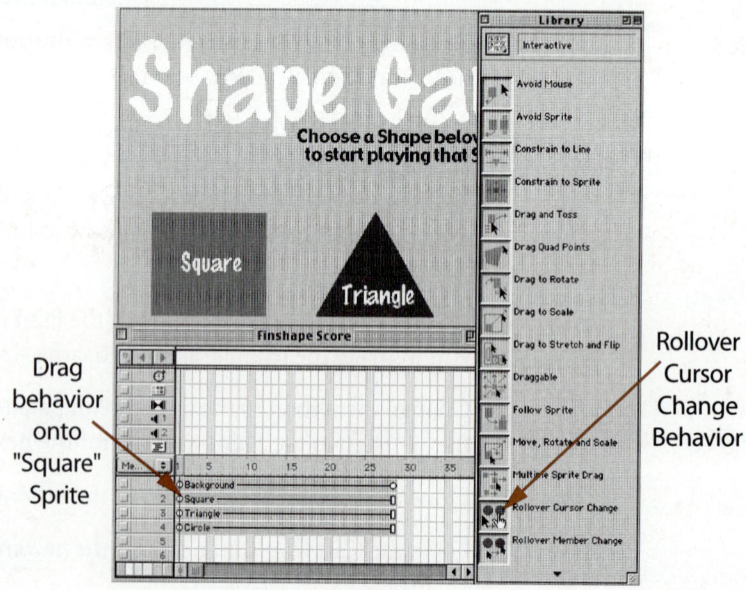

14. In the dialog box that appears, select Cursor member from the first drop-down menu. Select the correct Cast Member from the Cursor member drop-down menu (it should default to the correct one since you've made only one). The box should look similar to the example below. Ignore the Built-in cursor menu for now.

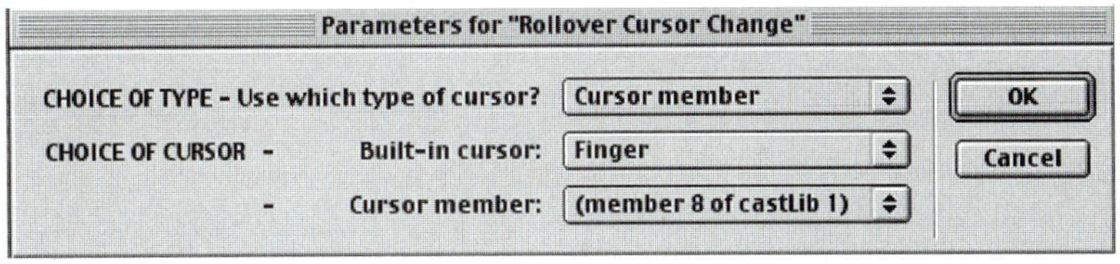


15. Repeat steps 12-14 for the "Triangle" and "Circle" Sprites and to finish creating the cursor animation.

16. Highlight the "Background" Sprite in your Score. Apply the Rollover Cursor Change behavior to it. However, set up the Parameters box a little differently (see the example below). From the first drop-down menu, select Built-in cursor. Set the Built-in cursor menu to Pencil. Ignore the Cursor member menu. Click OK.

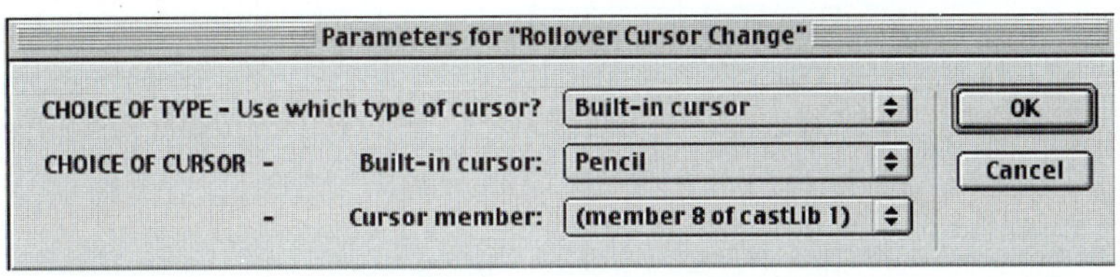


17. Make certain that your Control Panel is set to loop your movie.

18. Rewind and play your movie. Move your cursor around. When you glide over the triangle, circle, or square, you should see your animated cursor. When you are over the background, you should see the pencil cursor.

19. Quit Director without saving.

***Complete Project E: ABC's***

## Notes:

# CHAPTER 12

# COLOR: SETTINGS, PICKERS, PALETTES AND CYCLING

## CHAPTER OBJECTIVE:

To learn about the types of color and the bit depths that can be used in Director 8 and how they can affect the playback of Director movies. To learn about color cycling and how it can be used to animate graphics or for special effects. In Chapter 12, you will:

- Gain an understanding of the types of color used in Director 8.
- Explore the Color Palettes window.
- Learn which color pickers to use and which to avoid.
- Learn how to create a custom Color palette.
- Learn how to get your new Color palette to display in the Paint window so that you can use it to create Cast Members.
- Experiment with color cycling.
- Learn how to apply the Color Cycling behavior to Sprites in the Score.

## PROJECTS TO BE COMPLETED:

- Magic Carpet Tours (Project A)
- Redi-Base (Project B)
- Digital Portfolio (Project C)
- Emily's Photo Album (Project D)
- ABC's (Project E)

# Color: Settings, Pickers, Palettes and Cycling

This chapter is devoted to color and what choices you must make concerning color in Director. The color settings required for your movie or presentation are entirely dependent on where you will ultimately play your movie. For instance, the movie might be need to be viewed on the Web and at an interactive kiosk. How would you create or configure your colors so that they would work in both instances?

Another issue to look at is which platform the Director movie will be played on. Windows machines tend to show most colors darker than Macintosh machines do. If you are creating a movie for one platform only, you can adjust for this. If you are creating one that will be viewed on both platforms, you will just have to preview things on both platforms and tweak the colors as necessary.

If the movie is to be viewed only on the computer it was created on, you have an advantage because you either already know or can easily find out all your computer's specifications, including how powerful it is and what kind of monitor it has.

These are just a few of the many considerations concerning color that must be taken into account before creating a Director piece. Plan your project carefully to prevent unwanted color issues later.

## Color Settings

There are some general color settings you should look into before beginning your project so that you are aware of what they are currently set to and can decide whether to leave them alone or change them to better suit your project.

### General Preferences (for Macintosh only)

Before you begin your project, check the color options in the General Preferences dialog box. Make certain that the Reset Monitor to Movie's Color Depth check box is checked. (This option is not available from within Director to those on the Windows plaform. Windows users must go into Windows' Control Panel to change this option.) This option resets monitors to match the movie's color depth so that the colors are not skewed or modified. For instance, if you produce your movie to use thousands of colors and the monitor you are viewing it on is set to only 256 colors, your movie's wide range of colors will be converted to 256 and will look quite different.

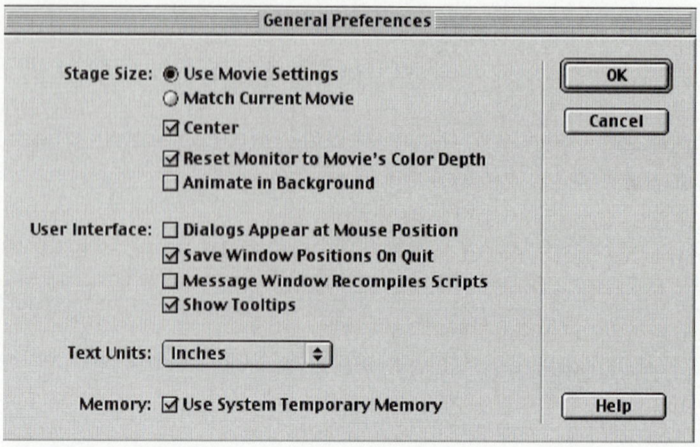

## Movie Properties

The Movie Properties tab of the Property Inspector is where a movie's color settings can be found.

For color mode you have two choices: RGB and Palette Index. Director typically defaults to RGB. When RGB is chosen, a two-digit number is assigned for each of the red, green, and blue values to make up the color. These are called hexadecimal values. They end up as six-digit numbers and provide consistent and accurate results.

When you choose Palette Index, the color is named by its number in the list within the palette. If it is the fifth color across in the first row, then it is color 5. Choosing the Palette Index option is fine as long as you move this particular color palette along with you wherever you go and don't disturb the order of the colors. If color 5 is blue and, later, you rearrange the colors to make 5 olive green, then that's what color your Sprite becomes.

Palette Index colors are still RGB colors, but there are only 256 of them available in the Index palette at any one time, unlike when you choose the RGB option, in which colors are available in the thousands or millions.

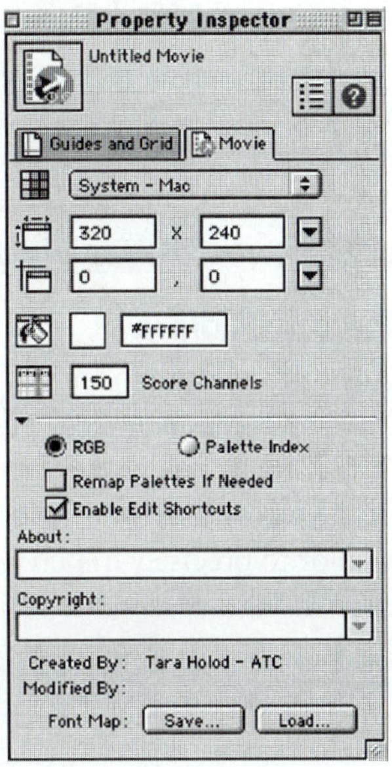


You have the ability to set your default Color palette. For productions being displayed on a single workstation, the System-Mac or System-Win selection is fine, depending on which platform you are using. These options offer 256 RGB colors on either platform and ensure consistent presentations on both.

If you are presenting on the Web and want to be absolutely sure that everything remains exactly the same no matter what machine you are viewing it on, select the Web 216 palette. These 216 colors are made up of the 216 RGB colors that the Macintosh and Windows system palettes share out of the 256. They are called the Web-Safe colors, because no matter what type of machine you view them on, they always look the same, albeit darker on Windows and lighter on Macintosh. The Web-Safe palette also helps keep file sizes to a minimum, keeping download time more reasonable for the average user.

## Color Pickers

The Macintosh version of Director contains different Color Pickers, which are ways to choose new colors. This section will show you the preferred color pickers and ways to reach and manipulate them.

Though unfortunate for Windows users, different color pickers are not available in the Windows version of Director. What Windows users will see when they open up the Color Palettes window is a palette like the one shown below. This is the standard Windows color picker and has nothing to do with the Director software.

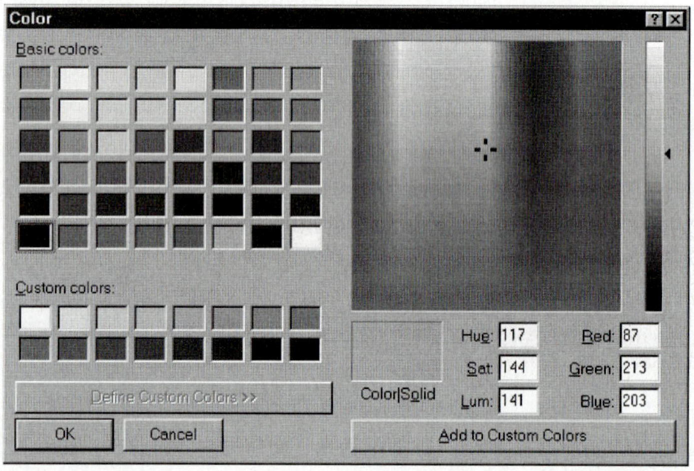


### Favorite Colors

Although we have been working with the Paint window and its many available options, it has a few areas related to customizing your Color palette that we have not discussed yet. When a new color is selected, either the hexadecimal equivalent or a Palette Index number at the top of the Color palette is provided. This is helpful for those times when you require a color to precisely match one that was previously used.

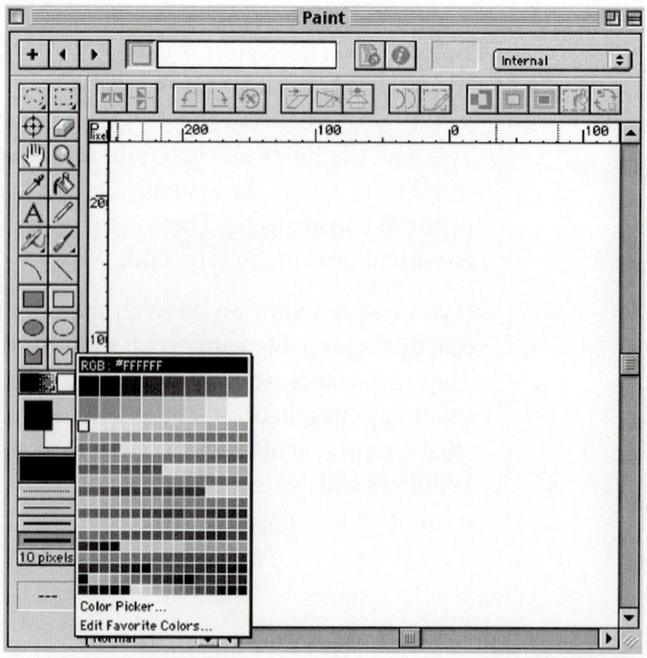

At the top of the Color palette is a series of 16 colored squares, referred to as Favorite Colors. These colors can be changed in the Edit Favorite Colors window, which is opened by selecting Edit Favorite Colors from the bottom of the Color palette. In this window, you must first select the Favorite Color you want to change. Then you can either click the Color Picker button to display the Color Picker dialog box, or enter the exact hexadecimal color value or Palette Index number and click OK.

## The Color Picker Box

Selecting Color Picker from the bottom of the Color palette opens a window where you can change colors and even create a custom palette if you wish (custom palettes will be explained later).

If you opened the Color Picker dialog box, shown below (Macintosh only), scroll through the list on the left side of the box to view the various options available. The color mode that is highlighted on the left is the one currently displayed in the main dialog box.

Remember, Windows users will not see a box like this where they can select different types of color pickers. Instead, when they click the Color Picker button, the Windows color picker, as shown in the previous section, will open.

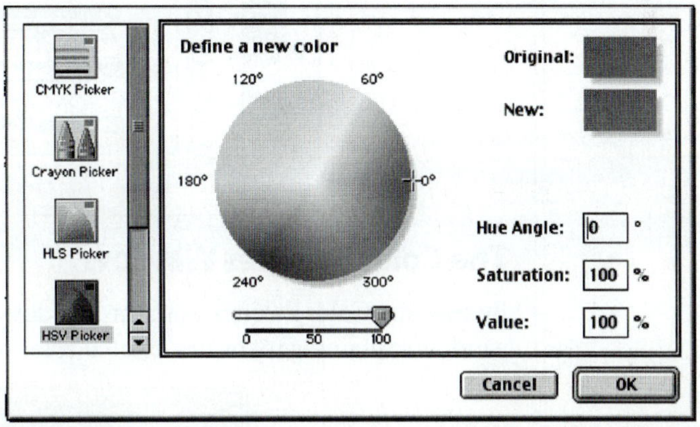


## Suitable Color Pickers

Two color pickers are most commonly used by Director users. The first is the RGB Picker. Here, you can create colors by moving the Red, Green, and Blue sliders back and forth. RGB is the best option for productions that will be previewed on both the Macintosh and Windows platforms. It is rapidly becoming the preferred color mode because of higher Internet bandwidths, faster modems, and more-advanced computers.

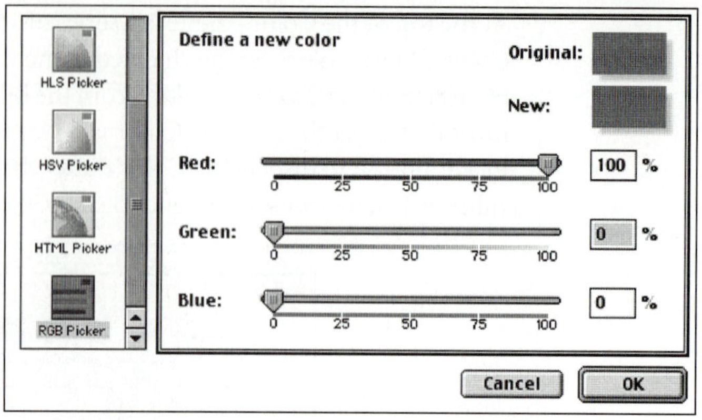


RGB color comes in three bit depths: 8, 16, and 32. Which bit depth is chosen can significantly alter the file size of your images. Try to use the lowest bit depths possible for each of your images to keep them as small a file as possible. The bit depth of bitmap Cast Members can be altered in the Modify>Transform Bitmap dialog box.

The HTML Picker provides RGB sliders to create colors too. However, it will allow you to stop only on certain values — the 216 Web-safe colors. This picker also provides the hexadecimal value of the color. In the image below, the color's hexadecimal number is FF0000.

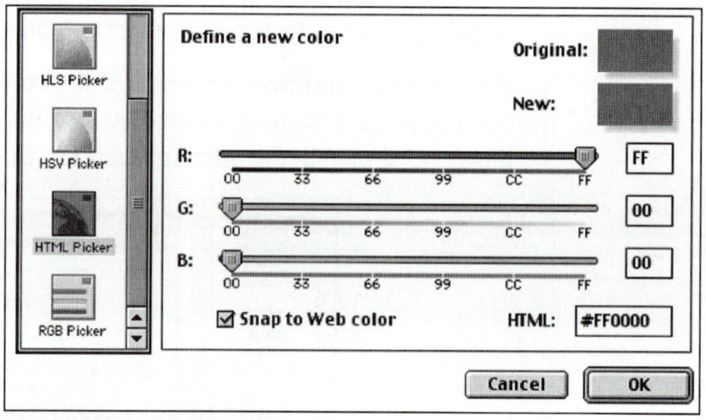


## The Color Palettes Window

By selecting Color Palettes from the Window menu, you can open a moveable, independent window containing many pre-created color palettes.

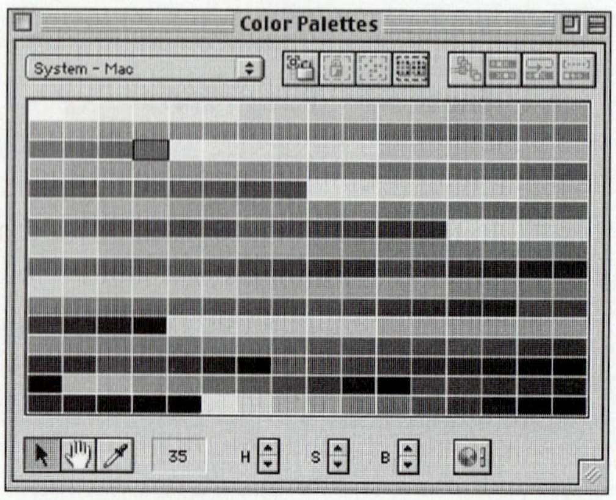

You can select a specific Color palette to meet your needs from the drop-down menu shown below. Among the most commonly used are the Rainbow and Metallic palettes. Additionally, there are collections of pastels and vivid colors available.

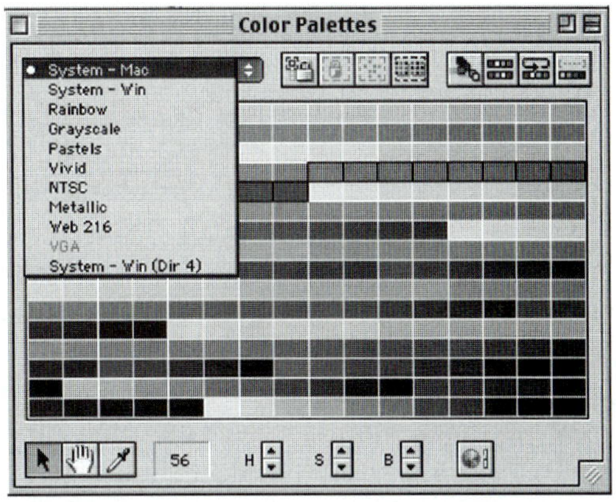


Director offers an Eyedropper tool that works much like Eyedroppers in other drawing and painting programs. The Eyedropper tool can be used to sample a color from an image and place it in the Color palette for use elsewhere. To do this, simply highlight the desired location in the Color palette, select the Eyedropper tool, and click on the color you want to reference.

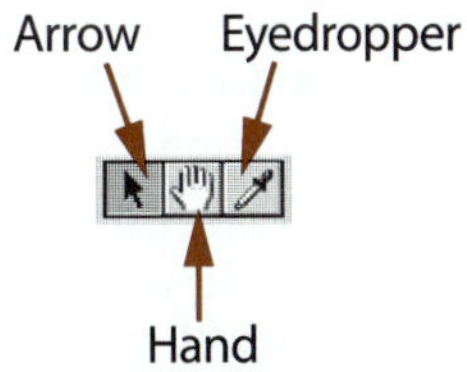


## Custom Color Palettes

To change any of the colors in a palette or to make a custom one, highlight the color using the selection (Arrow) tool, located at the bottom left of the palette. Then click the Color Picker button, shown below.

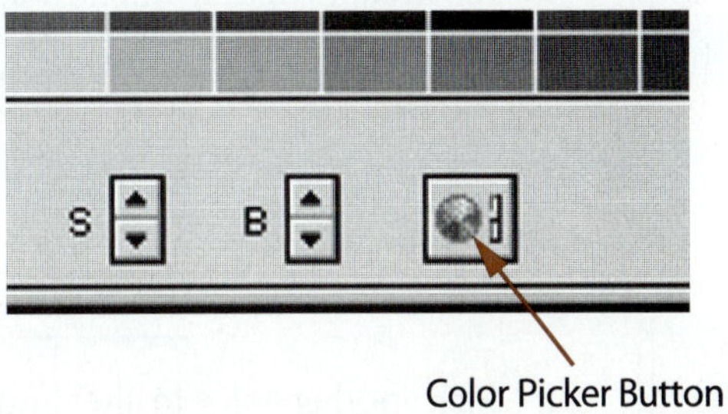


The controls for adjusting the hue, saturation, and brightness are identified with the corresponding H, S, and B spin boxes at the bottom of the Color palette. Adjust the arrows up or down to quickly alter and preview your color changes.

The order of the colors within the palette may be altered at any time by using the Hand tool, located next to the Arrow. Simply drag the colors around to rearrange or duplicate them. A prompt comes up asking you to save and name your New Custom palette. The palette must be saved before you can move anything. When you are done with your changes, the new palette appears in the Cast.

## The Color Palette Channel

The Color Palette channel is located in the Special Channels section of your Score. This channel is where you load your different Color palettes. Each frame of a movie can run off a different Color palette, and a Color palette, like any other Sprite, can be extended to cover several frames.

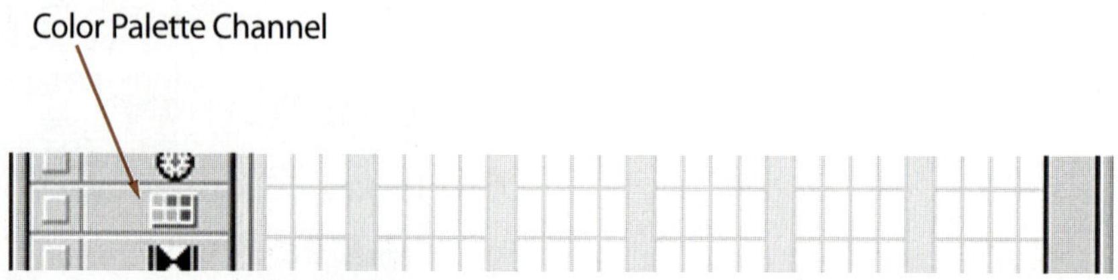


You might import an image that has different colors than the movie you have created. This image imports its own custom Color palette, containing the colors it used. When you place the image in your Score, notice that Director automatically places the image's custom Color palette in the Color Palette channel starting on the same frame as the image.

To make different frames use different color palettes, highlight the frame in the Color Palette channel and select Modify>Frame>Palette to choose the palette you want the movie to work with.

### *Creating a Custom Palette*

1. With Director open, select Window>Color Palettes.
2. Click on any color you wish to change. Now select Color Picker from the bottom-right corner of the Color palette. Save the new palette as "New Palette" and click OK.
3. The Color Picker window should now be displayed. Scroll to the RGB Picker and manipulate the sliders to create a different color (Windows users, just pick a new color from the Windows color picker). Click OK. Notice that the new color has replaced the old. It will now appear in the Cast.

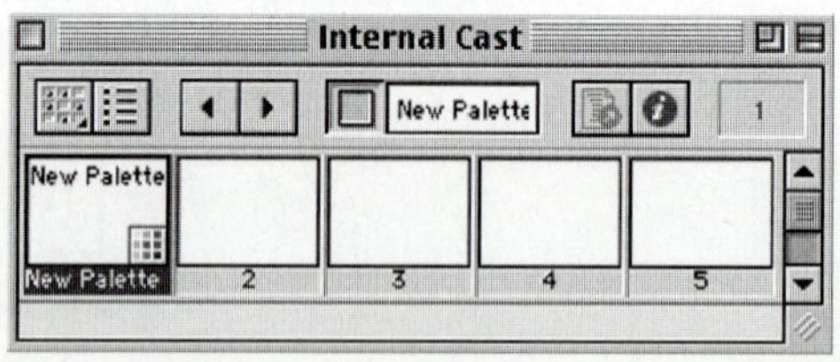


4. Pick another color to alter and repeat the process. Keep an eye on your new colors. You will need to remember their location later.
5. Using the HTML Picker, create two new colors (Windows users, pick two new colors from the Windows color picker). Now you have four new colors.
6. With the Hand tool, at the bottom left of the Color Palettes window, click on each color (one by one) and drag it to the top-left corner of the Color palette. When you are finished, all four colors should be in positions 1-4 of the Color palette.

*You will not be able to make your new Color palette appear in the Paint window unless you paint a little something in the window first. This is a minor inconvenience, as you can quickly paint a stroke with a paintbrush and erase it later.*

7. To force your new Color palette to appear in the Paint window, select Modify>Transform Bitmap. Set the Color Depth to 8 bits. Now you can select New Palette from the Palette drop-down menu. Click Transform and then OK. Notice how New Palette is available in the Paint window, ready to use.

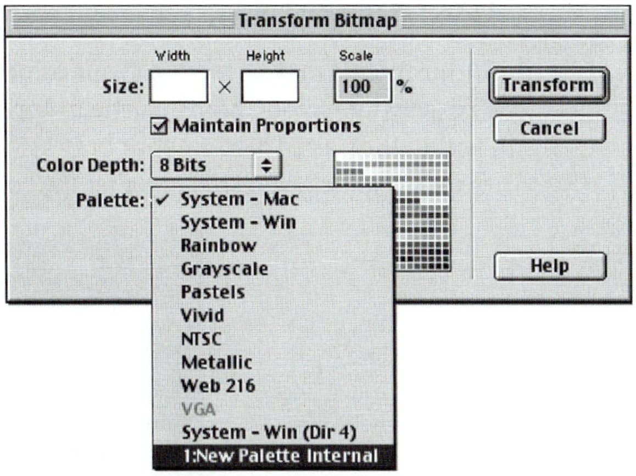


8. Quit Director without saving.

## Color Cycling

Color Cycling is a Color palette special effect. A series of colors taken from the current Color palette can be displayed quickly to show a range of colors in a sequence. You can set the Sprites to cycle through the colors, making them appear animated. For example, color cycling could be used to make the lights surrounding a spaceship blink. Color Cycling can be applied through the Frame Properties palette or through a behavior from the Library palette, both of which will be discussed below.

### Frame Properties Palette

To apply color cycling to an entire frame or multiple frames, double-click in the frame of choice in the Color Palette channel. Make certain that your monitor is set to 256 colors or else this method won't work.

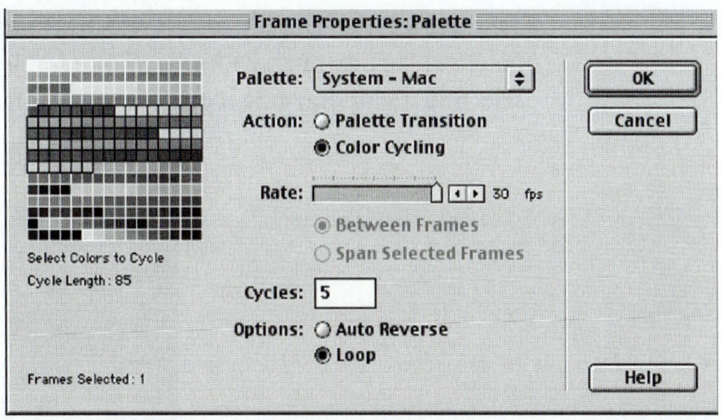


Then, pick a Color palette, set the action to Color Cycling, set the rate at which you want it to cycle, set the number of cycles you want it to complete, and choose whether you want the frame to loop or auto reverse when it reaches the end of each color cycle.

To select the colors you want to cycle, drag across them in the Color Swatch box, in the top left of the dialog box. They become outlined in black once they are selected. (see the image below)

Color cycling affects anything in a frame that contains the selected color or colors. If you select greens and blues, then greens and blues will be the only two colors that cycle.

Adjustments may be made to your color cycling selection within the Color Palettes window. To get your Color Cycling palette to appear in this window, you can double-click on it from within the Cast. There are four buttons in the top-right section of the Color Palettes window to help you select or alter the colors.

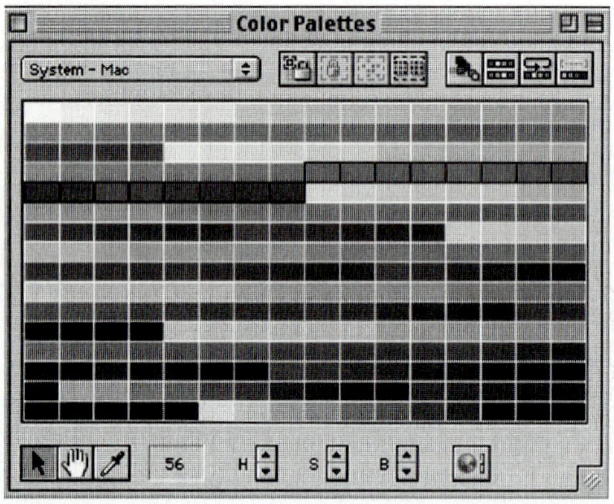


The buttons do not become active unless more than one color in the palette is selected. The first button allows you to sort your selected colors based on hue, saturation, or brightness. The second button offers you the flexibility to be able to reverse the order of the colors that you have selected.

The third button shifts the colors back one space, making what *was* the first color the last.

The fourth button is used to create animated gradients/blend effects. Clicking it takes the first and last colors you selected and blends the two across the color spaces between them.

### The Library Palette

The second way to apply color cycling is to use the Color Cycling behavior in the Library palette. Like other behaviors, the Color Cycling behavior can be attached to a Sprite(s) by selecting it and dragging it onto the Sprite in the Score.

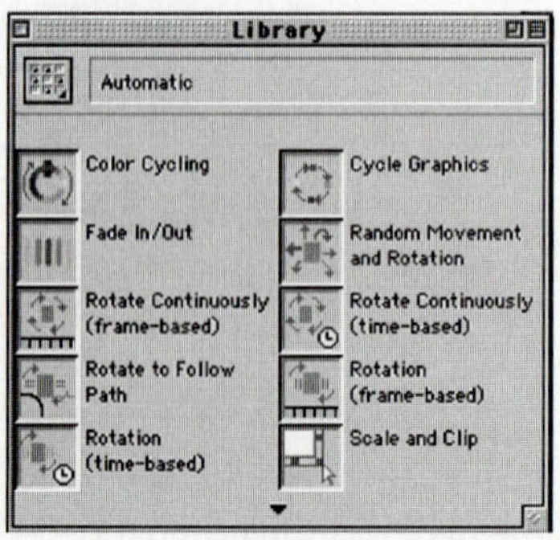

After you have applied the behavior to the Sprite, a Parameters dialog box appears.

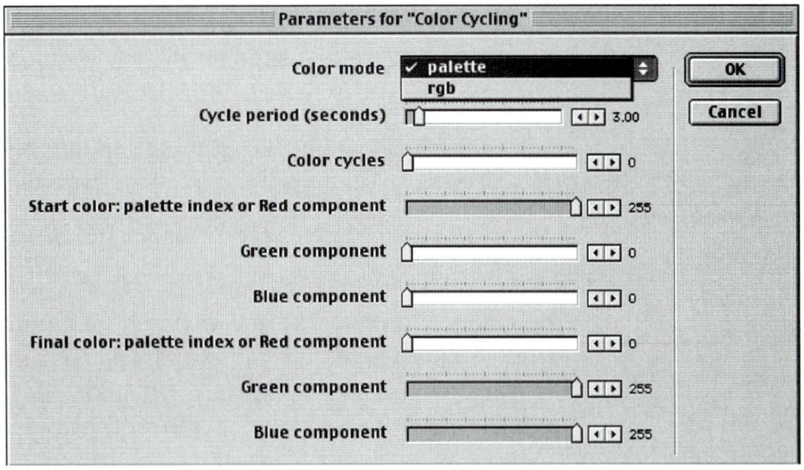


If you choose the Palette mode from this dialog box, you will need to set your monitor to 256 colors. If you choose the RGB mode, you do not need to alter your monitor settings.

## *Color cycling*

1. Open the **Color.DIR** file from the **SF-Director** folder.
2. Switch your monitor's color depth to 256 colors. Most monitors default to thousands or millions of colors. The following method of applying color cycling does not work if your monitor is not set to 256 colors.
   - If you have a relatively new Apple computer, you can change your monitor's setting right in the Control Strip.
   - If your computer is older, you may not have a Control Strip, so go into the Control Panels folder located inside your System folder and double-click on the "Monitors" or "Monitors and Sound" control panel. Adjust the setting to 256.
   - If you are running Windows 95/98, go to Start>Settings>Control Panel>Display Properties and then click on the Settings tab to bring up your color choices. Adjust the setting to 256 colors.
3. Go to the Color Palette channel in the Special Channels section of the Score and double-click on frame 1. It should display the Frame Properties palette, shown below.

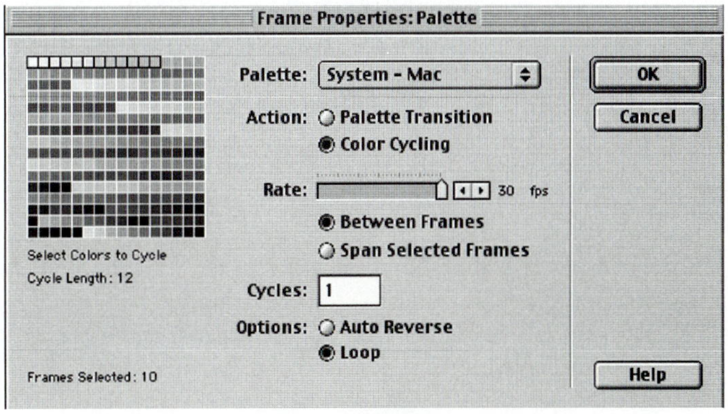

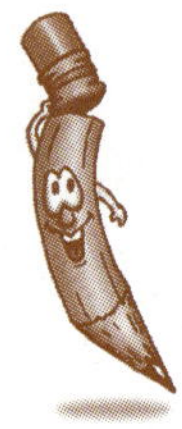

*When using frame-based color-cycling, you might also see the menu bars, window frames and dialog boxes in the background on your monitor cycling through the colors also. This is because everything on your screen is using the same palette.*

4. Click the Color Cycling radio button, next to Action:. This allows you to access the colors within the Swatch box.
5. Highlight the first 12 colors in the top row. Make certain that your palette is set to System-Mac or System-Win, depending on your system.
6. Double-check that the rest of the options match the previous image and then click OK.
7. Extend the Sprite in the Color Palette channel of your Score to cover frames 1-10.

If you rewind and play the movie at this point, you'll notice the background cycles through the colors (yellows, pinks, and oranges), but the shapes do not. This is because we have selected a portion of the Color palette that contains the same color as the background — yellow. If we had picked a portion containing the same green as the circle, it would have cycled instead. If we had picked the whole palette, all the Sprites would cycle.

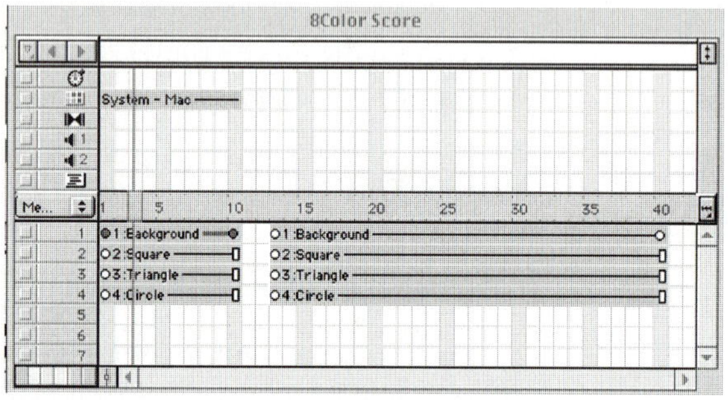


8. In the section of the Score containing Sprites (13-40), you will make the three individual shapes cycle. First open the Library palette by selecting Window>Library Palette. Choose Animation>Automatic from the drop-down menu.

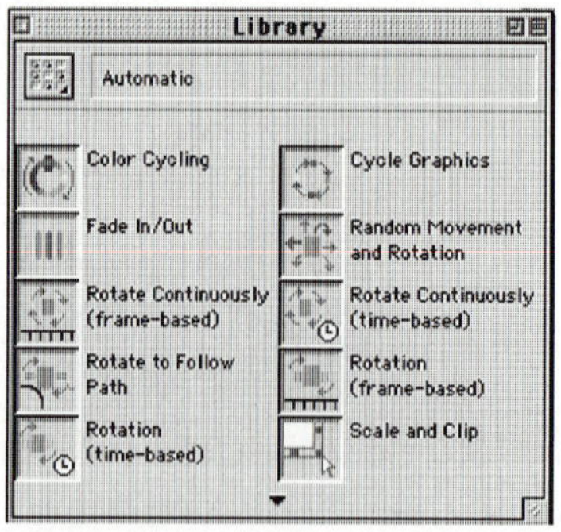


9. Highlight the "Square" Sprite, covering frames 13-40, in the Score. Drag a copy of the Color Cycling behavior from the top left of the Library palette onto the Sprite in the Score.

*We could have chosen RGB instead of palette for the color mode, allowing you to run cycling without your monitor set to 256. However, since the monitor was already set to 256 for the previous few steps to work, we decided to leave it as is.*

10. The Parameters box appears. Match the settings to those in the following image if they don't match already and then click OK.

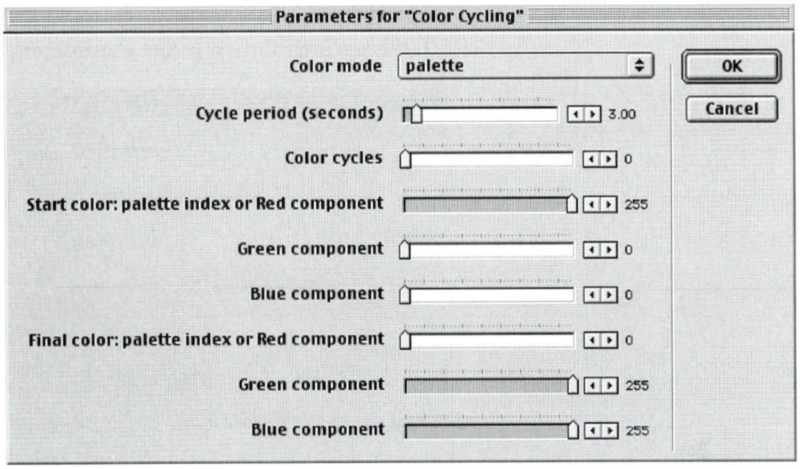


11. Highlight the "Triangle" Sprite, covering frames 13-40, in the Score. Drag a copy of the Color Cycling behavior from the top left of the Library palette onto the Sprite in the Score.

12. Match the settings in the Parameters box below and then click OK.

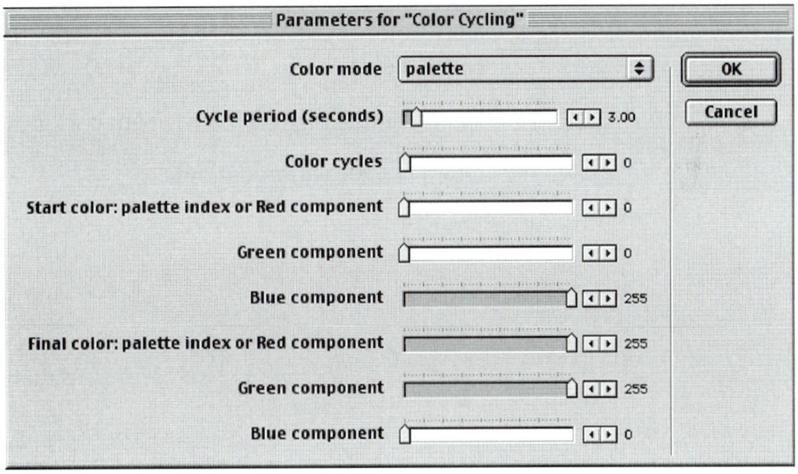

13. Highlight the "Circle" Sprite, covering frames 13-40, in the Score. Drag a copy of the Color Cycling behavior from the top left of the Library palette onto the Sprite in the Score.

14. Match the settings shown in the Parameters box below and then click OK.

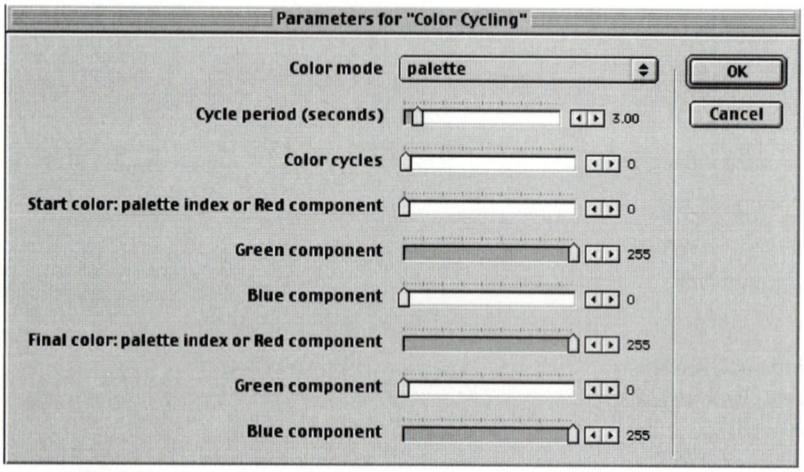


The parameters were set differently for the shapes in order to retain their color. You can choose a Start and End Color for each Sprite. You can set the parameters so that the Start Color of each Sprite is its screen color. For instance, the red square had a Start Color of 255 in the red component (100% red) and 0 in the green and blue components.

15. Rewind and play your movie. Your background cycles first, followed by the shapes.

16. Quit Director without saving.

# CHAPTER 13

# LINGO BASICS

## CHAPTER OBJECTIVE:

To understand the basics of Lingo, Director's scripting language, and the different types of scripts that you can write. In Chapter 13, you will:

- Learn what Lingo is and why it is so powerful.
- Learn about the different scripts you can write using Lingo.
- Become familiar with the hierarchy of scripts.
- Learn about a script's anatomy.
- Learn about event handlers.
- Find out where to go to find prewritten sections of Lingo.
- Learn about the various Lingo instructions.
- Adjust your Script window preferences.
- Learn how to troubleshoot basic script errors.
- Use the Debugger window.
- Practice using the Message window.
- Learn some valuable tips for working with Lingo.

## PROJECTS TO BE COMPLETED:

- Magic Carpet Tours (Project A)
- Redi-Base (Project B)
- Digital Portfolio (Project C)
- Emily's Photo Album (Project D)
- ABC's (Project E)

# Lingo Basics

Lingo, Director's scripting language, allows you to provide Director with specific instructions to follow. Using Lingo is an easy way to customize your production and add interesting features that would otherwise require a much more in-depth knowledge of programming to accomplish.

## Scripts

Each set of instructions written for Director to follow is called a script. Multiple instructions, or commands, may be placed in each script by listing them in the order that you want them carried out. To avoid confusing those of you who are new to programming or scripting, we have limited each practice script in this chapter to only one instruction.

There are four different types of scripts that can be written: Cast Member, Score, movie, and parent.

### Cast Member Scripts

A script can be attached to a Cast Member. In the example below, a script is attached to Cast Member 2 that says "continue." These type of scripts typically start off with the *on mouseUp* handler, which indicates that the task should be initiated when the mouse-click is coming back up after someone clicks on the Cast Member. When you click on the Cast Member, the movie starts playing.

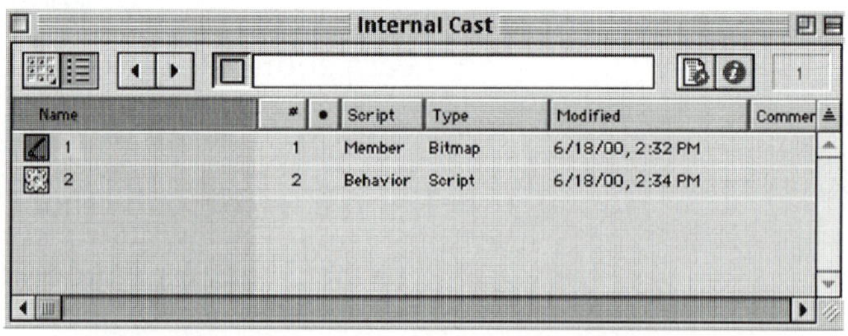


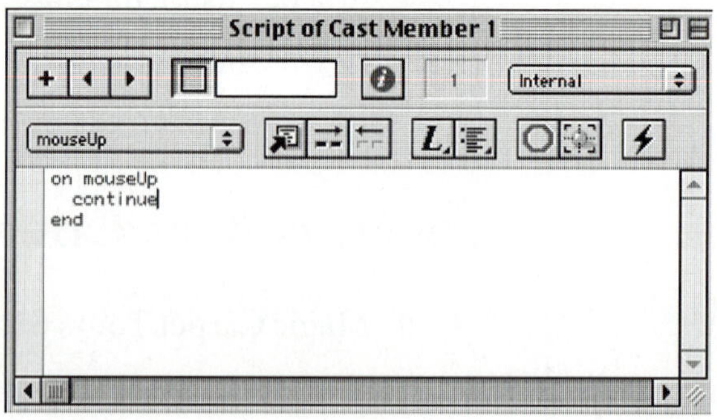

## Score Scripts

There are two types of scripts that can be in the Score. Score scripts are also known as behaviors. You can assign the behaviors as many times as you want and to as many scripts as you desire. As you create these scripts/behaviors, they are immediately added to the list available from the Behaviors drop-down menu on the top-left side of the Score. You can choose from this list and apply them as needed.

Frame scripts are to be placed in the Script channel. Double-clicking on any frame in the Script channel displays the Script dialog box. The following is an example of a Frame script, which is located in frame 1 of the movie. Frame scripts start off with *on exitFrame me*, telling Director that as soon as the Playback Head starts to leave this frame, follow these instructions.

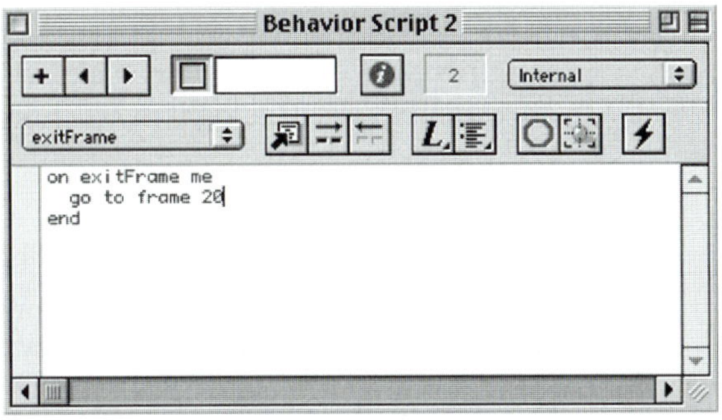


Sprite scripts can be attached to any Sprite in the Score. They can be created through the Behavior Inspector or by using the Library palette to apply an already written behavior to a Sprite. You can apply multiple scripts or behaviors to a Sprite.

## Movie Scripts

Scripts that contain instructions that apply to an entire production are called Movie scripts. An example might be a scenario in which you want the movie to begin only after the user has met certain criteria. Director keeps processing the instructions until they are completed, and then the Playback Head begins.

## Parent Scripts

Parent scripts are complex, and require a solid knowledge of object-oriented programming to use them effectively. Parent Scripts are not covered within this book.

## Script Hierarchy

Director processes Scripts in a definite order as the Playback Head moves through your movie. The process typically begins with small Sprite scripts and works up to Movie scripts. As the Playback Head rolls onto frame 1, Director looks for Sprite scripts and then executes and/or continues to look for any Cast Member scripts. The general order is:

A. Sprite script

B. Cast Member script

C. Frame script

D. Movie script

It is important to have a general idea of the order in which Scripts are executed so that you are certain to place the right instructions into the appropriate type of script.

## Script Anatomy

Lingo scripts are built like a present: The present itself, the Script's instructions, is nestled inside a box that describes the present in detail with a "To: Mom" name tag on it. In a Lingo script, the box and tag are known as Event Handlers.

### Event Handlers

*On mouseUp* and *end mouseUp* are examples of event handlers. Event handlers always travel in pairs, with a starting and ending statement, and trigger Director to watch for instructions. The instructions that Director is to follow must be written between these two statements.

Director understands many different event handlers. A few of the more common ones are listed below.

- on mouseUp — when the mouse is on its way back up from being clicked.
- on exitFrame — when the Playback Head prepares to leave the current frame.
- on mouseDown — when the mouse button is pressed.
- on mouseEnter — when the mouse pointer enters a Sprite's boundaries.
- on mouseWithin — while the pointer is still within a Sprite's boundaries.
- on mouseLeave — after the pointer leaves a Sprite's boundaries.
- on startMovie — before the Playback Head starts moving.
- on endMovie — at the end of the movie (after the Playback Head stops).
- on beginSprite — when the Playback Head hits the first frame of a Sprite.
- on endSprite — when the Playback Head leaves the last frame of a Sprite.

When a Score or Cast Member script is opened, Director displays a default event handler. The default is set to whichever handler is used most frequently. The cursor appears where you are to type your instructions.

Often, a script will pop up with no handler; instead, the word "Global" will appear at the top of the dialog box. Other times, you may wish to change the handler. To access Lingo code, simply click on the italic "L" menu button in the center of the second row of buttons. The drop-down menu that appears contains the different Lingo handlers and instructions listed alphabetically. If you are looking for *on mouseUp*, as shown below, you would go to the Mo to Move section and then choose that handler from the list. A space appears between the event handlers in the script window for you to type your commands.

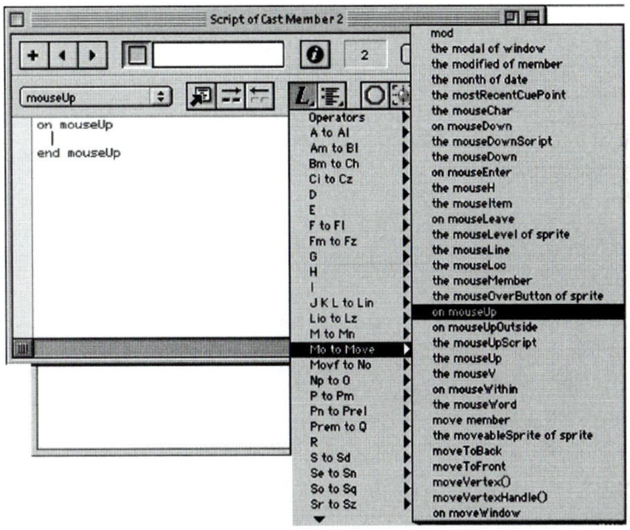


The button to the right of the "L" menu button displays a drop-down menu that lists Lingo in various categories. If you know what you want Director to do but don't know the name of it, go into the appropriate category. You will likely find what you are looking for.

If you already know the type of Lingo you want to use, feel free to delete the default words and type in what you want, rather than looking it up.

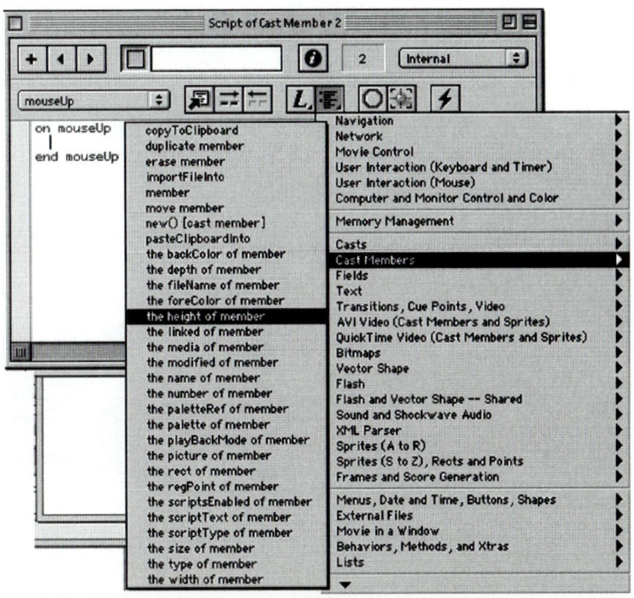

## Dissecting Lingo Instructions

Lingo is made up of many parts. It's a lot like the English language. In English, sentences may comprise nouns, verbs, pronouns, adverbs, prepositions, conjunctions, and adjectives. Lingo may comprise Commands, Keywords, Operators, Functions, Constants and Properties. Below is a brief explanation, along with a few examples, of each component.

- Commands — *continue, pause, quit, halt, go.* Commands tell Director to do something. The examples are self-explanatory.
- Keywords — *the, on, end.* Certain words that have a special meaning in Director. For instance, *on* means "listen up, instructions are coming." *The* means that a property comes next.
- Operators — >, <, +, -. Operators are ways to manipulate values (numbers). Director can do basic math.
- Functions — *date, time, key.* These are questions that Director is prepared to answer. If you use *date*, Director displays the current date (as per your computer's clock). If you use *key*, Director can display which key or combination of keys you pressed last.
- Constants — *return, true, empty, false.* Constants never change; they always mean the same thing within Director. *True* and *false* are used often in Lingo to determine if a condition is met within "If, Then, Else" statements (if a condition is true, then do this; otherwise, do that).
- Properties — *locV, locH, width.* Properties are the attributes of an object. Italic and 12 pt. are attributes of type. They help describe or define the object. *LocV* is vertical location; *locH* is horizontal location.

It is important at this point that you have a general understanding of how Lingo instructions are built by combining the parts listed above. It is not important that you memorize everything mentioned so far. Lingo is complicated, so another book would be needed to discuss it in full.

### Script Window Preferences

Director has a Script Window Preferences box, where you can assign different colors to different parts of your Lingo scripts. This should make Lingo a little easier to understand. Here, you can set some standards and even choose the font in which your scripts appear. Access this dialog box by going to File>Preferences>Script.

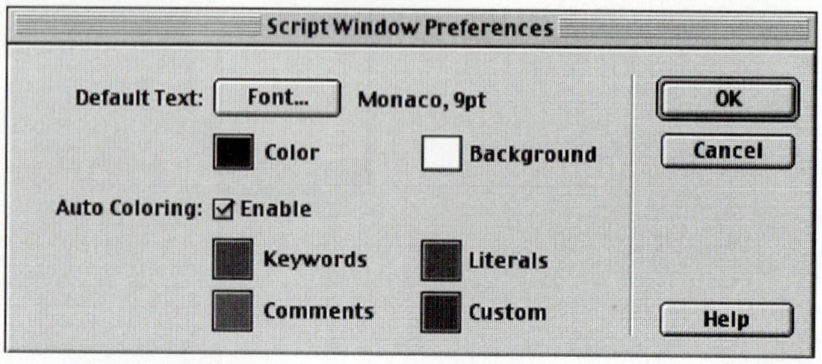

## Script Errors

If you don't formulate your instructions clearly, a warning box appears.

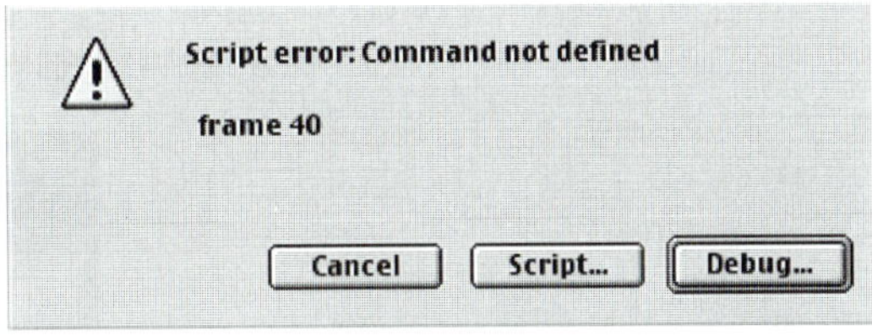


The warning box shown above lets you know that the command was not defined. The instruction in the script just says *frame 40*; it should say *go to frame 40.*

You have the option to cancel, but cancelling won't fix the problem. The Script button takes you straight to the offending script. This is great if you know what is wrong and how to resolve the problem. If it is a long Script or you don't know where the problem is, press the Debug button, which displays the Debugger window.

There are times when the Debug button will not be available. If it isn't, the script is more than likely incomplete.

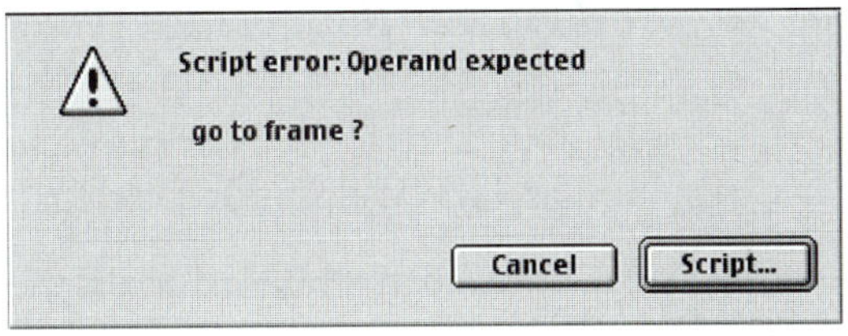


### The Debugger

The Debugger identifies the offending line so that it can be fixed. In the example below, you can see that the arrow is pointing to the error in the script. Once the problem has been identified, you can go back to the script and make your changes. For long and complex scripts, the Debugger utility is incredibly valuable. You can access the Debugger by selecting Window>Debugger.

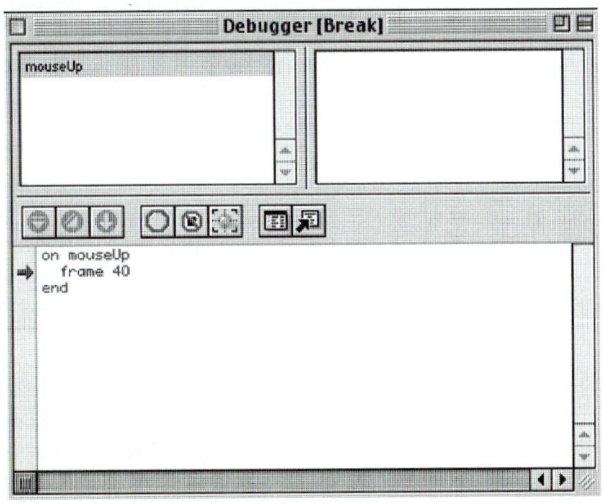

## The Message Window

The Message window allows you to see how Director works and processes scripts step by step. Director refers to dispatching steps as "sending messages" to different areas within itself. You can use this window to test scripts and verify that they are running as planned.

### *Working with the Message Window*

1. With Director open, select Window>Message to display the Message window. It displays "Welcome to Director" at the top of the window.
2. There are five buttons across the top. Click the Trace button, which is the middle one. It keeps a running list of all the messages that it runs.
3. Type the word *beep* and press the Return/Enter key. You should hear a beeping sound. It is the system beep on your machine. You wrote a script, minus the handlers, and ran it to test it. Let's try another one.
4. Type *put the date* and press the Return/Enter key. The current date, as per your computer's clock, is displayed. Take a look at the steps. The first line is your instruction, the second line is the message as it was executed, and the last line is the result.

   If you want the results to appear in the Message window, you must type the word "put" before your Lingo instructions. Without this extra word, Director might still execute the instruction, but you will have no way of confirming that it is working correctly.
5. Type *put 5+5* and press the Return/Enter key. You should see the line where it sends the message and then the line containing the answer, 10. Compare your Message window with the one below. They should look identical.

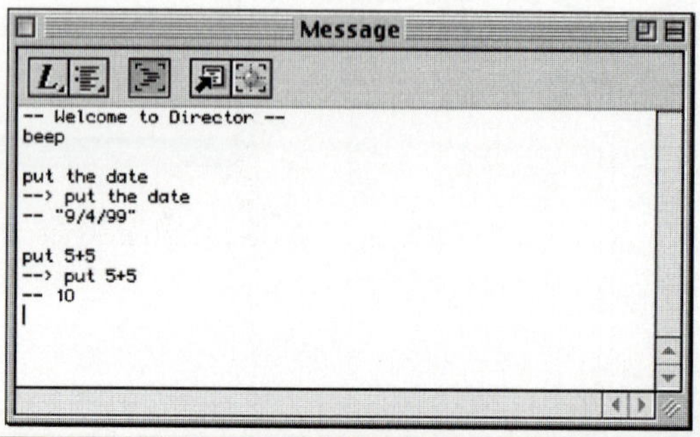

6. Close the Message window.
7. Keep Director open for the next exercise. However, you do not need to save this movie.

## Menu Commands

Under the Control menu, there are several commands that refer to scripting. For now, let's focus only on the Disable Scripts option. As you gain experience and begin to generate long scripts in several places to accomplish different functions, the scripts can get out of hand. There may be times when you have conditions set up in such a way that you can never see one of the alternative endings play out in real time unless you disable the scripts.

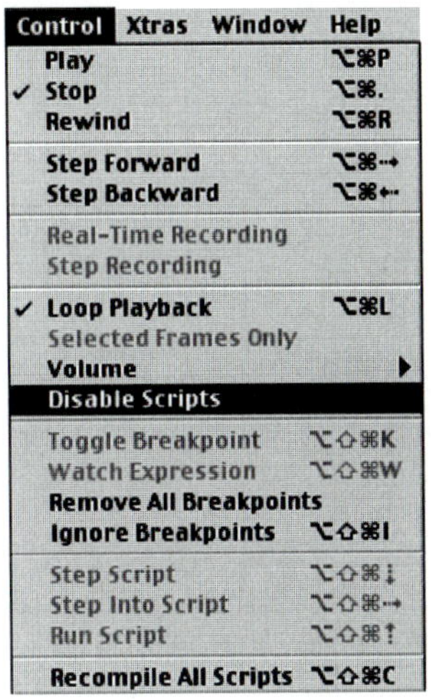

### *Working with Lingo*

1. Select File>New Movie. Make certain that the Special Channels section of the Score is open. If it is not, click on the Hide/Show button on the right edge of the Score to open it.
2. In frame 40 of the Script channel, double-click to display the Frame (or Behavior) script. Your cursor should be blinking between the *on exitFrame me* and *end* event handlers. Type *go to frame 1* and close the window.

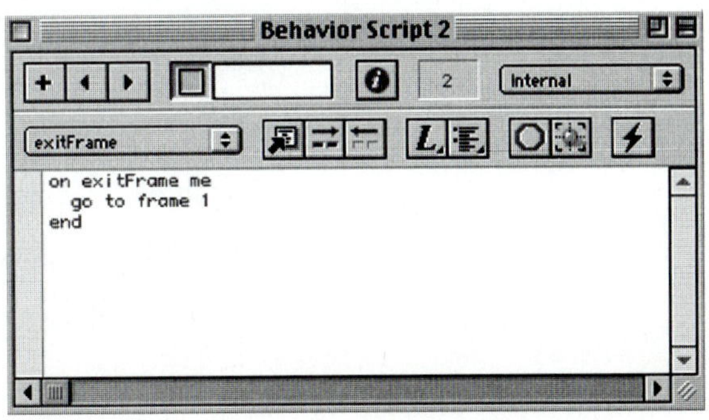

3. Open the Paint window and draw a filled rectangle. Create the phrase "Click Me" with the Text tool. Select the text and drag it on top of the rectangle. You have now created a Click Me button. Let's add a script to it to make it work.

4. While you are still in the Paint window or from within the Cast, click on the Script button to open up the script of Cast Member 1. The script should have the *on mouseUp* and *end* event handlers showing, and the cursor should be blinking between them. Type in *go to frame 40* and then close the window.

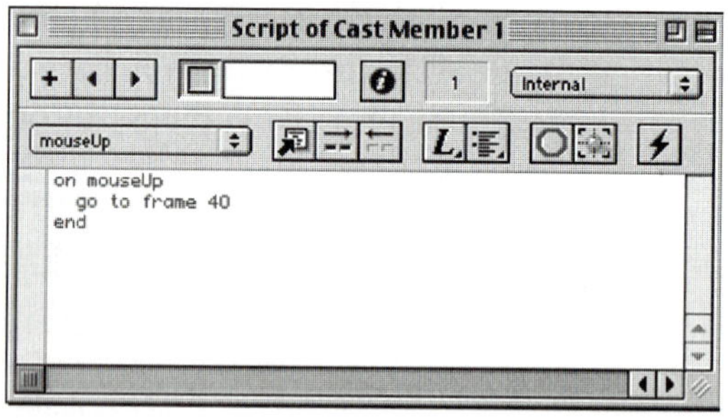


5. Open your Message window by selecting Window>Message. Make certain that the Trace button is pressed in.

6. From your Cast, drag a copy of Cast Member 1 into channel 1, frames 1-28 of the Score.

7. While watching your Message window, rewind and play your movie. Click the Click Me button quickly, making the movie jump to frame 40 and then to frame 1. Stop the movie. It should look like the example following.

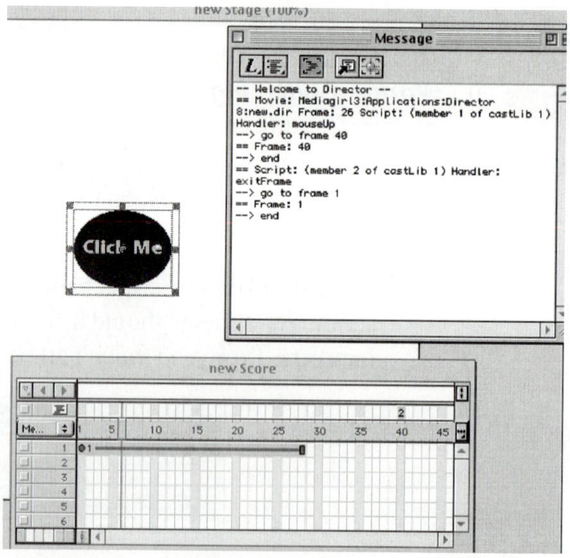


Take a look at the messages and see if you can follow them.

8. Let's mess up a script on purpose.

Go back into the Cast Member script attached to the Click Me button. Delete the words *go to* so that the instruction just reads *frame 40*. Close the window and play your movie. Click the Click Me button on the Stage and an error message appears.

9. Click the Debug button to open the Debugger window. The offending script line is displayed in the bottom window with an arrow pointing to it.

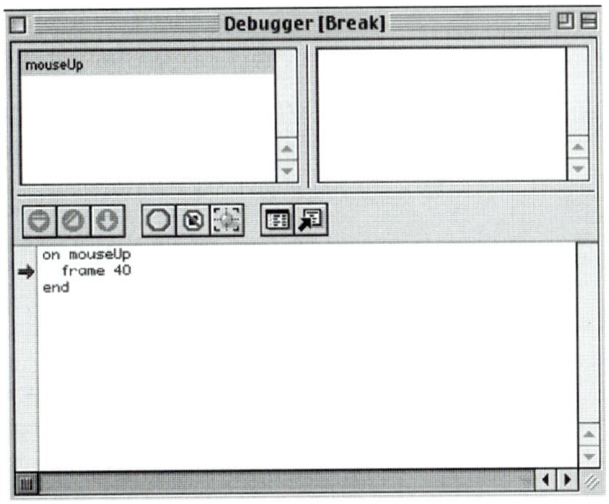


10. To fix the problem in your script, click the Go To Handler button in the Debugger window, shown below, and it will open the script and place a cursor in front of the offending line. Fix the script so that it says *go to frame 40*. Rewind and play the movie to make certain that it works this time.

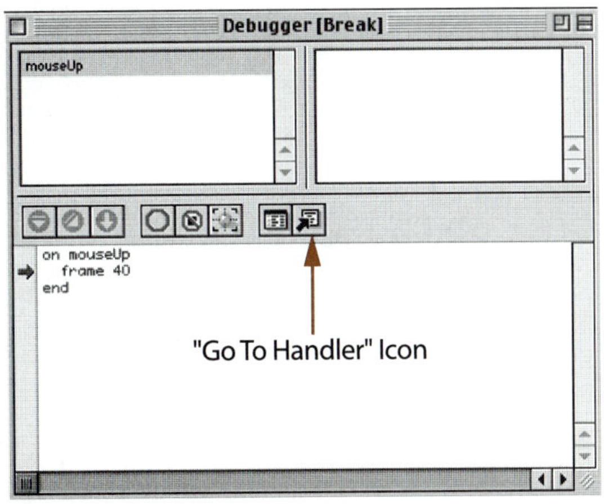


11. Quit Director without saving the movie.

## Lingo Tips

- Lingo instructions and messages must be surrounded by event handlers.
- Watch out for typos. Director doesn't respond to words it doesn't understand, and those include misspelled words. If you aren't good at spelling, carry a dictionary and double-check everything. Have someone else proofread your scripts as a backup.
- Use your Copy and Paste commands to cut down your workload. When you have to create many scripts that are similar, type the script once and then copy and paste it. Make small, individual changes to minimize the possibility of errors creeping in. Another option is to use the drop-down lists that contain Lingo in chunks — let Director write the scripts for you.
- Keep an eye on your Message window if something is not working right.
- Make certain that proper names, such as a marker name or the name of a file, are placed within quotation marks and spelled correctly. Watch the uppercase and lowercase letters too — Director is case-sensitive.
- If you are going to do a lot of scripting, customize your script colors so that they are soothing to the eyes.

### Frequently Used Lingo Scripts

The following is a list of frequently used scripts to get you started with Lingo. Most of these can work with many different event handlers.

| Instruction | Definition |
|---|---|
| pause | pauses a Director movie (stops all sound, transitions, and video as well) |
| continue | continues a paused movie |
| quit | stops movie and closes Director |
| halt | stops movie on its current frame but doesn't quit Director |
| beep | makes a system beep |
| alert "message" | displays an alert dialog box with your message on it — type your message between the quotes |
| go to frame | allows you to jump to a specified frame number or replace the frame number |
| go to the frame | loops Director continuously on the current frame |
| go to "nameofmarker" | allows you to jump to markers — fill in name of marker between the quotes (case-sensitive) |
| go to movie "name.dir" | allows you to jump to another Director movie — type the file name in between the quotes |
| go loop | jumps the Playback Head to the first marker to the left |

# CHAPTER 14

# PREPARATION AND DELIVERY

## CHAPTER OBJECTIVE:

To learn how to compress and prepare your finished project for distribution through various methods. In Chapter 14, you will:

- Learn how to prepare your product for delivery.
- Learn about what a projector is and its benefits.
- Learn how to create projectors and practice using them.
- Gain an understanding of how and when to use Shockwave compression.
- Learn how to create a projector that will run using Shockwave Player.
- Become familiar with which types of projectors produce the smallest files.
- Learn how to "publish" a movie to the Web.
- Learn about streaming Shockwave movies and how to create them.
- Investigate the various print options available for printing out pieces of your Director project.

## PROJECTS TO BE COMPLETED:

- Magic Carpet Tours (Project A)
- Redi-Base (Project B)
- Digital Portfolio (Project C)
- Emily's Photo Album (Project D)
- ABC's (Project E)

# Preparation and Delivery

There are two different ways you can deliver a finished Director project. The first is to create a self-contained version of your project called a Projector for distribution via CD or disk. The viewers do not need to have a copy of Director on their computer. A projector can be viewed by double-clicking on the file.

The Internet is an alternative way to distribute a Director project. To prepare a final project for the Web, it must be saved as a Shockwave movie (now referred to as "publishing" your movie). Through the Publish settings, Director will automatically generate an HTML page for your Shockwave movie to reside in on the Web. The Director movie can then be viewed in many standard Web browsers, such as Microsoft Internet Explorer and Netscape Navigator.

It is important to do everything possible to make your movie file as lean as possible before you finalize your production for distribution. The following list identifies a few ways to streamline your files.

- Use Background Transparent only when necessary. Use Matte instead.
- Delete any unused Cast Members and linked files from your Score.
- Keep your bitmap Cast Members as small as possible. Go to Transform Bitmap to reduce them to 8-bit images if you can. Make a copy of the image and try to transform the copy just in case you don't like the result. Remember, you cannot undo a Transform Bitmap command.
- Use vector images whenever possible. Bitmaps may be re-created as vector images in the Vector Shape window.
- For distribution on the Web, keep the Stage size at less than 640 X 480 pixels (500 X 440 will work fine) since the Internet browser takes up lots of room at the top and the left and right sides of the monitor.
- For projects that won't be viewed on the Web, work with 640 X 480 pixels unless you know for certain that your viewers have large monitors and fast machines.
- Audio and video created in other software applications should be compressed using a format such as Cinepak. Make these files as compact as possible.
- Don't use video for Shockwave projects. Video does not cross platforms reliably when used in this way.

## Projectors

As stated earlier, projectors are self-contained versions of Director movies. The viewer simply double-clicks the movie's icon, and the movie opens and plays. A copy of the Director software is not necessary.

Since projectors are self-contained, they need to incorporate some system-specific resources. For instance, if you create your movie on a Macintosh, it can run only on a Macintosh. If you want a projector that runs on a Windows computer, an additional version must be opened and saved on that platform.

Macromedia offers the projector free for distribution purposes. Each time a projector file is opened or closed, a "Made with Macromedia" splash screen will appear.

For specifics about the projector-distribution agreements, locate the Made with Macromedia folder inside your Director 8 folder. Here you will find a Read Me document that explains all the details.

When you are ready to make your projector, select File>Create Projector.

A dialog box will appear that is similar to the Import dialog box. Find your project in the box on the left and then add it so that it appears in the box on the right. If your project contains multiple movies linked together, be certain to add all of them.

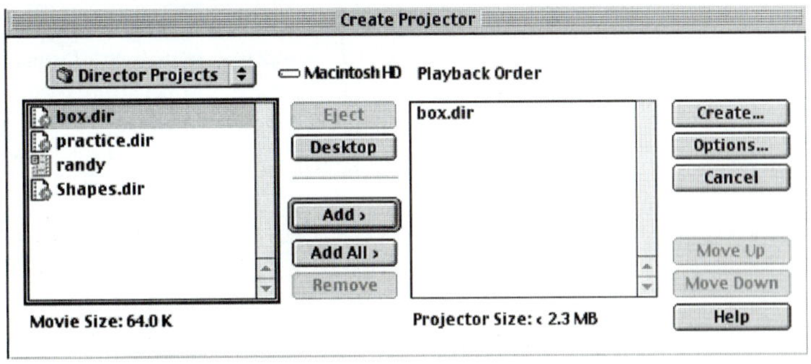


After you have added the necessary movies, click the Options button to adjust your projector's settings. The Projector Options dialog box is shown in the following image. Here is a brief explanation of each option.

- There are two playback options. Play Every Movie is relevant if your project is made up of more than one Director movie. Animate in Background allows your movie to continue to play even if two files are open at once.

- Full Screen fills in the monitor with the same color as the background of the movie. Show Title Bar allows the Title bar to show across the top of your Stage.

- Stage Size offers several options. Use Movie Settings uses whatever movie settings you specified for each Director movie. Match First Movie makes all the movies in your project match the settings of the first one that plays. Center ensures that your Stage is centered on the monitor, no matter what size monitor it is playing on. Reset Monitor to Match Movie's Color Depth automatically resets any monitor to match the movie's color depth, whether it is 256 colors or millions of colors, assuming that the monitor can handle it.

- Media allows you to compress your movie as a whole using the Shockwave format. This will decrease file size.

- The Player section allows you to choose from three types of players (how the player code is included in the projector). A Standard player uses no compression, allowing it to be the fastest but largest file. A Compressed player will compress the player code but not the file as a whole, as the Media compression option does. Shockwave instructs the Director movie to play through Shockwave Player. It does not include Shockwave Player in the projector file, however. The viewers need to have a copy of this plug-in installed on their system. If they try to play a Shockwave projector and do not have the plug-in, they will be asked whether they would like to download it (for free) from Macromedia's Web site, www.macromedia.com.

- Use System Temporary Memory is a Macintosh-only option. It allows Director to borrow memory from the Macintosh system when required.

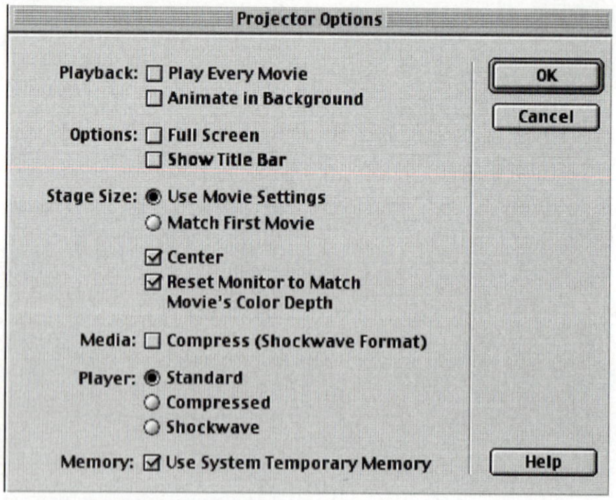

When you are finished, click OK. Then click the Create button to make the projector. Next, a Save dialog box appears. Name the file, put it where you want it, and click Save.

While the projector is being made, a Creating Projector dialog box with a status bar will appear. The status bar shows which files it is adding and how long the process will take.

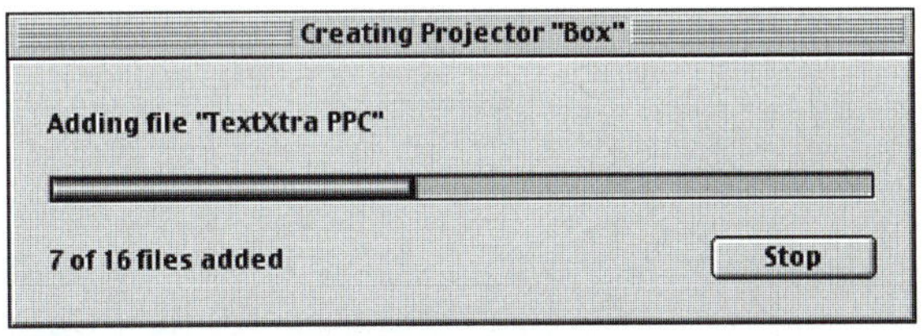


The projector, when shown in icon form, is in the shape of a diamond with the Director 8 colors and logo on it, like the icon shown below named Box.

When viewed in a list, the projector looks like an application. Under "Kind" it will be called an "application program", as seen below.

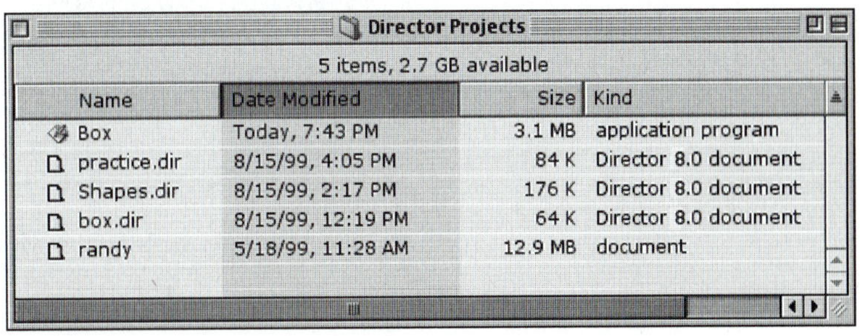

## *Creating different types of projectors*

Some of the file sizes generated in this exercise may not be exactly the same as the ones shown in this exercise. This is because of all the different computer configurations out there. Instead of using these numbers verbatim, please use them as a general estimate to scrutinize the relationship between the different types of projectors and the file sizes they create.

1. Create a new folder on your desktop and name it "Director Projects".
2. Open the **FinAmthe.DIR** file in the **Finished Exercises** folder within your **SF-Director** folder.
3. Select File>Create Projector. Find the **FinAmthe.DIR** file in the left list and then click Add so that the file displays in the right box. (Windows users will see the boxes stacked on top of each other rather than side by side.)

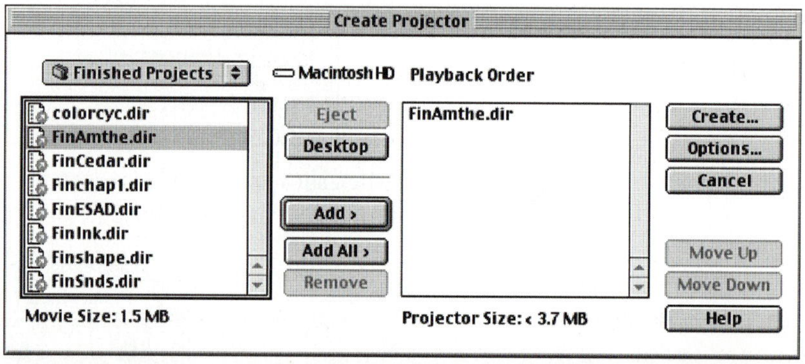


4. The first type of projector you are going to make is a compressed projector (a projector in Shockwave format, not a projector that requires Shockwave Player). Click the Options button. Make the options match those in the following example and then click OK.

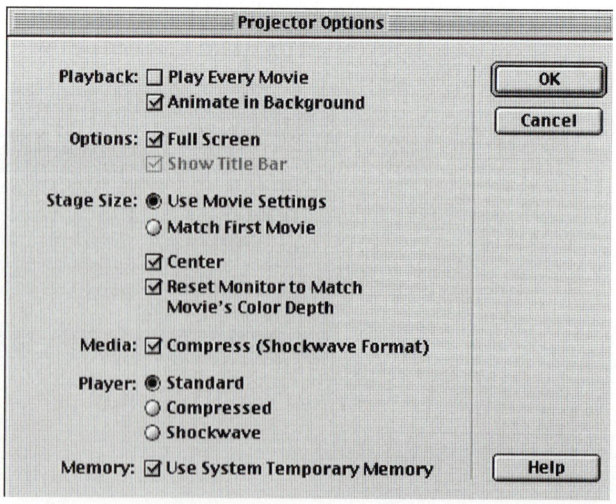

5. Click Create. A Save As dialog box appears. Select the Director Projects folder that you just created. Name the projector "Theatre1" and click Save.

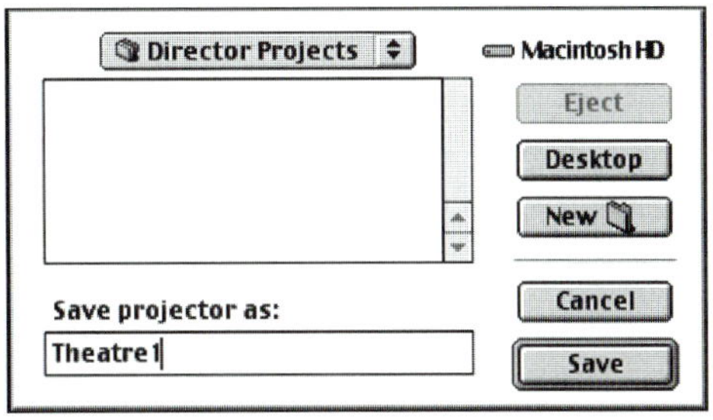


6. The second projector you are going to create is an uncompressed one. Select File>Create Projector and add the **FinAmthe.DIR** file again. In the Projector Options dialog box, uncheck the Media Compress (Shockwave Format) option and then click OK.

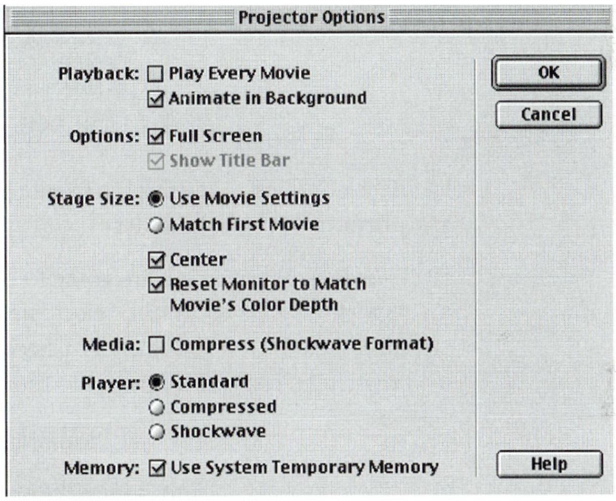


7. Click the Create button to create the projector.

8. Save it as "Theatre2" and place it in the **Director Projects** folder you created.

9. Stop for a moment and take a quick look at the folder that contains your projectors. Choose View>List to see them in list form. Notice how much smaller the compressed projector is. It is about 3.3MB; the uncompressed one is 3.8MB.

10. The third projector you are going to create is an uncompressed projector that runs off Shockwave Player, not its own resources. It will require Shockwave Player to run. Select File>Create Projector, add the **FinAmthe.DIR** file, and click the Options button. Select the Shockwave option in the Player section. Match the rest of the options to the following example.

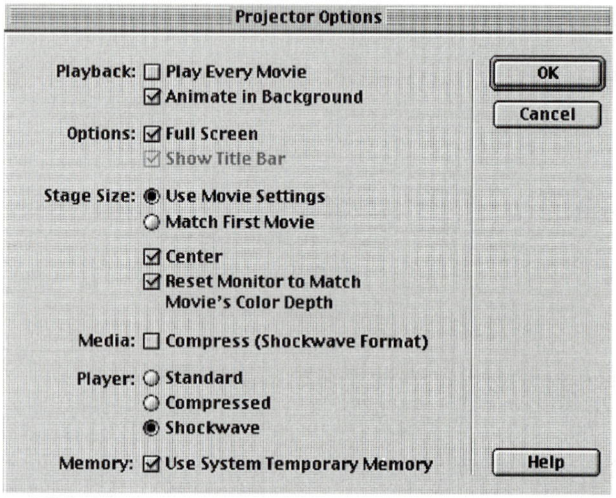


11. Click OK and then click the Create button. Name it "Theatre3" and place it in the **Director Projects** folder.

12. The last projector you are going to create is a compressed projector that requires Shockwave Player to run. Select File>Create Projector, add the **FinAmthe.DIR** file, and click the Options button. Check the Compress (Shockwave Format) option and match the rest of the options to those shown below.

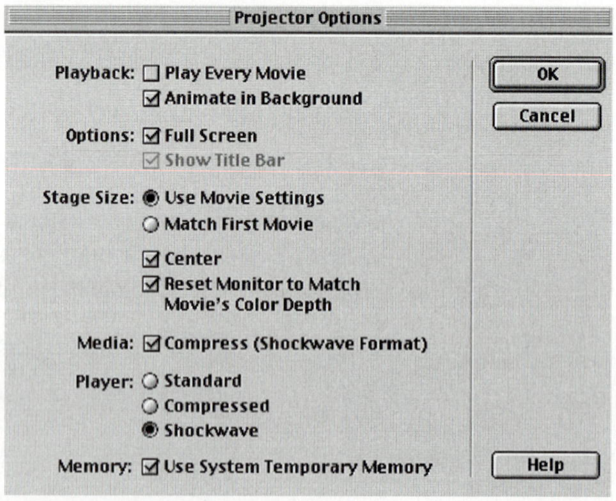


13. Click OK and then click the Create button. Name the projector "Theatre4" and save it in the **Director Projects** folder.

14. Go to the **Director Projects** folder and look at all four projectors. Notice that projectors made to run through Shockwave Player are smaller files. This is because Director doesn't need to save the whole projector inside the file. The project may be accessed on both the Macintosh and Windows platforms.

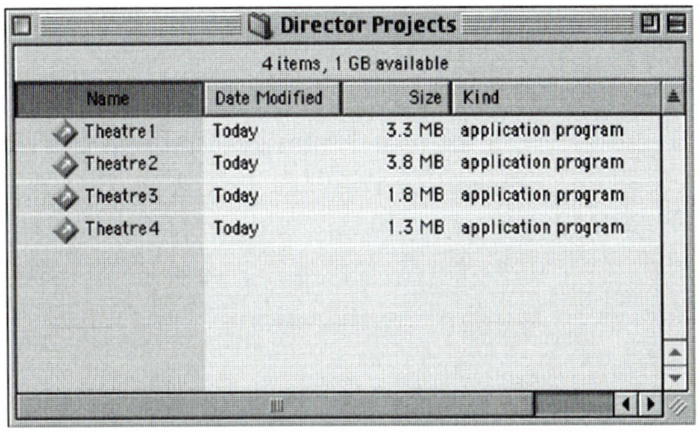


15. Double-click on the projectors one at a time and make certain that they work. The last two, unless you have Shockwave Player installed on your computer or you clicked the Web Download if Needed option, cause an error message to appear.

    The first two projectors are application programs, but the last two require Shockwave Player. If you have a fast Internet connection, download a copy of Shockwave Player and try to play the last two projectors.

16. Don't forget to take your video clips — in this case, Sol and Emily — with you in the same folder wherever you go. A projector does not embed video clips. You need the originals for your movie to play correctly. Select File>New Movie for the next exercise.

## About Shockwave Movies

Shockwave movies are not projectors and are not self-contained. They are compressed using the Shockwave compression scheme, and at the same time, they generate the HTML coding necessary to play on the Web. The extension .DCR is attached to the end of the new Shockwave file. A separate .HTML file containing the HTML coding is generated as well.

A browser with the Shockwave plug-in is necessary to view Shockwave files on the Web. The first versions of Internet Explorer to contain the Shockwave plug-in are version 3.0 for Windows and version 4.01 for Macintosh. The first version of Netscape Navigator to contain the plug-in is version 3.0 for both platforms. Newer versions of these applications include the plug-in.

If your browser is newer than the above-mentioned versions but didn't come with the plug-in, go to Macromedia's Web site, www.macromedia.com, and download a free copy.

You can also view Shockwave movies with Macromedia's Shockwave Player. A free copy of the application may be downloaded from the Macromedia Web site.

Shockwave files may not be edited. If changes are required, the edits must be made to the original Director movie, and the Shockwave file must be re-created. The fact that this type of file cannot be edited offers you the flexibility to distribute Shockwave movies over the Internet without the concern of viewers who own a copy of Director altering your work.

It is not recommended that you use video clips in a Shockwave movie, because they are not reliable across platforms. If you choose to do so, however, be certain to place all the video files in one folder within the same folder as your projector and name it "dswmedia". This will instruct the Shockwave plug-in or player where to find these files when it runs on Windows workstations.

### Streaming Shockwave Movies

There are a couple of steps you must do to set up your files correctly for the Internet. The first step is to select Modify>Movie>Playback and be certain to check the Play Movie While Downloading option. Set the frames to download before playing to 5, causing five frames of the movie to be preloaded into the computer's memory so that the movie is ready ahead of time. This is known as Streaming a movie. When a movie is streamed, each part is loaded just before it is needed. Match the rest of the settings to those shown in the image below.

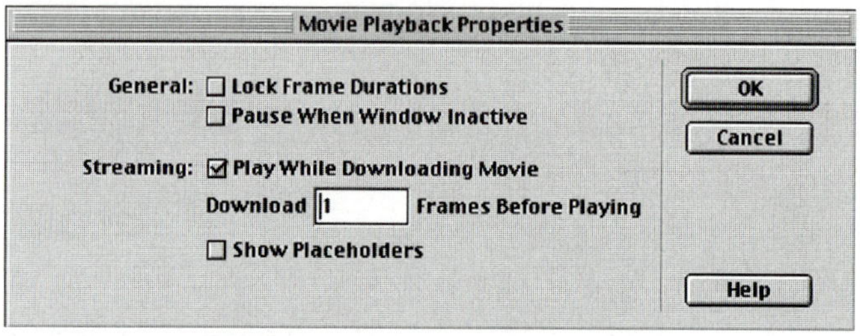


The next area to check is the Publish Settings dialog box, which is accessed through the File menu. The dialog box has five tabs. The Formats tab will show you the HTML file and Shockwave file that using the Publish command will create.

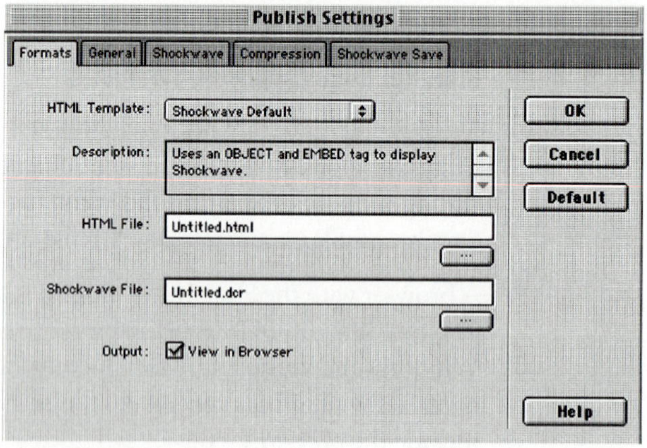

The next tab, the General tab, shows which dimensions the movie will open up with in the browser window. It will also allow you to pick a background color for the Web page just in case your movie doesn't fill the entire browser window.

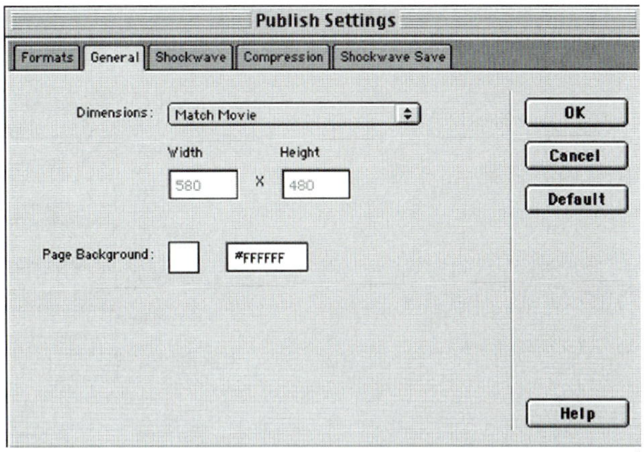


Next is the Shockwave tab. For the time being, the default options here will be fine.

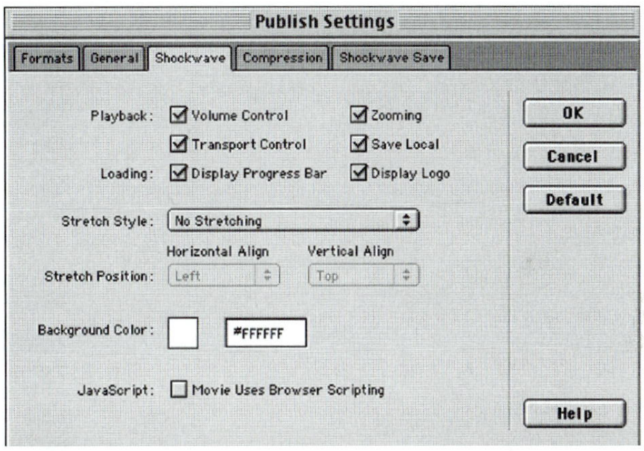


On the Compression tab, you can set an overall JPEG compression level for your Shockwave movie by choosing JPEG and adjusting the slider. The higher the number, the better the image quality and the larger the file size.

Shockwave Audio compression is also available on this tab. Choose Compression Enabled and select a speed. There is a Convert Stereo to Mono option, which will reduce audio file sizes when selected. Typically, Mono is used only for voice-overs.

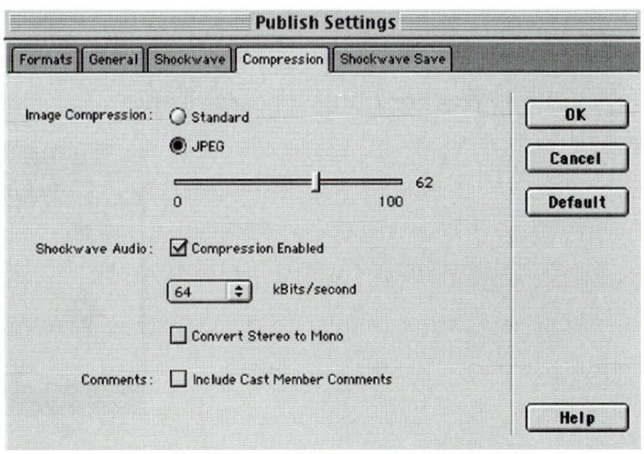

The final tab holds the Shockwave Save settings. These settings need to be adjusted only when creating a file for playback with Macromedia's Shockmachine. Here, you can give your movie a category and a title, among other things.

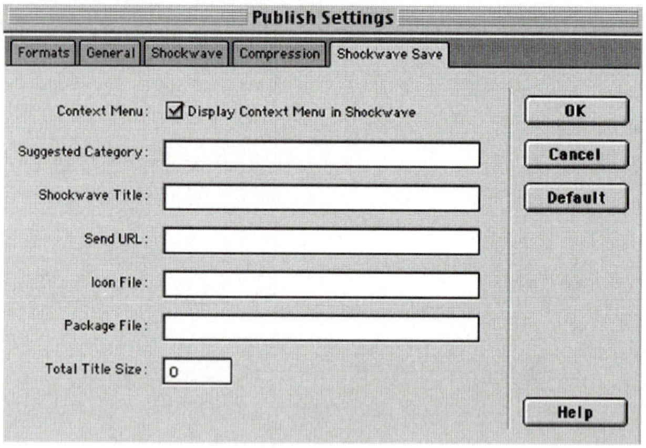


After you have checked these tabs, it is time to create your Shockwave movie. The Publish command is located under the File menu.

In the example below, you can view how both the Shockwave file (box.dcr) and the HTML file (box.html) appear as icons.

When viewed in a list, you can see from the following image that they are just documents. The Shockwave file is listed as a Director 8.0 document, and the HTML file is listed as a Netscape Navigator document.

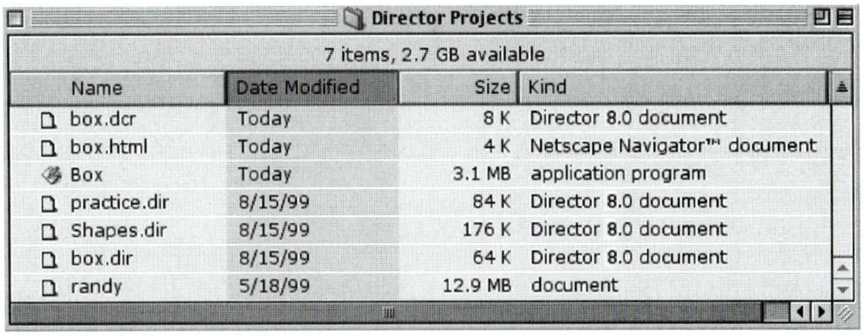

## *Creating a Streaming Shockwave Movie*

1. Locate the **FinSnds.DIR** movie in the SF- Director>Finished Exercises folder. Save a copy of this file in your **Work in Progress** Folder and name it "Stream.DIR".
2. Open the **Stream.DIR** movie you just created.
3. Check to see that the Shockwave Audio settings are correctly set because this movie contains sounds. Select File>Publish Settings>Compression and then match the settings to those below.

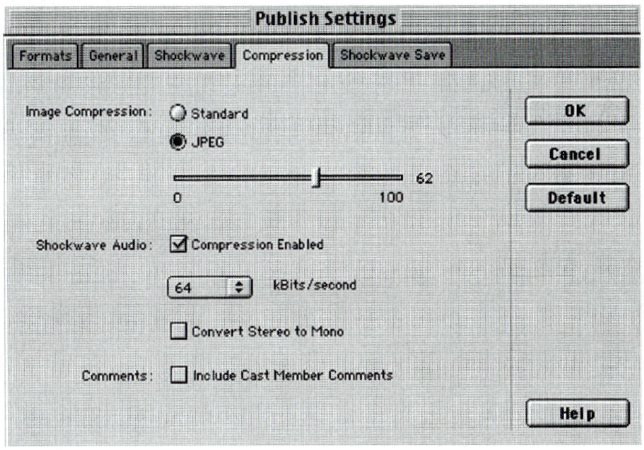


4. Select File>Publish and Director will automatically generate the HTML and DCR files for you.
5. After the files have been created, go to the **Director Projects** folder and you will see the Shockwave .DCR file and the .HTML file.

If you have the Shockwave plug-in included in your browser, feel free to double-click on the .HTML file and view it in the browser. If you do not have the newest Shockwave plug-in, you may go to www.macromedia.com and download a copy for free. Please keep in mind that it will take 15 or 20 minutes to download at 28.8KBs.

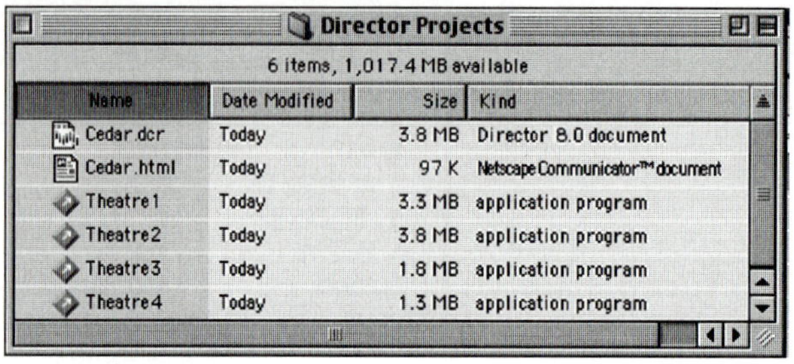


6. Quit the Director application.

## Printing Screens

On occasion, it will prove necessary to print out various portions of your production. Maybe you need to show a client new art at various stages, to pin up thumbnails of your Cast Members, or to print out your screens to keep a running storyboard.

Director provides numerous printing options to choose from. You can print the Stage, Cast Members, Scripts, or other movie components. You can even choose to print parts of the Score or certain frames, such as those with artwork changes only or those with markers only.

The image below shows all the options available when you choose the Print Stage option.

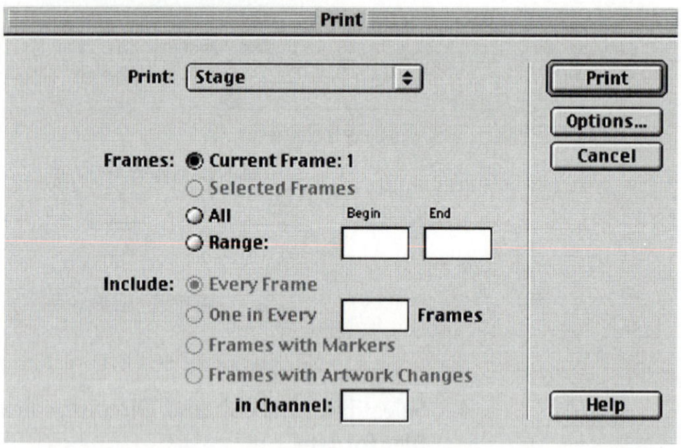

The next image shows all the Print categories available. Notice that some of the options available change when the category is changed.

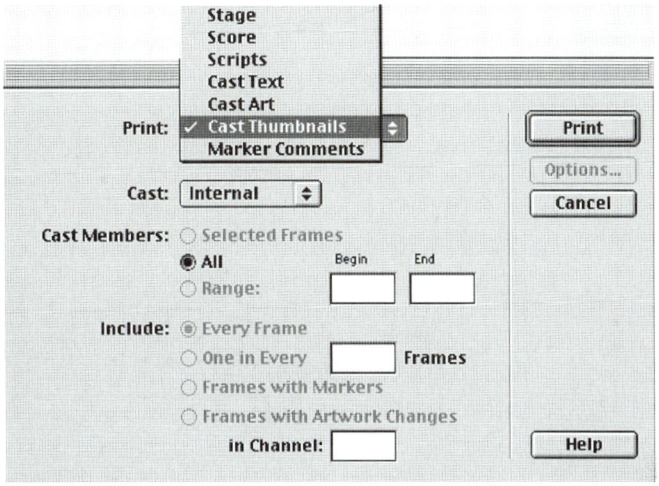


Other options can be found by clicking on the Options button. These include the ability to scale your output and the ability to choose whether you want certain identifying marks to show on each of your pages.

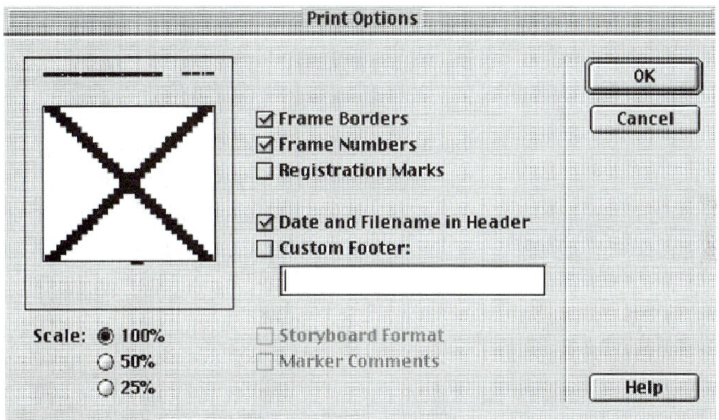

## *Printing Parts of your Presentation*

1. Open the **CH9befin.DIR** located in the Finished Exercises folder on your Director CD.
2. Go to File>Print, choose the Stage category, and then print frames 10-15 at 50% with Frame Numbers and Registration Marks turned on.
3. Choose the Cast Thumbnails category and print out the entire Cast as thumbnails.
4. Choose the Scripts category and print out the scripts for Cast Members 15-17.
5. Go to File>Quit and quit Director.

## Notes:

# Project Assignment #2

## Assignment

Your local Director-users group is sponsoring a contest. The first prize is a three-day, all-expenses-paid trip to the Macromedia Developers Conference in San Francisco. All the winner has to do is develop a great game in 10 days or less.

Your assignment is to create a shooting gallery, complete with targets that move on a horizontal track and fall down when they're shot. If you've ever been to a carnival or seashore amusement park, you've probably seen one like it. In its most basic form, the game would be good practice for someone who needed to polish their eye-hand-mouse coordination.

## Applying Your Skills

Be sure to:

- Create an introductory splash screen with an animation to introduce your game.
- Use the Paint window to develop an eye-catching background for the doomed ducks, tin cans, or whatever target items you choose to create.
- Create a custom cursor that looks like the crosshairs in a rifle sight, and make certain that it's active all the time.
- Create Cast Members to shoot at using any combination of the Paint, Text, or Vector shape windows. There can be different targets that move faster or slower depending on their type.
- Utilize film loops in at least two of your animations.
- Mix and match behaviors, being certain that you apply at least four different ones to keep the game interesting.

## Specifications

| | |
|---|---|
| Stage Size: | 640 x 480 pixels |
| Required Sections: | Introduction |
| | Rules |
| | Game Body |
| | Tally |
| | Reward |
| Required Components: | Custom cursor |
| | Animals or other targets |
| | Credits |
| | Background |
| | Rollover Cursor behavior |
| | *go to frame* scripts |
| | Frame scripts |
| | Cast Member scripts |

Construct the game around a central theme. We designed a sample project using an under-the-sea theme. To view our sample, open the "Project2.DIR" file which can be found on the student CD in the SF-Project Assignments folder.

Create an introduction, complete with an animation and rules on how to play. Then create animated objects and different levels to progress to. Work out a way to keep score. Show some type of a "You Win" screen at the end as a reward.

## Publisher's Comments

This is a great opportunity to show off your Director skills and use your imagination to create a fun game. If you're sensitive about shooting at little tin rabbits, come up with something that is OK to shoot at. Remember, it's all in fun.

Be certain to test the game and verify that when you click, the target falls. Some games are set up so that if you make a less-than-direct hit, the target falls only part of the way. You can accomplish this in a variety of ways — for example, making two different hotspots on each target, one that results in a kill and another that only damages the target a little bit.

# Review #2

## Chapters 8 Through 14:

In Chapters 8 through 14, you practiced creating Masks for Alpha Channels. You learned about Director's Library Palette, filled with pre-written behaviors. You learned about creating Film Loops and Custom Cursors. Various Color palettes were discussed, and you learned how to create a custom Color palette and make the colors cycle for effect. You were introduced to Lingo and learned some basic scripts. Several ways of delivering your final product were discussed, and you learned how to print out pieces of Director projects. After the second half of this course, you should:

- Have an understanding of the various masks and be able to create basic masks for use as alpha channels.
- Be familiar with the more frequently used behaviors that can be applied to Sprites through the Library palette. You should understand the different categories of behaviors and the usefulness of the Behavior Inspector.
- Know how to manipulate Sprites via the Property Inspector. You should be familiar with creating film loops and understand their benefits.
- Be comfortable creating and using custom cursors. You should also know how to create animated cursors and apply behaviors to them to create special effects.
- Be comfortable with the different types of color and bit depth that can be used in Director and how they can affect the playback of Director movies. You should have learned about color cycling and how it can be used to animate something or to create special effects.
- Understand the basics of Director's scripting language, Lingo, and the different types of scripts that you can write. You should have an overall understanding of the necessary pieces of a script and have practiced writing a few.
- Know how to compress and prepare your finished project for distribution through various methods. Whether your project is going to be distributed on CD or disk or over the Internet, you should understand the variety of specific options regarding distribution methods.
- Be familiar with the different print options available to print various parts of your Director projects.

# Project A: Magic Carpet Tours

The Magic Carpet Tours project is for a typical information-filled travel kiosk. Jill Hantz, a student at the Allentown Business School, created this presentation for her class project, designing, all the images and text within it.

The purpose of this project is familiarize you with a working Director file. This particular production makes use of sound and various graphics and transitions. Although you will not be creating this movie, it is important to browse around and become familiar with the pieces that were used to make it.

## Getting Started

1. Navigate to the **Norleans.DIR** file in your **SF-Director** folder and drag a copy into your **Work in Progress** folder. Work from this file for the remainder of the project.
2. Open the Control Panel by selecting Window>Control Panel.

3. Click the Play button to start the Director production.

*Be sure that you have installed the ATC fonts from your student CD. This production makes use of the ATC Tradewinds font. If the fonts are installed properly, this production will run smoothly.*

4. Work your way through each of the three sections (Sights to See, N'awlins Eateries, and Hotels) to familiarize yourself with the whole project and how to navigate through it. Make certain that you check out all the buttons.

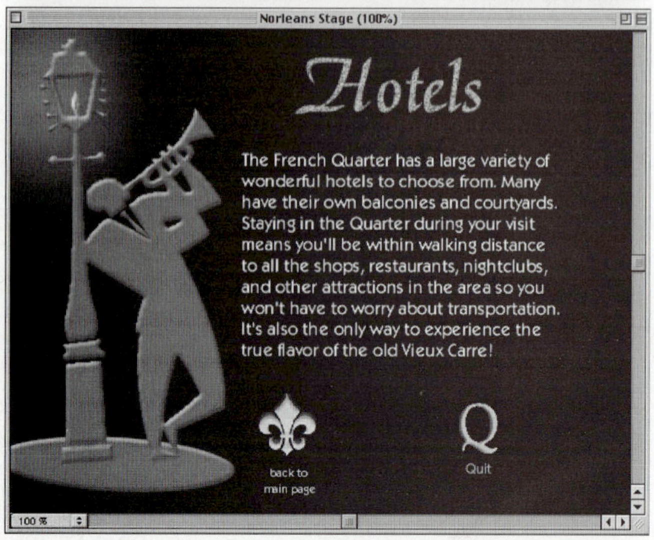

5. Select Window>Cast to open your Cast. Scroll down through the different Cast Members and take a look at them.

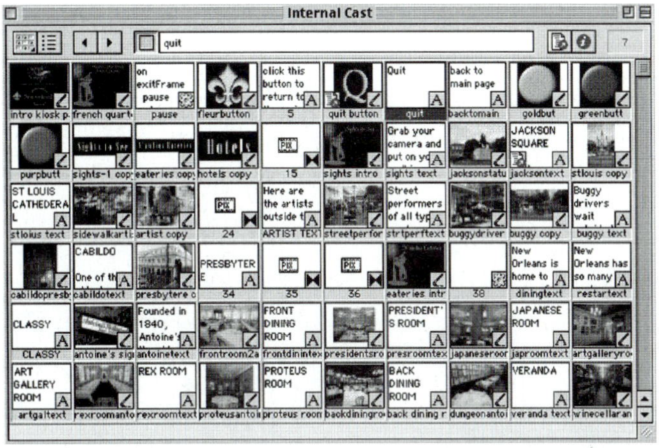

6. Open the Score (Window>Score). Scroll to the right and take a look at the names of the Sprites and where they are placed. See if you can figure out what is going to happen in the movie just by looking at the Score.

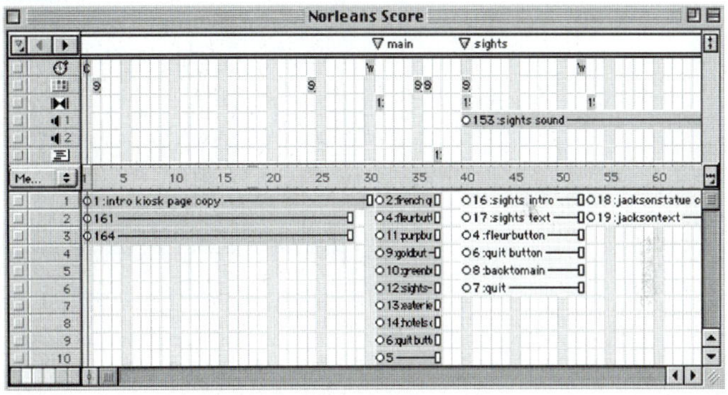

7. Drag the red Playback Head to the section of yellow Sprites, which make up the Sights to See area. The pink Sprites, next in line, make up the N'awlins Eateries section, and the light-blue Sprites make up the Hotels section.

8. Click on any Sprite that is currently located under your Playback Head. Notice that the image of the Sprite is highlighted on the Stage.

9. Click on another object on the Stage and take note that the corresponding Sprite in the Score is highlighted, allowing you to easily identify which image belongs with which Sprite.

   You should have noticed by now that there are big chunks of unused space (frames) between the sections of Sprites. With the use of Lingo, Director's scripting language, we will be able to jump from one group of Sprites to the next.

10. Scroll to frame 143 (after the yellow section) and double-click on the single Sprite in the Script channel (the channel located just above the frame numbers). You will see a Script appear containing the words *go to the frame* in it. This script is telling the movie to stop on frame 143 until something else happens.

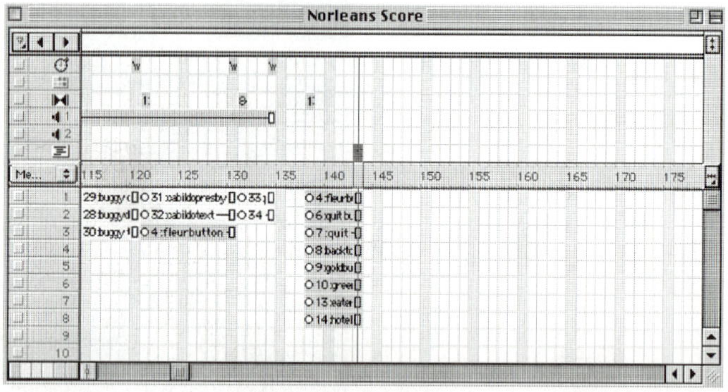


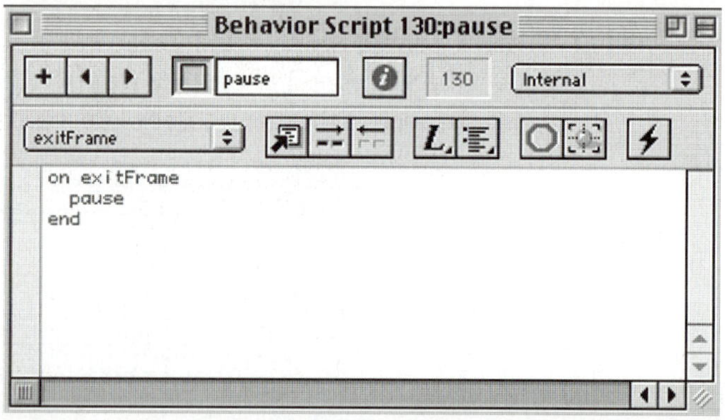


Notice that there are buttons on the Stage. Each of these buttons has a script attached to it, so when it is clicked, Director will begin reading and executing its script. Click on the N'awlins Eateries button and you will be sent to frame 206. Frame 206 is the first frame in the pink section.

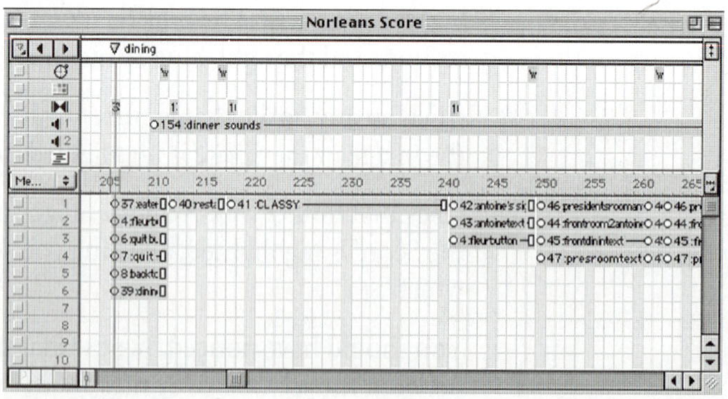


11. If you are not already there, drag your Playback Head to frame 143. With your Score open so that you can see frame 206, click Play on the Control Panel to resume playing the movie from this point. Next, click the N'awlins Eateries button and watch the Playback Head jump to frame 206.

    Director works in a linear fashion, one frame after another. You do, however, have the option to interrupt a movie and provide alternative instructions through the Lingo scripting language.

12. Press Command/Control-period to stop the Director movie. Click on the "Q" button. It is a Quit button. This particular production will continuously run on a touchscreen computer in a tourism rest area, where visitors can access it any time. Ms. Hantz made her Quit button advance the movie to a credits/thank-you screen and then rewind it to frame 1 so that it is ready for the next person.

Please take the time to work with this file. There are all sorts of things you can do: move Sprites around, double-click on Cast Members, add more Sprites to the Score, rearrange the pages in the Score, change the graphic layout of the pages on the Stage — the options are endless. Try doing all of the above at least once. Have fun and explore. The more you poke around, the more familiar you will become with Director.

## Notes:

# Project B: Redi-Base

Redi-Base will be featured and sampled at an upcoming food festival. Our job is to create a presentation that could be used by sales representatives to market the product. This project will be accomplished by working with keyframes and using Director's frame based timeline. In this project we will also practice moving and extending Sprites.

## *Getting Started*

1. Launch Director 8.0 and open the **RediBase.DIR** file located in your **SF-Director** folder. Choose File>Save As and save a copy of the file in your **Work in Progress** folder. Name the copy with the same name, "RediBase.DIR," and work with it for the remainder of the project.

   Familiarize yourself with the items that appear in the Cast. The first thing you will do in the next section is label your Cast Members. By doing so, it will be easier to read your Score later.

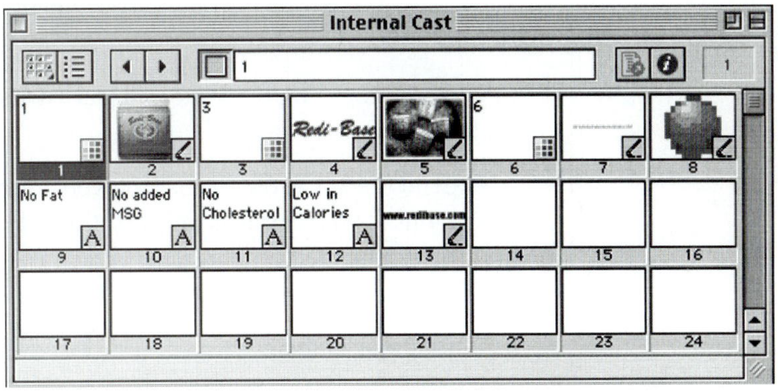


## *Naming Cast Members*

1. Starting with Cast Member 1, highlight each Cast Member one at a time by clicking once in the name area at the top of the Cast. As the last member becomes highlighted, type in its new name and press the Return/Enter key.

| | |
|---|---|
| #1 Jar Palette | #8 Button |
| #2 Jar | #9 No Fat |
| #3 Logo Palette | #10 No added |
| #4 Logo | #11 No |
| #5 Photo | #12 Low |
| #6 Slogan2 | #13 Website |
| #7 Slogan | |

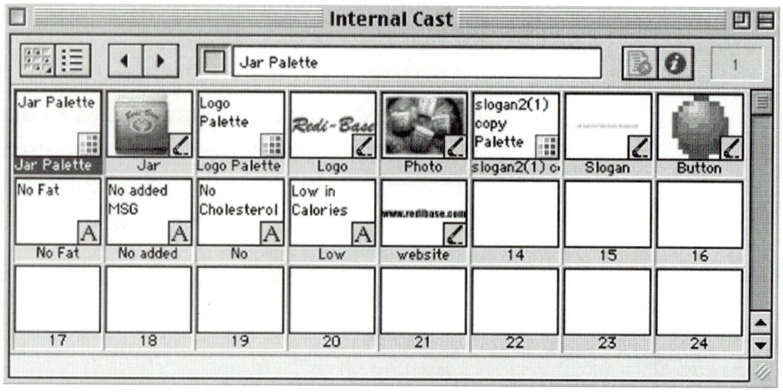


## *Creating the Animated Introduction*

1. Drag a copy of the "Logo" Cast Member to the Score and place it in frame 1, channel 1.

   As images are put in the Score, each will automatically bring along its own Color palette, which is placed in the Palette channel. The palettes appear in your Cast because these Cast Members are 8-bit and you are working in a higher bit depth than that.

2. Center "Logo" on the Stage and place it about one-third of the way down from the top.

3. Extend the Sprite out so that it covers frames 1-166 using one of the following options: if your Sprite is only one frame long, hold down the Option key and drag the right side of the Sprite until you reach frame 166; if your Sprite is more than one frame long, drag the right side of the Sprite out until it reaches frame 166.

   This Sprite, which is the product's logo, will stay on the Stage throughout the presentation.

4. Drag a copy of the "Slogan" Cast Member to the Stage and center it under the logo. In the Score, it should have automatically been placed in channel 2. Extend Slogan out so that it covers frames 1-166, again, using the appropriate method.

5. Highlight both Sprites in the Score and click on the light-yellow rectangle in the bottom-left corner of the Score. Changing the Sprites' color to yellow will make it easier to differentiate them from things that will change throughout the movie. Save your changes.

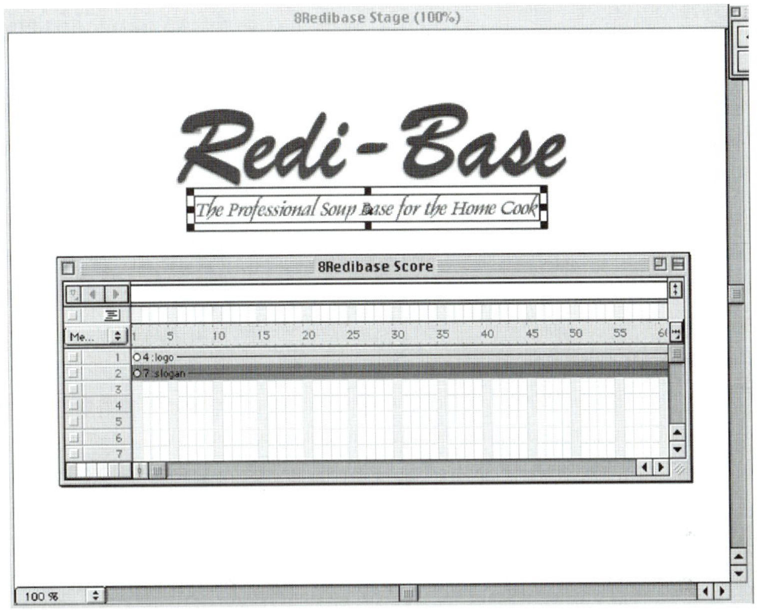


6. For the first 30 frames, we are going to display a jar of the product so that people can see its container size, type, and contents. Drag a copy of "Jar" to the Stage and center it under the slogan. Leave about 1-1/2″ between the top of the jar and the bottom of the slogan. Make certain that the "Jar" Sprite is in channel 3 and extend it out to cover frames 1-30. Leave the jar blue.

## Creating Animated Bullet Points

After you complete the next few steps, the following should happen: Once "Jar" reaches frame 30, four bullet points ("Button" Cast Members) are going to appear under the slogan(and replace the Jar). Words will now begin sliding in from the right side, one by one, and stop next to the bullet points.

1. Drag your Playback Head to frame 31 in the Score. Then drag a "Button" Cast Member to your Stage and place it about 1" below the slogan. Align it with the 'd' in the Redi-Base logo. Drag "Button" to channel 5, frames 31-135 of the Score.

2. Drag another copy of the "Button" Cast Member down to the Stage and place it about 1" below the first one. Place the Sprite in channel 7, frames 31-135 of the Score.

3. Drag another copy of the "Button" Cast Member down to the Stage and place it about 1" below the last button. Place it in channel 9, frames 31-135 of the Score.

4. Finally, drag down the fourth copy of the "Button" Cast Member and place it about 1" below the third one. Move it to channel 11, frames 31-135 of the Score. Save your changes.

5. Highlight all four "Button" Sprites in the Score and change their color to pink so that it will be easy to identify them.

You may want to use the Alignment palette, located under the Modify menu, or turn on the grid overlay or use guides (both are located in the Property Inspector under the Grids & Guides tab) to help you accurately align the rest of the buttons .

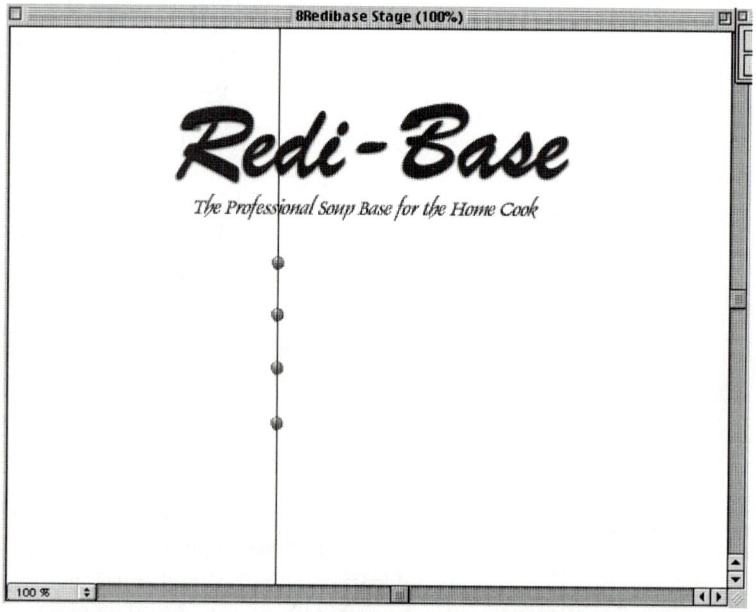


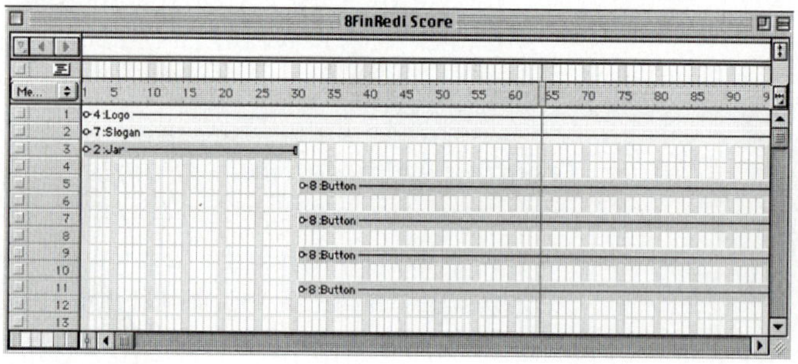


Now let's work with keyframing and set the text to slide into place.

6. Take the "No Fat" Cast Member and drag it next to the first button on the Stage. Put it in channel 4, frames 31-135 of the Score.
7. Insert a keyframe at frame 46 (highlight channel 4, frame 46, and then choose Insert>Keyframe). Now you have three keyframes, one at the beginning, one at the end, and one at frame 46.
8. Highlight the first keyframe by clicking on it. Then, while holding down the Shift key, drag the text off the right side of the Stage. The Shift key will make certain that the animation path stays straight.

What you have done in step 8 is tell the first keyframe that you want it to start from off the right side of the Stage. When the Playback Head reaches the second keyframe (frame 46), the text phrase should be sitting next to the bullet. When the Playback Head reaches frame 136, it should disappear.

9. Add the next text phrase, No Added. Place it on the Stage next to the second button. Put the Sprite in channel 6, frames 46-135. This text phrase is starting at frame 46 because you want the second phrase to start moving onto the Stage just as the first one is done moving next to the button.

10. Highlight frame 62 of the "No Added" Cast Member and insert a keyframe, just as you did in step 7.

11. Repeat step 8. Save your changes.

12. Add the third text phrase, the "No" Cast Member. Place it next to the third button. Put the Sprite in channel 8, frames 62-135 of the Score.

13. Highlight frame 78 of the No Cast Member and insert a keyframe.

14. Repeat step 8.

15. Add the last text phrase, the "Low" Cast Member. Place it next to the fourth button. Put the Sprite in channel 10, frames 78-135 of the Score.

16. Highlight frame 94 of the "Low" Cast Member and insert a keyframe.

17. Repeat step 8.

    Take a moment to rewind and play your movie. You will find that the text slides into place, one phrase at a time. If you have any trouble with this, you may want to open the finished version to check your progress and figure out any mistakes you may have made. The finished version is called **FinRedi.DIR** and is located in the **Finished Projects** folder inside the **SF-Director** folder.

18. Highlight the four text-phrase Sprites in the Score, one at a time, and change their color to green to identify them as text Sprites.

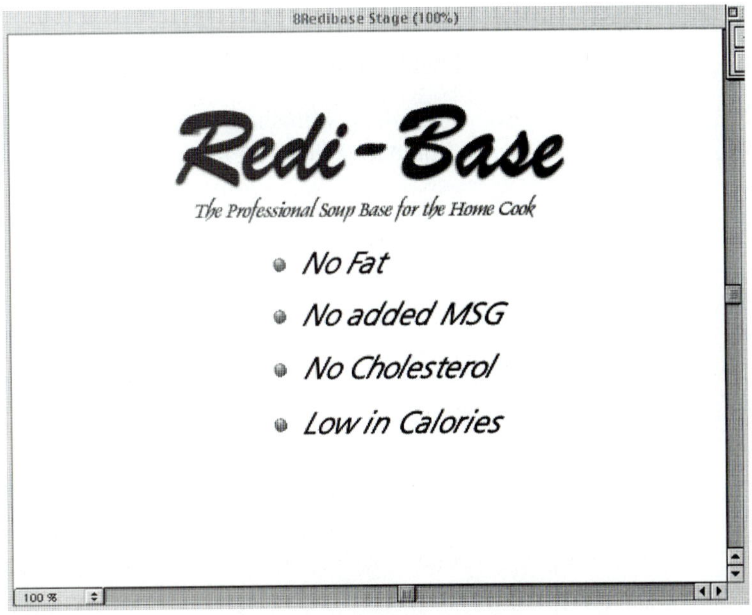

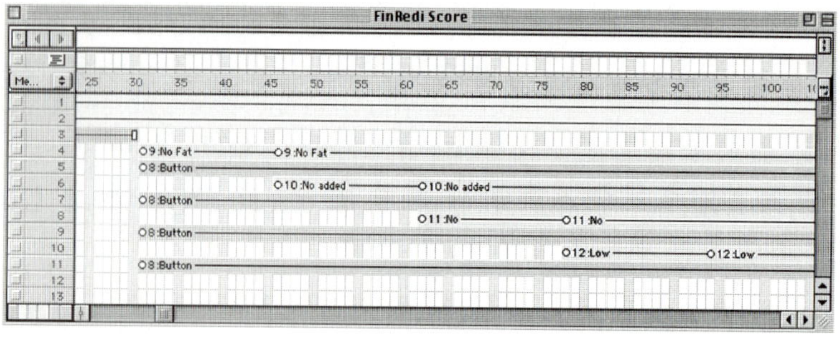


## *Creating the Ending*

1. The last section of the production will display a photo and the company's Web site address. First, drag a copy of the "Photo" Cast Member into channel 3, frames 136-166. Center it horizontally. Vertically, it should start an inch or two below the baseline of the slogan — whatever looks visually pleasing to you.
2. Now drag a copy of the "Website" Cast Member to the Stage and center it about 1" beneath the photo. Place it in channel 4, frames 136-166. Save your changes.
3. Highlight frame 150 of the "Website" Sprite and create a keyframe.
4. Highlight the first keyframe of the "Website" Sprite. While holding down your Shift key, grab a corner of the selection box on the Stage and size it down (drag your arrow toward the center of the Sprite) until it is the size of just a small dot. Then, while the first keyframe is still highlighted, use your Arrow keys to center it under the photo.

   By reducing the "Website" Sprite in the first keyframe and leaving it the correct size in the last keyframe, you have told it to start out as a small dot and zoom in until it is back to its original size at keyframe 150.
5. Highlight the "Photo" and "Website" Sprites in the Score and make them orange.
6. You are now finished with your presentation. The final Stage and Score sections should look like the examples provided below. Rewind and play the production.

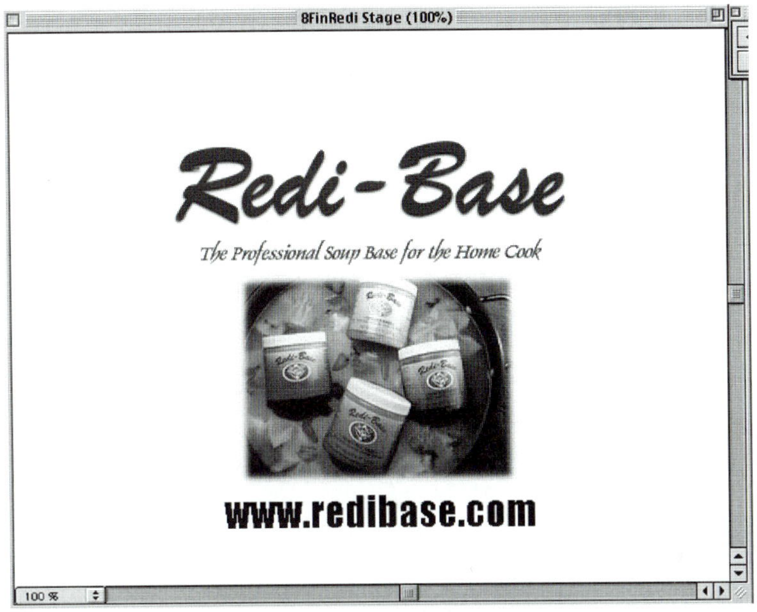


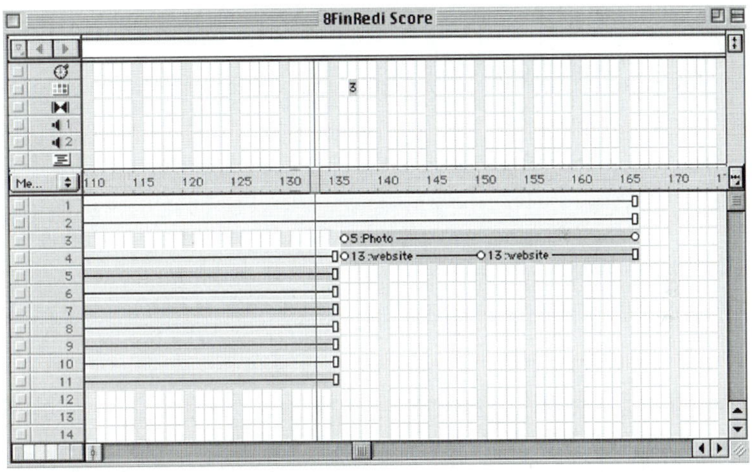


7. Save your changes and quit Director.

## Notes:

# Project C: Digital Portfolio

One of the most important aspects of a student's career path is the creation and compilation of a dramatic, compelling portfolio of work. This project — designed for a kiosk — was selected from just such a portfolio. Elizabeth Beecher, a student from Allentown Business School, was kind enough to contribute some of her work as a starting point for your own learning experience. This project is a fun and colorful assignment. To complete it, you will add a section on Web Design and another on Fine Art.

## *Getting Started*

1. Locate and move the **Start.DIR** and **X.MOV** files from your **SF-Director** folder to the Work in Progress folder on your desktop. Now, open the **Start.DIR** file that you just moved. It will run much more quickly off your hard drive.

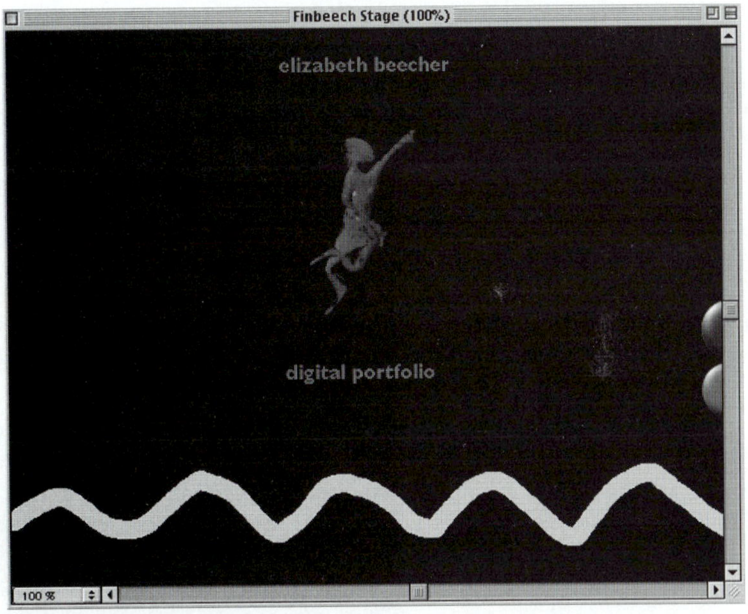


2. Open the Control Panel and play the movie. It will run through an introduction and stop on the Main menu, which offers some options. Browse and experiment with these features and see how they work.

### *Adding Buttons to the Main Menu*

1. Using the Control Panel, stop your movie. Let's place a few additional buttons that will direct the user to the Web Design and Fine Art areas of the electronic portfolio. Open your Score and scroll over until you can see frames 30-70.
2. Open your Cast and drag a copy of "Eliza Port Button" (Cast Member 1) to the Score. Place it in channel 2, frames 36-63. Position it on the Stage so that it is horizontally even with the graphic art button and on the right side of the icon in the center.
3. Drag a copy of "Fine Art Button" (Cast Member 36) to the Score and put it in channel 6, frames 36-63. Go to the Stage and drag the text so that it is placed to the right of the white button and even with the graphic art button.
4. Drag a copy of "Purple Button" (Cast Member 4) to the Score. Put it in channel 5, frames 36-63. Position it on the Stage so that it is horizontally even with the animation button and on the right side of the icon in the center.
5. Drag a copy of "Web Design Button" (Cast Member 46) to the Score and put it in channel 9, frames 36-63. Go to the Stage and drag the text so that it is to the right of the purple button and even with the animation type.

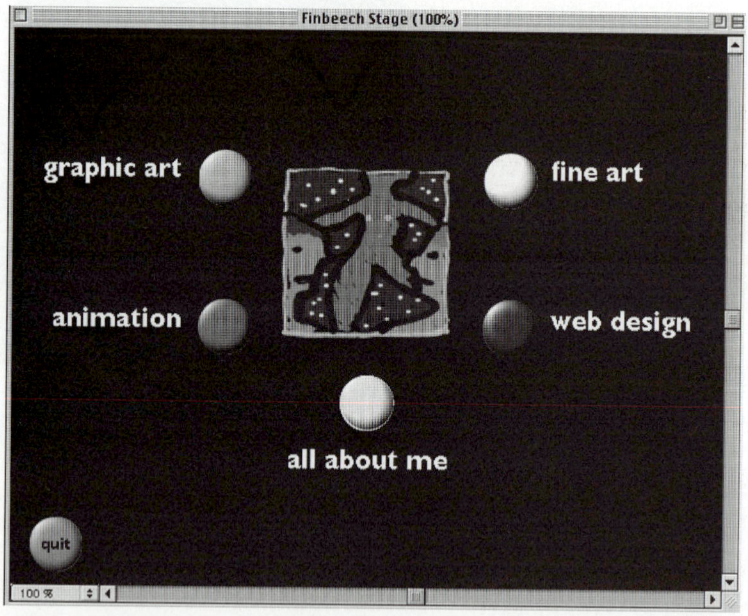

## *Making the Buttons Work*

It's time to make the buttons do their thing. The fine art button must jump the viewer to frame 64 in the Score to get to the appropriate location.

1. Save your changes.
2. Go to your Cast and highlight "Eliza Port Button" (Cast Member 1) and click on the Script button in the top-right corner of the Cast. The script for that Cast Member should appear and your cursor should show up between *on mouseUp* and *end* or *end mouseUp*. Start typing right where your cursor appears active and type *go to frame 64.* Then close the Script window.

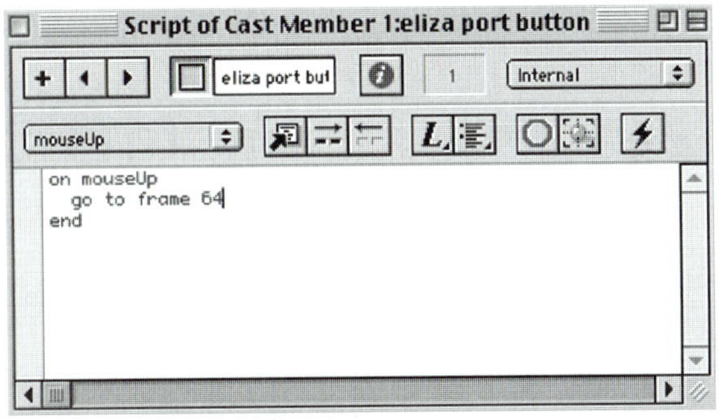


3. Go to the Cast window again and highlight the "Purple Button" (Cast Member 4). Click on the Script button and type *go to frame 572.* Close the Script window and rewind and play the movie. Click the buttons and watch the Score to make sure that they jump the movie to frames 64 and 572 respectively. Don't forget to stop your movie when you are finished.

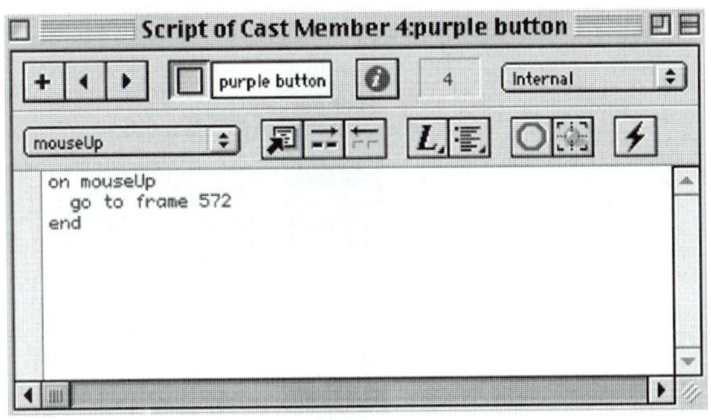

## *Creating the Web Section*

1. Go to frame 572 by highlighting the current frame number in the Control Panel. Type "572" and press the Return/Enter key. You will build the Web Design page first since it has only one example of work. The page will have two buttons on it when you open it, a Main Menu button and a Quit button.

2. To activate the Quit button, go to the Cast window and highlight the orange button (Cast Member 53). Click on the Script button, type *Quit*, and close the box. Don't test this button until you are completely finished with this project as it will quit the Director application entirely. *Halt* may be substituted for *Quit* if you would prefer that Director just stop rather than quit entirely. Now every Quit button in this project will work because they were all Sprites generated from Cast Member 53.

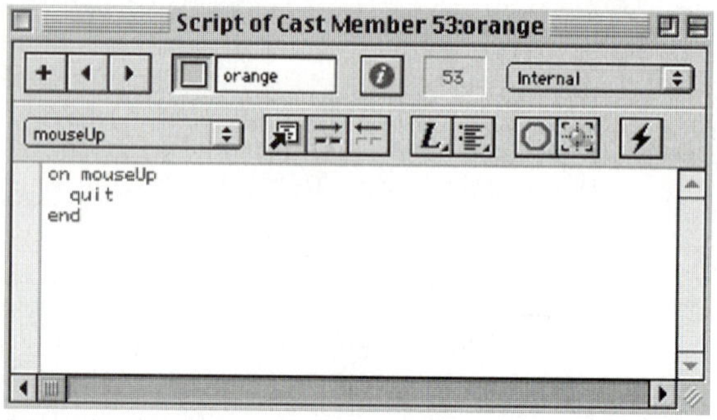


3. The Main Menu button already works, so let's get the artwork in place. Go to the Cast and drag a copy of the "Web Page" Cast Member (160) to the Score and place it in channel 1, frames 572-577. On the Stage, place it in the top-right corner (it should be to the right of the red button).

4. Next, put in a transition so that the switch from the Main menu to this page is not so harsh. Go to your Score and open the Special Channels section (click the small button at the top-right edge of the Score with the up and down arrows on it). Now go to the Transition channel of frame 572 and double-click on it to bring up the transition options. Choose Center Out, Square. Leave the duration set to two seconds for this as well as all the remaining transitions. Maker certain that the Changing Area Only option is selected and then close the Transition dialog box.
5. Let's put in some way to stop the movie in this area so that the viewer can browse at their leisure. For this exercise we will use the *pause* script. Go to your Score and double-click in the Frame Script channel of frame 572. The Frame Script channel is the channel just above the frame numbers where the Playback Head is. Type *pause* and close the box.
6. Go back to the Main menu and try this section of the project. Make sure the transition and the Pause command work correctly. Save your changes.

## Creating the Fine Art Section

1. For the Fine Art section, use the Control Panel to go to frame 64 your Score.
2. Put a *pause* script in the Frame script of frame 64.
3. This section has a splash of color and a painting on each page. Go to the Cast and drag a copy of "Red Blob" (Cast Member 57) to channel 1, frames 64-91. On the Stage, move the blob so that it extends off three sides of the Stage — the top, right, and bottom. Enlarge it by grabbing the corners of the Sprite on the Stage and pulling it if necessary. Apply the Matte Ink effect to the Sprite by highlighting the Sprite in the Score and choosing Matte instead of Copy from the Ink Effect menu in the Property Inspector. There should be black showing on the left side and under the Main menu and Quit button.
4. Go to the Cast and drag a copy of "Beachgirls" (Cast Member 7) to the Score and place it in channel 2, frames 64-91. On the Stage, move the painting on top of the red blob so that the top-right edge of the painting abuts the top-right edge of the Stage.

5. A description of the painting needs to be placed on the Stage. Go to the Cast and get "Beachgirls" (Cast Member 80) and bring it down to channel 9, frames 64-91. On the Stage, move it to the bottom-left corner of the painting so that a little bit of it is on the painting and most of it is on the red color. Set the ink effect of this Sprite to Background Transparent.

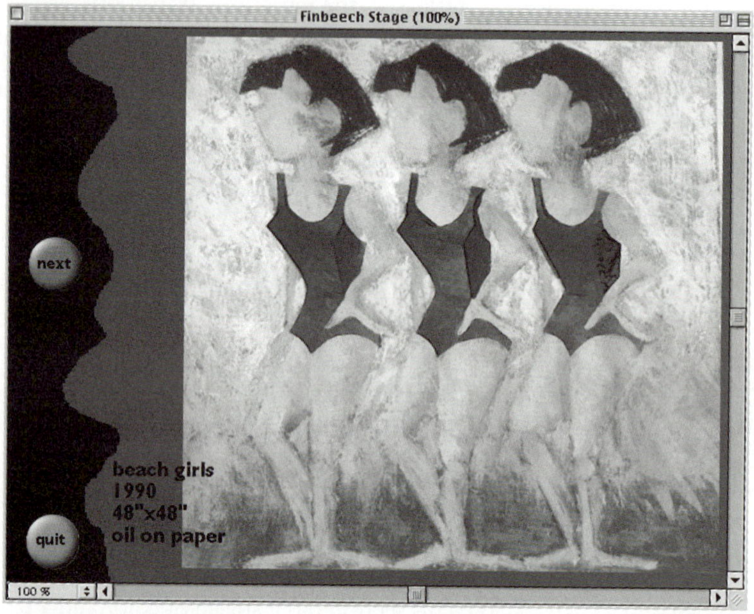


6. Put a Cover Down transition in frame 64 (double-click on the Transition channel in frame 64). Save your changes.

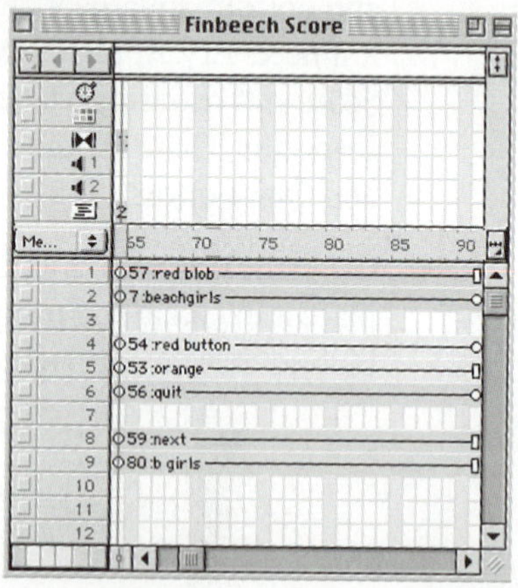


7. Go to the Cast, highlight Cast Member 54, and click on the Script Button. Type *go to frame 148* and then close the box. This button will jump the viewer to the next page of artwork.

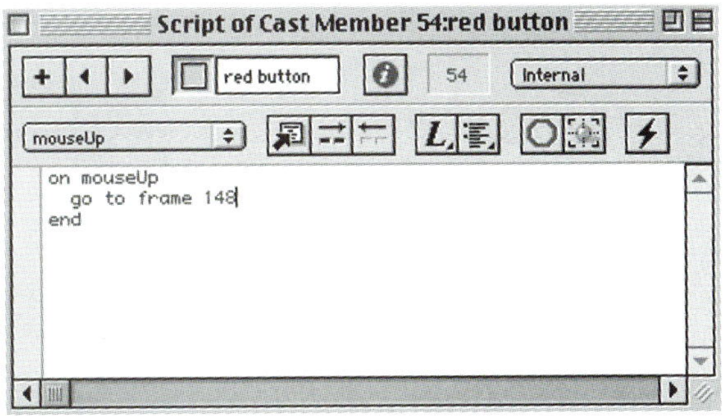


To make sure it works, drag the Playback Head to frame 62 and play your movie. Click the "Next" button. The Playback Head should go to frame 148 in the Score.

8. Put a *pause* script in the Frame script of frame 148.

9. This time the splash of color is violet. Go to the Cast and drag a copy of "Violet Shape" (Cast Member 10) to channel 1, frames 148-175. On the Stage, move the blob so that it extends off three sides of the Stage — the top, right, and bottom. Set the ink effect of this Sprite to Matte. There should be black showing on the left side and under the Main menu and Quit button.

10. Now put the painting on the violet color. Go to the Cast and drag a copy of "3Nudes" (Cast Member 6) to the Score and put it in channel 2, frames 148-175. On the Stage, move the painting so that the top-right edge of the painting abuts the top-right edge of the Stage. Resize if necessary by holding down the Shift key (to maintain proportions) and drag toward the center of the painting.

11. For the description of the painting, go to the Cast and get "Nudes Type" (Cast Member 65) and bring it down to channel 9, frames 148-175. On the Stage, move it to just underneath the bottom-left corner of the painting. Set the ink effect of this Sprite to Background Transparent.

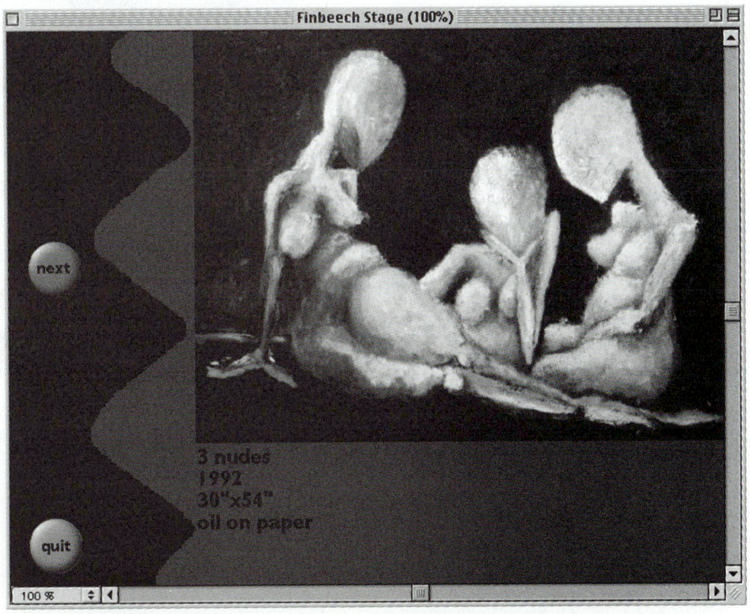


12. Put a Dissolve Patterns transition in frame 148. Save your changes.

12. Put a Dissolve Patterns transition in frame 148. Save your changes.

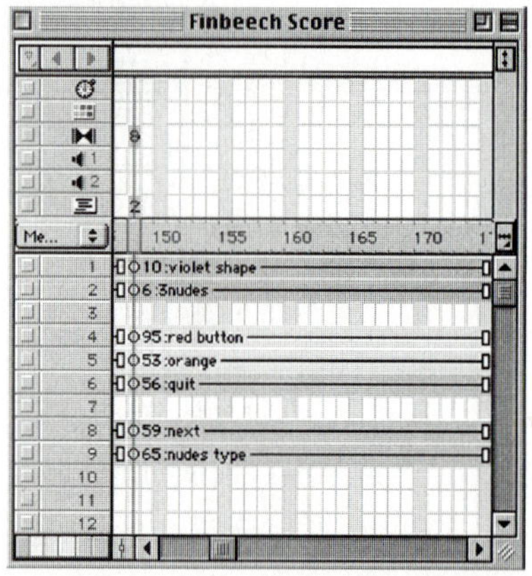


13. Go to the Cast and highlight Cast Member 95 and click the Script button. Type *go to frame 176* and then close the box. This button should jump the veiw to the next page of artwork.

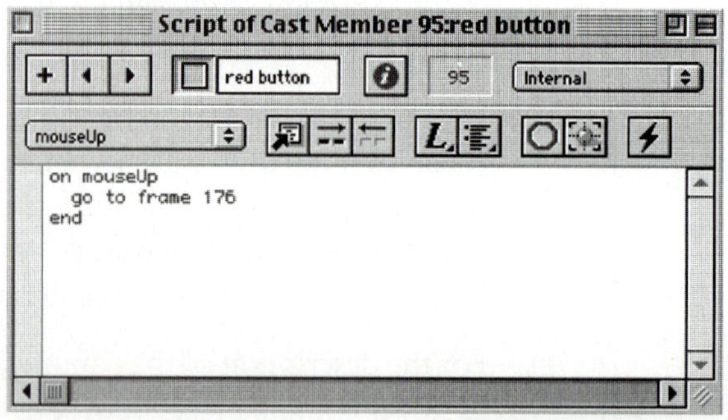


14. The third piece of art needs a *pause* script placed in the frame script of frame 176.

15. This time the color is green. Go to the Cast and drag a copy of "Green Shape" (Cast Member 66) to channel 1, frames 176-203. On the Stage, move the blob so that it extends off of three sides of the stage — the top, right, and bottom. Set the Ink Effect of this Sprite to Matte. There should be black showing on the left side and under the Main menu and Quit button.

16. Now put the painting on the green color. Go to the Cast and drag a copy of "Clique" (Cast Member 29) to the Score and put it in channel 2, frames 176-203. On the Stage, move the painting so that the top-right edge of the painting abuts the top-right edge of the Stage.

17. For the description of the painting, go to the Cast and get "Clique Type" (Cast Member 67) and bring it down to channel 9, frames 176-203. On the Stage, move it to the bottom-left corner of the painting so that it matches the following image. Set the ink effect of this Sprite to Background Transparent.

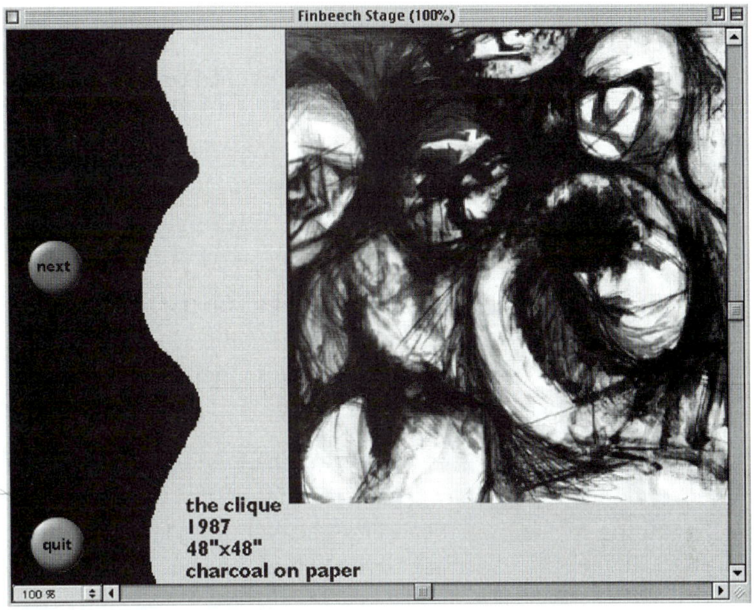


18. Put a Wipe Left transition in frame 176.

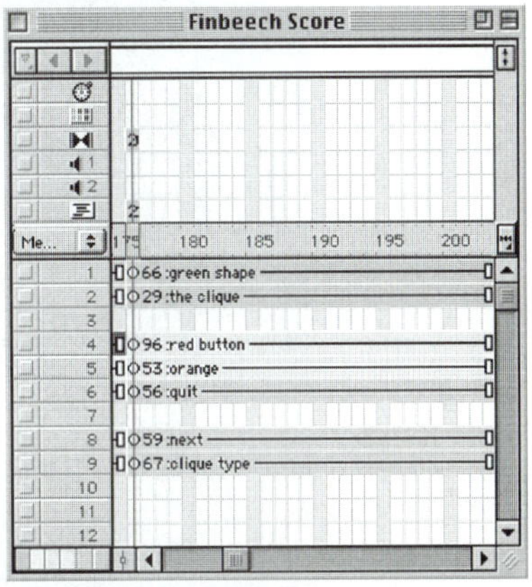


19. Go to the Cast, highlight Cast Member 96, and click the Script button. Type *go to frame 204* and close the box. This button should jump the movie to the next page of artwork.

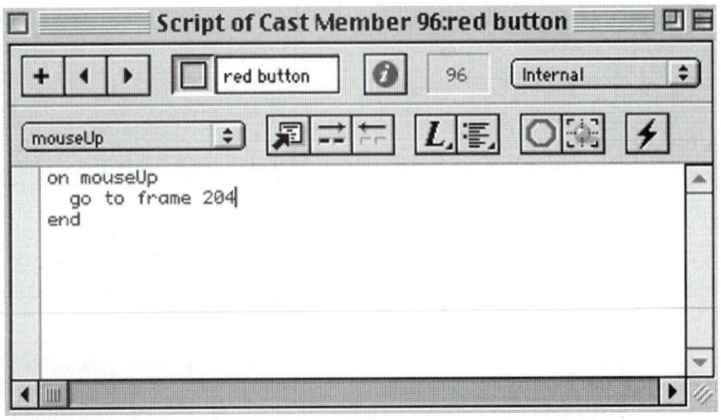

20. The last piece of art needs a *pause* script put in the Frame script of frame 204.

21. This time the splash of color is pink. Go to the Cast and drag a copy of "Pink Shape" (Cast Member 68) to channel 1, frames 204-231. On the Stage, move the blob so that it extends off three sides of the stage — the top, right, and bottom. Enlarge it by grabbing the corners of the Sprite on the Stage and pulling it if necessary. Set the ink effect of this Sprite to Matte. There should be black showing on the left side and under the Main menu and Quit button.

22. Now put the painting on the pink color. Go to the Cast and drag a copy of "Be A Girl" (Cast Member 13) to the Score and put it in channel 2, frames 204-231. On the Stage, move the painting so that the top-right edge of the painting abuts the top-right edge of the Stage.

23. For the description of the painting, go to the Cast and get "Girl" (Cast Member 81) and bring it down to channel 9, frames 204-231. On the Stage, move it to the bottom-left corner of the painting so that it matches the image that follows. Set the ink effect of this Sprite to Background Transparent.

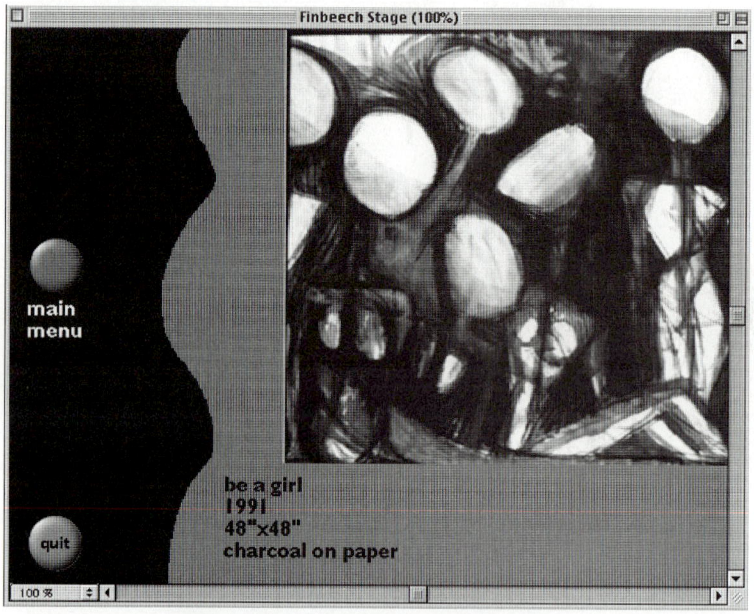


24. Put a Random Columns transition in frame 204.

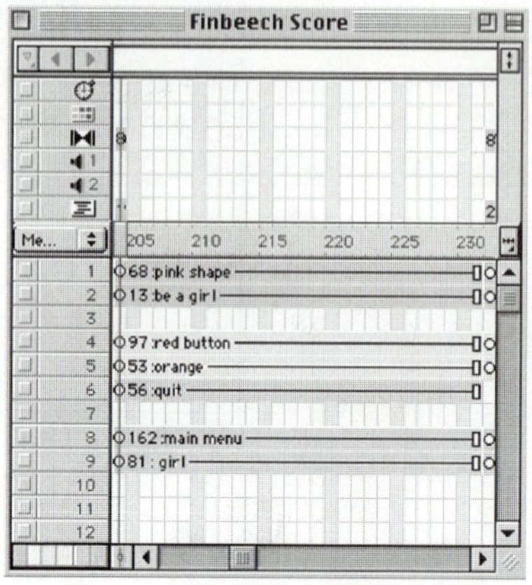

25. The red Main Menu button works already because it is the same Main Menu button you used in the Web Design section.

26. Now rewind the movie and play it through again. See how your changes enhanced the project. To compare your work with a completed version, see the **Finbeech.DIR** file by selecting **SF-Director>Finished Projects**.

27. Save the file and Quit Director.

## Notes:

# Project D: Emily's Photo Album

An interactive photo album is the basis for this project. Although we have provided images, video, and sound files, you may choose to use your own components to complete the production.

The specifications for the project call for various screens that display photographs of the first four years of Emily's life. The final production should have an introductory screen followed by imagery that shows Emily as she matures. To view the sample of our completed project, select **SF-Director>Finished Projects>Emily.DIR**.

## *Getting Started*

1. Locate the **StartEm.DIR** and **Cake.MOV** files in the **SF-Director** folder and copy them into your **Work in Progress** folder. Open the **StartEm.DIR** file and browse around to see what items are in the Cast and what you have to work with.

2. Since you moved the files from their original location, you will need to relink the movie. Highlight Cast Member 12 (the Cake.MOV Cast Member) and select File>Import. Navigate to your Work in Progress folder, highlight it, click Add, and then click Import. This will re-establish the link.

## *Creating the Main Menu*

1. Using the Vector Shape, Paint, and Text windows, create an introductory screen for the production. The name "Emily's Photo Album" should appear somewhere on this screen. The following image is a sample that we created.

2. Create the Main menu with four buttons. It should somehow contain the four ages for which we have pictures of Emily — from zero through three years of age.

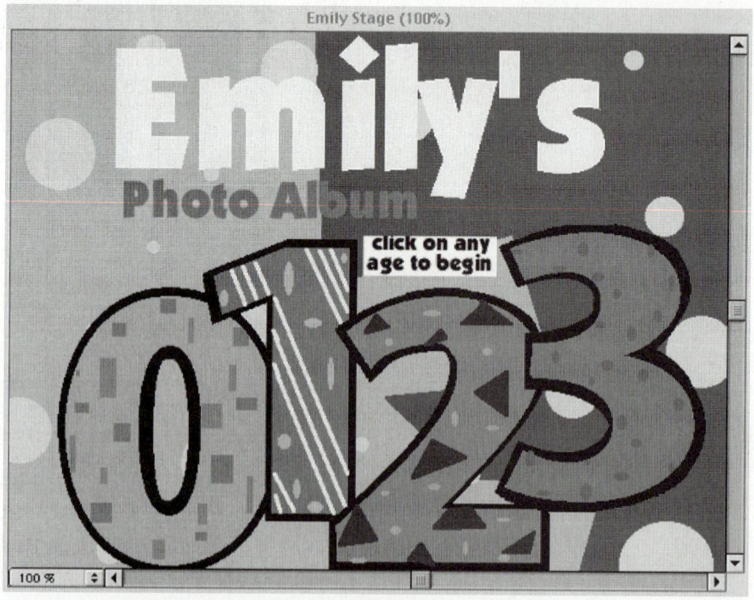


3. Give each of your four buttons a script that will send the viewers to the frame in the Score where each section starts.

## Creating the Age 0 Section

1. Create a page for the pictures of Emily in her first year of life, from birth to 12 months. It should contain all the images that have a "0" after the name. These images can be accessed from the Cast. Be sure to create a button to get back to the Main menu. Add a transition between the Main menu and this page. The transition should be put in the Transition channel of the first frame of the Sprite that you are transitioning to.

2. Double-click on the Script channel and put in a *pause* for the age 0 page so that it will stop moving.

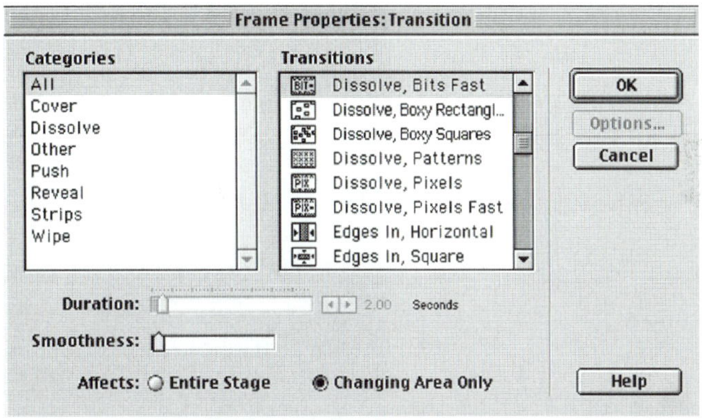


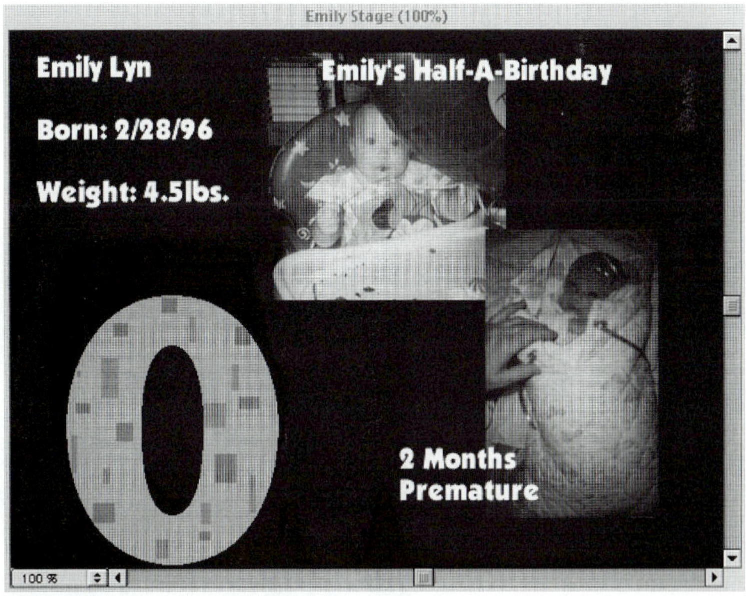

## *Creating the Age 1 Section*

1. Create a page for the pictures taken of Emily between her first and second birthdays. Keep the pages consistent with one another. For this page, use all the images with a "1" after their names.

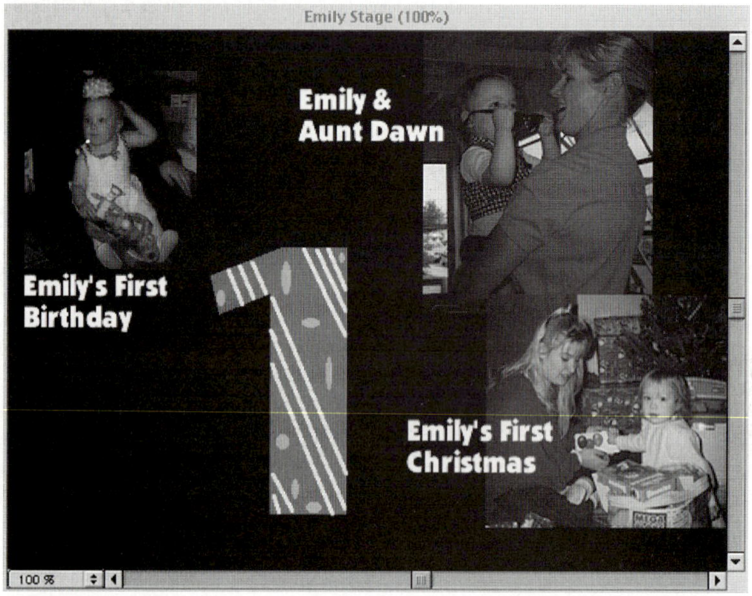


## *Creating the Age 2 Section*

1. Create a page for the photos taken of Emily between her second and third birthdays. For this page, use all the images that have a "2" after their names.

## Creating the Age 3 Section

1. Create a page for the photos taken of Emily between her third and fourth birthdays. For this page, use all the images with a "3" after their names.

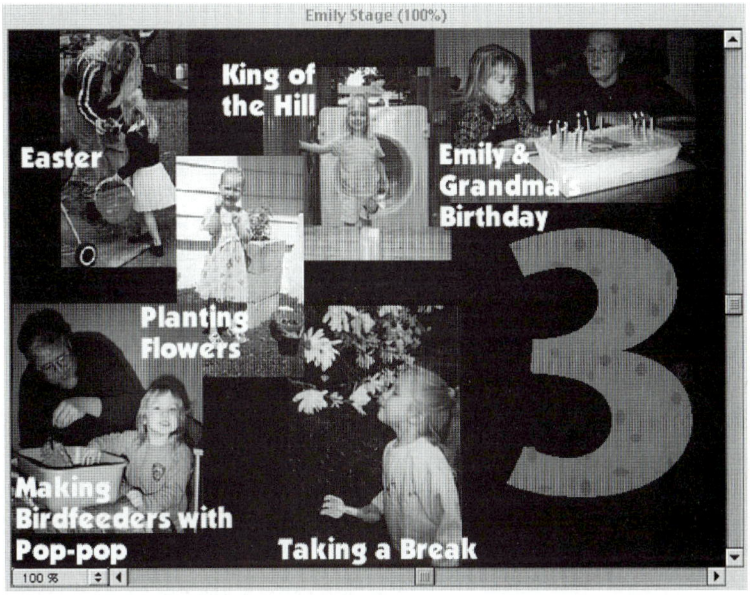


## Adding Music

1. Add the music clip called "Runrun." It is Cast Member 17. Determine exactly where you want to place it and then drag it to Sound channel 1 of the Score and extend it as needed. In the example below, it is placed in the introduction.

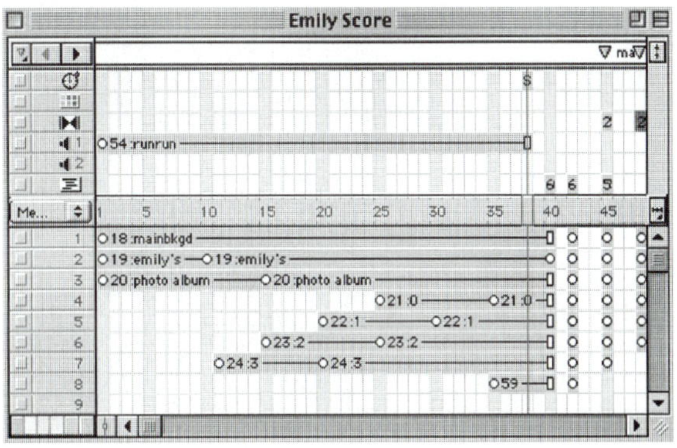

2. Highlight the sound Cast Member in the Cast and click the Cast Member Properties button to access the Sound tab of the Property Inspector. Take a look at your options and set them as you wish.

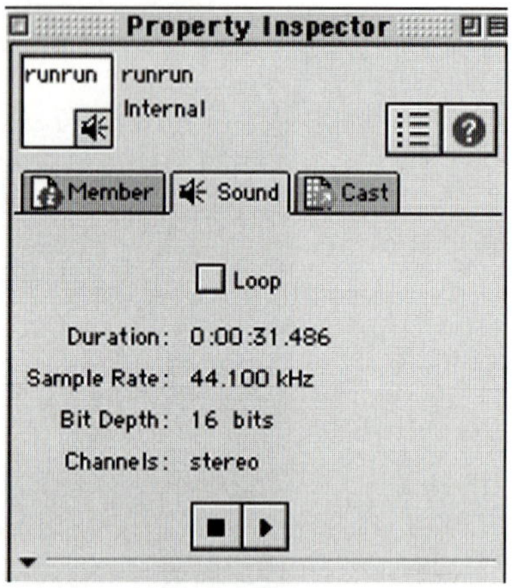


In addition, you may wish to look at the Cast Member properties a sound has by selecting the Member tab of the Property Inspector, shown below.

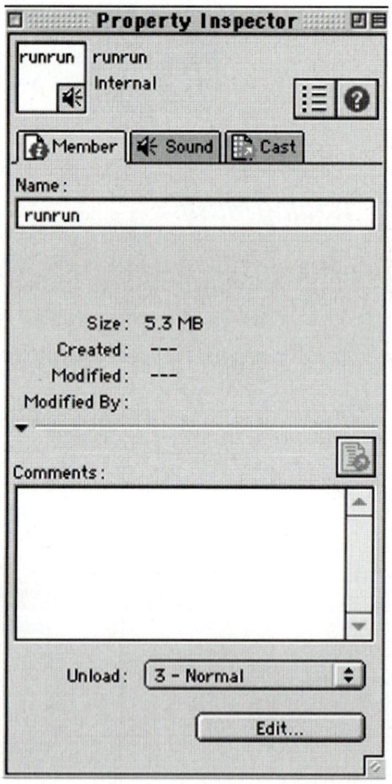

3. Go to the Tempo channel in the Score. Double-click in the Tempo channel the last frame that the "Runrun" Sprite occupies (the Sprite can be any length). The Frame Properties: Tempo dialog box will appear.

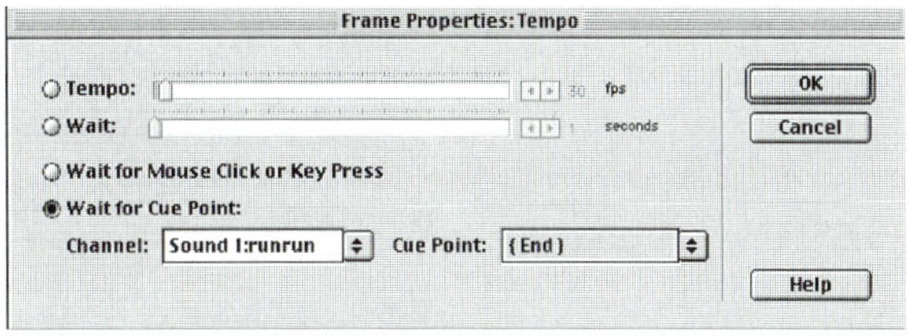


4. Click the Wait for Cue Point radio button. Set the Channel option to Sound1: runrun. Set the Cue Point to End. When the Playback Head reaches that frame, it will pause until the music is done playing.

## *Adding a QuickTime Movie*

1. Double-click on your movie (Cake.MOV) in the Cast and a QuickTime Player window will appear. Preview the movie.

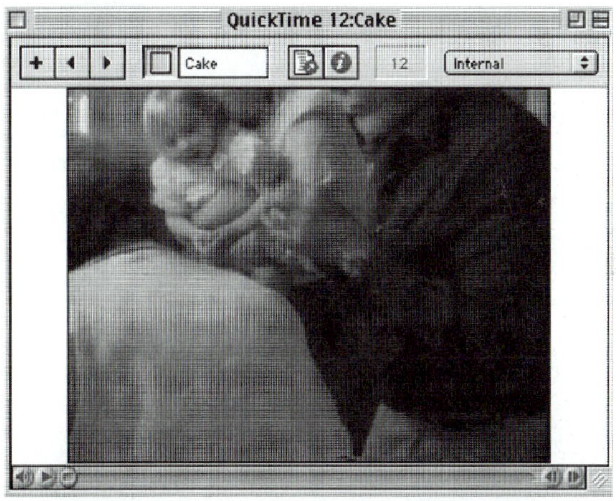


2. Place your movie in the section containing the images with a "2" after them. Select an area and then drag the movie into the appropriate Visual channel and frames. In the example, the movie is placed in channel 6, frames 98-110.

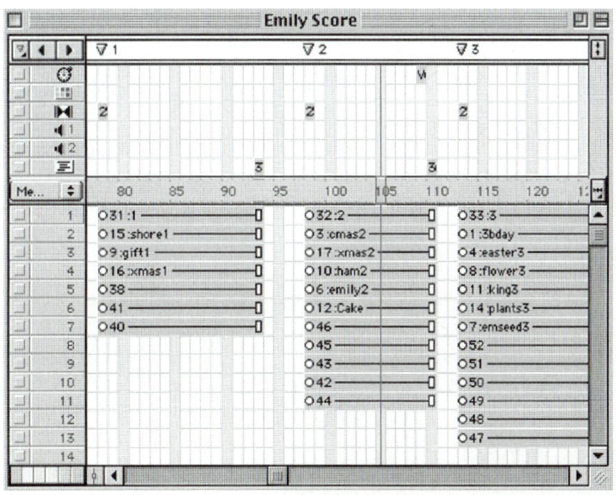

3. Double-click the Tempo channel and then click the Wait for Cue Point radio button. Set the Cue Point to End.

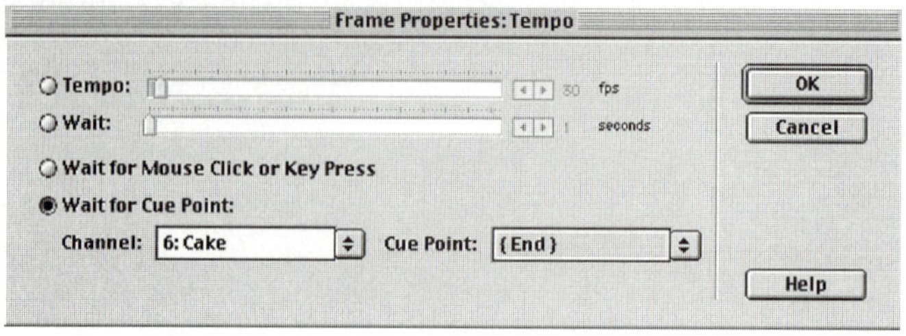


4. Highlight the movie in the Cast and click the Cast Member Properties button in the top-right corner. Check out the movie's Member properties in the Property Inspector.

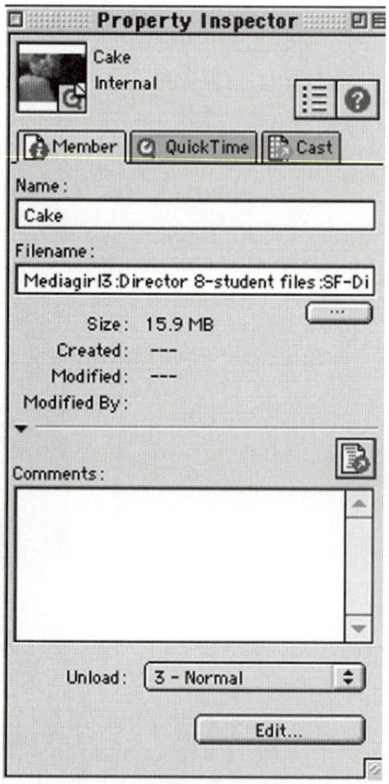

5. Select the QuickTime tab in the Property Inspector. The QuickTime Xtra Properties box will appear. Choose any options you feel would be appropriate for this video.

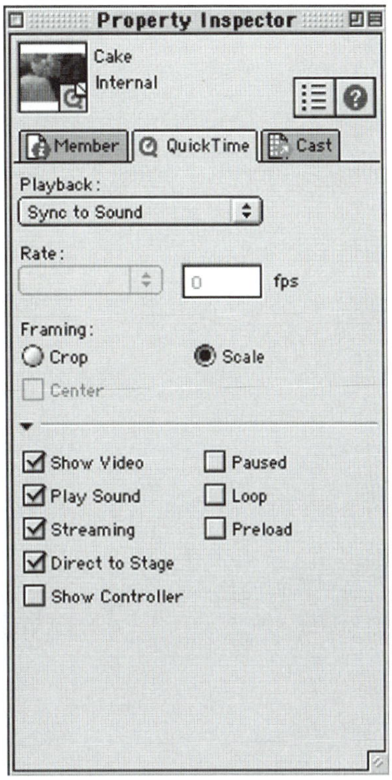


6. Rewind and play your movie. Tweak it if necessary.

7. The project is now finished. Save and quit Director.

## Notes:

# Project E: ABC's

The ABC's presentation is an example of using multimedia for educational purposes. In this project you will practice assembling the various parts of an animation and turning them into film loops. In addition, some fun and playful behaviors will be used.

Before starting this project, please open and view the finished version that has been supplied for you. Seeing the end result should greatly enhance your understanding of what you are doing in each section and why you are doing it. The completed presentation is called **Alpha.dir** and is located in the **Finished Projects** folder inside your **SF-Director** folder on the enclosed CD.

## *The Introduction*

1. Copy the **Starter.DIR** movie from the **SF-Director** folder to your **Work in Progress** folder. Double-click on the copy to open the file.
2. Design the introduction screen, which will cover frames 1-14 (see sidebar). Use Cast Members 21, 22, 23, 25, 26, and 28 to create the image shown below.

3. Double-click in frame 2 of the Tempo channel and put in a Wait for Mouse Click or Key Press command.

*The introduction (along with several sections that follow) could be done in one Frame; however, it might be better to leave the Sprites longer so that there is more room for their names to be spelled out.*

## Creating the Main Menu

1. The Main menu will cover frames 15-42 and contain Cast Members 13-20. Make the Main menu look like the sample that follows.

2. Highlight the B, C, And D letters on the Stage one at a time, go to the Property Inspector and check the Highlight When Clicked box on the Bitmap tab. This will make each of the buttons become highlighted when they are turned into interactive buttons later in the project.
3. Put a Dissolve, Bits transition in the Transition channel of frame 15. This will allow the introduction to dissolve into the Main menu.
4. Put a marker at frame 15 and name it "MenuA-D" (don't type the quotes when naming).
5. Put a *go to the frame* script in the frame script (Script channel) of frame 42 to pause your movie on the Main menu so that users will be able to make their choices. Save your changes.

## Making the Buttons Work

1. Let's make the letters interactive so that they advance the movie to their corresponding page each time they are clicked. We will skip the letter A since it will not be active. In the Cast, highlight "B/scr" (Cast Member 14) and click on the Cast Member Script button. Type *go to "Bunny"*. Don't forget the quotes. Markers are proper names and therefore require quotes around them. You will be adding a marker named "Bunny" a little later.
2. Do the same for the letter C (Cast Member 15). The script should read *go to "Cat"*. For the letter D (Cast Member 16), the script should read *go to "Dog"*.

## *Creating the Bunny Section*

1. The Bunny page will cover frames 50-64. First, however, you need to make a somewhat realistic bunny animation and then turn it into a film loop. First, we will put a couple of bunny heads in different positions in channel 1. To do this, first put Cast Member 1 in channel 1, frames 50-51. Put another copy of it in channel 1, frames 54-55.

2. Continue with the bunny heads by putting a copy of "Nose" (Cast Member 2) in channel 1, frames 52-53 and frames 56-57. Place a copy of "Left" (Cast Member 3) in channel 1, frames 58-60. Put "Right" (Cast Member 4) in channel 1, frames 61-64. That takes care of the head. Now, for the body ...

   Warning: Do not touch the Stage yet. All the pieces are perfectly aligned on top of each other because all the registration points are in the same spot. These points were set in the Paint window when the pieces were created so that they would be aligned.

3. Let's put a couple of different body positions in channel 2. Put a copy of "Arms Down" (Cast Member 5) in channel 2, frames 50-54 and another copy in frames 60-64. Put a copy of "Arms Up" (Cast Member 6) in channel 2, frames 55-59. Matte all the bunny-part Sprites in the Score. Now your Score should look like the following:

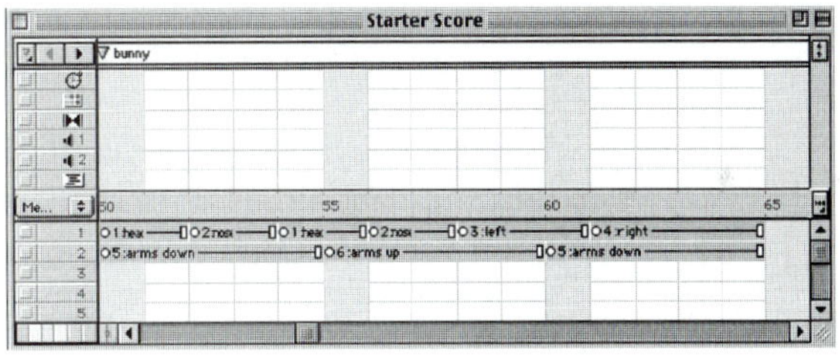


   Feel free to play this section of Sprites, and make certain that you like how the bunny will animate. Make any changes that you want before going on to the next step.

4. Highlight all the Sprites that the bunny is made of. Select Insert>Film Loop. Name the film loop "Bunny" and click OK. Be certain that you don't move or rename any of the bunny Cast Members in the Cast at this point, or the film loop will become problematic.

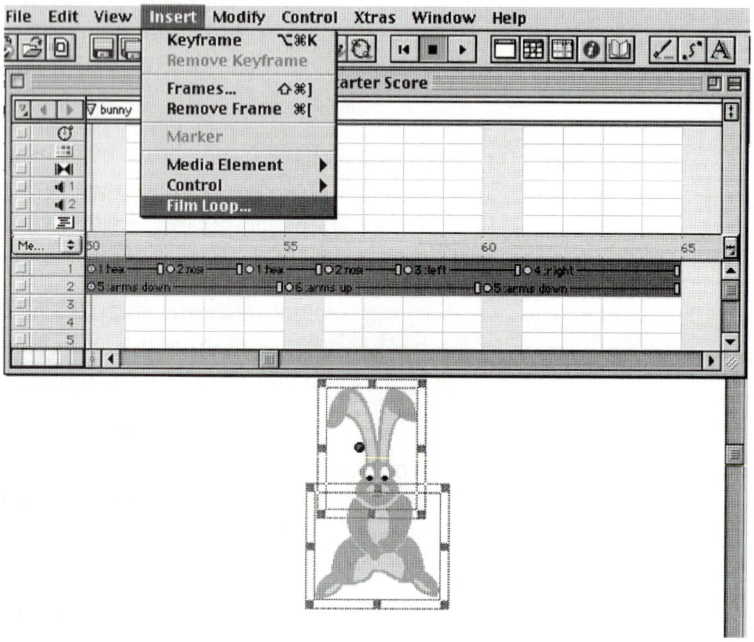


5. Delete the highlighted pieces of the bunny in channels 2 and 3 in your Score. Go to your Cast and drag a copy of the film loop into channel 3, frames 50-64. If you need to move your bunny anywhere on Stage, be certain that the whole Sprite is selected in the Score first.

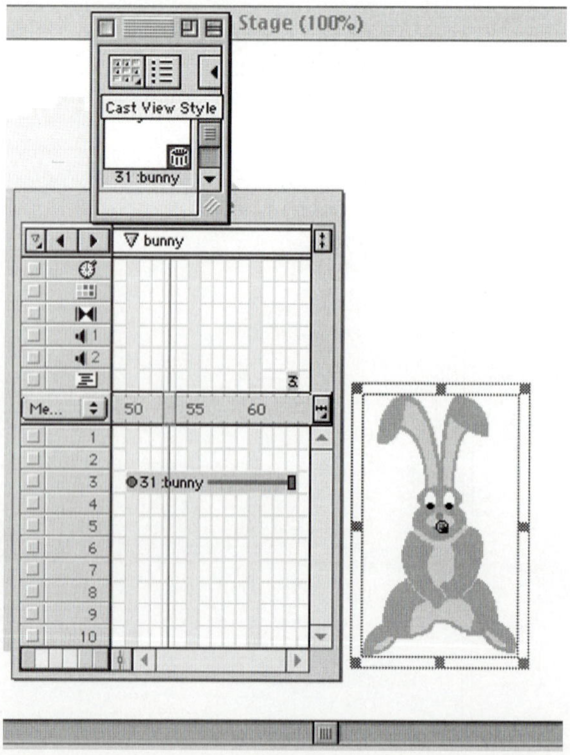

6. The rest of the page should contain Cast Members 22, 18, 33, and 37. Cast Member 37 is a Back button, which needs a script that reads *go to "MenuA-D"* (don't forget the quotes). Cast Member 33 is the big light-pink B. Cast Member 18 is the word "Bunny". Arrange your image so that it looks similar to the sample that follows.

7. Now for the little stuff. Put a marker named Bunny at frame 50.

8. Put a *go to "Bunny"* (with quotes) script in the Frame script (the Script channel) of frame 63.

## *Creating the Cat Section*

1. The next section is the Cat section, which should cover frames 65-78. Drag one copy each of Cast Members 11, 19, 23, 35, and 37 and two copies of 12 (the cat eye) to the Score one at a time and place them as seen in the sample that follows.

   Make certain that the cat eyes have the Matte ink effect applied to them and are in front of the cat (either use the Modify>Arrange menu item or arrange the Sprites in the channels of the Score).

2. Add a *go to "Cat"* script into the Frame script of frame 78.

3. Put a marker named Cat at frame 65.

4. Let's make the cat's eyes follow the cursor. Place the eyeballs on the cat (this should have already been done). Don't worry that the pupils are on the right side of the eyes and not at the bottom; they need to be this way in order for this Lingo script to work. Select Window>Library Palette.

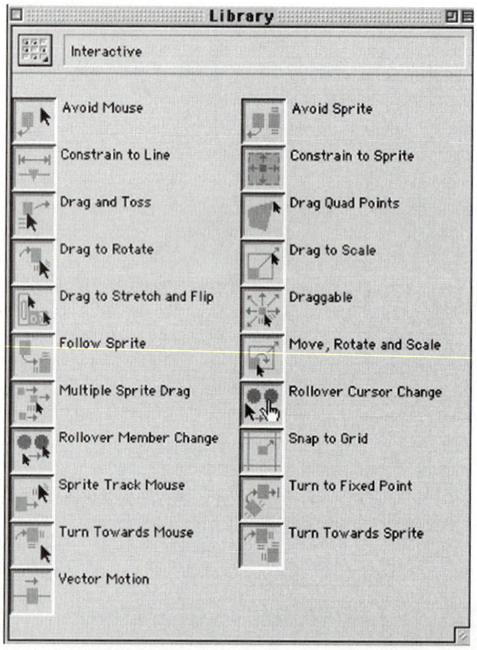


5. Select Animation>Interactive. Scroll down to Turn Toward Mouse and drag a copy of the behavior onto one of the eye Sprites in the Cast. In the dialog box that pops up, match the settings to the sample that follows. Click OK.

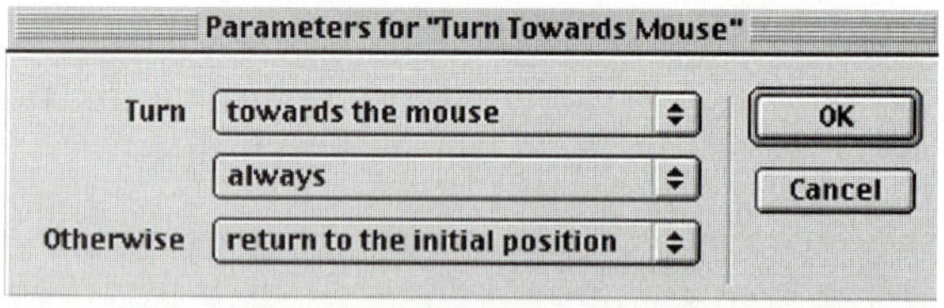


6. Complete the same steps for the second eye. The Sprites will now spin and give the illusion of following your cursor when you play your movie.

## Creating the Dog Section

1. The Dog section is the last section you will work on. The dog is a little easier to animate because he is made up of only one figure. Drag Cast Members 7, 8, 9, and 10 into channel 1, as shown in the following image. Cast Member 7 goes into frames 80-81, Cast Member 8 into frames 82-83, Cast Member 7 into frames 84-85, Cast Member 8 into frames 86-87, Cast Member 9 into frames 88-89, Cast Member 10 into frames 90-91, Cast Member 9 into frames 92-93, and Cast Member 10 into frames 94-95.

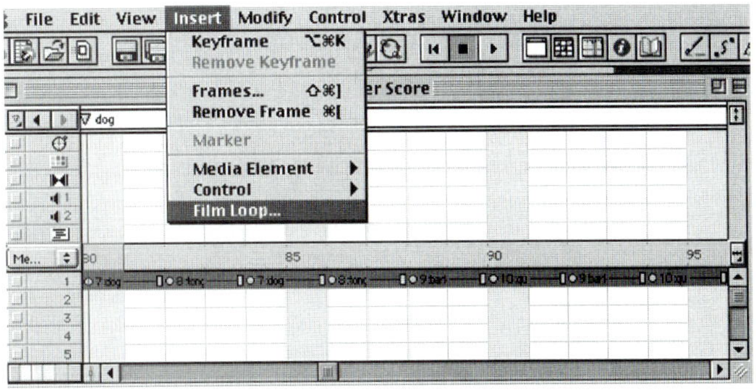

2. Highlight the dog pieces in channel 1 and then select Insert>Film Loop. Name the film loop whatever you like and click OK. Delete the original pieces from the Score and replace them with the film loop you just made. Put the loop in channel 2, frames 80-95.

3. Place the rest of the elements. Cast Members 20, 24 , 37, and 38 should match the sample that follows. They should each cover frames 80-95.

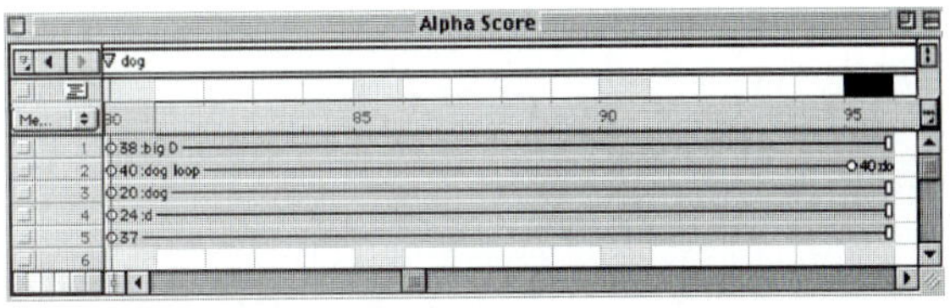

4. Put a *go to "Dog"* (with quotes) script into the Frame script of frame 95.

5. Put in the marker at frame 80 and name it "Dog".

## *Creating an Animated Cursor*

The next section will involve making an animated cursor and then applying it to a few Sprites using the Rollover Change Cursor behavior from the Library palette.

1. Select Insert>Media Element>Cursor.

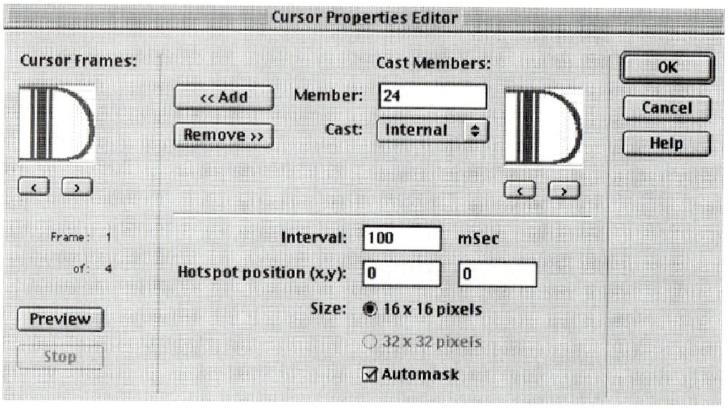


2. Click through the Cast Members section until you reach the letter A (Cast Member 21). Click Add to add Cast Members 21, 22, 23, and 24. Click the Preview button to view the animation. Click OK and it will show up as a Cast Member with a Cursor icon on it in the Cast.

3. Assign Rollovers to the letters A, B, C, and D on the menu page. Select Window>Library Palette again. Under Animation>Interactive, you will find the Rollover Cursor Change behavior.

4. Drag the behavior from the Library palette to the Score. Drop it onto one of the letter Sprites in the menu section of the Score. Do the same for all four letters. As you do, the following dialog box will appear. Match your settings to those shown below and click OK for each.

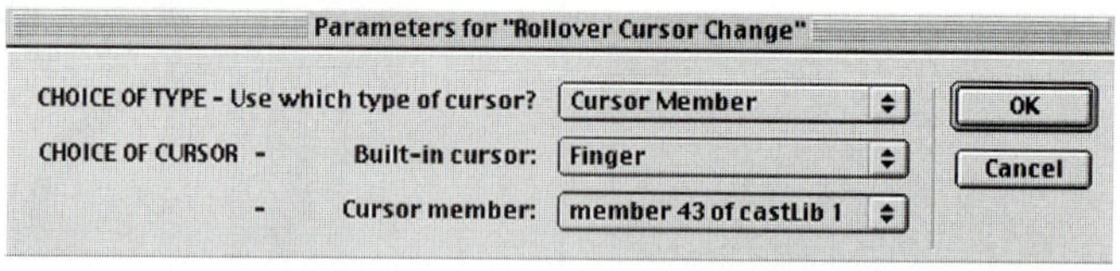

## *Adding Sounds*

1. The last thing to do is to add some music to the cat and the dog. Double-click on the cat and dog sounds one at a time in the Cast and check the Loop option, as shown in the following image.

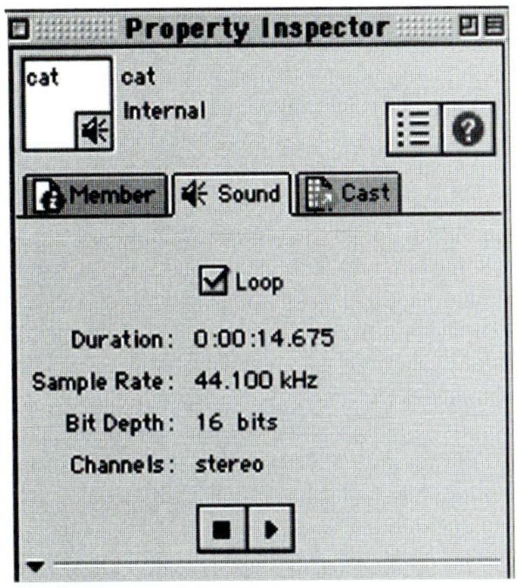


2. Drag a copy of the cat sound into the Sound channel of frames 65-78. Drag a copy of the dog sound into the Sound channel of frames 80-95.

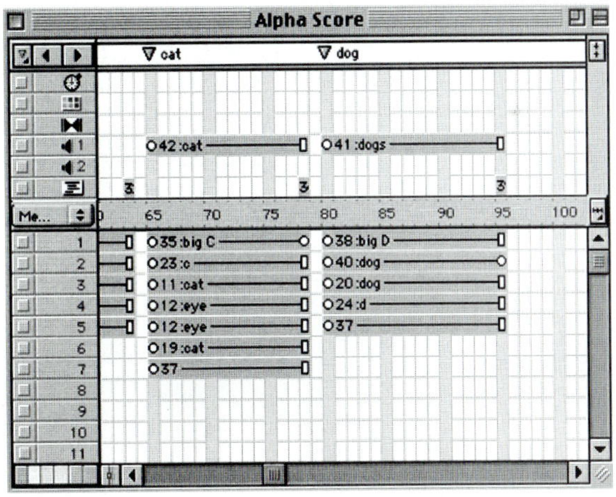


3. Rewind and play your production to see how you made out. If you have any questions, remember you can see a completed version of this production by selecting **SF-Director>Finished Projects>Alpha.DIR.**

4. Save and quit Director.

## Notes:

## Acrobat

This program by Adobe Systems, Inc. allows the conversion (using Acrobat Distiller) of any document from any Macintosh or Windows application to PDF format, which retains the page layout, graphics, color, and typography of the original document. It is widely used for distributing documents on-line because it is independent of computer hardware. The only software needed is a copy of Acrobat Reader, which can be downloaded free.

## Adaptive Palette

A sampling of colors taken from an image, and used in a special compression process usually used to prepare images for the world wide web.

## Adjacent Color

The eye will respond to a strong adjacent color in such a way as to affect the perception of the particular color in question. That is, a color having different adjacent colors may look different than it does in isolation. Also referred to as metamarism.

## Afterburner

The now-obsolete application used to convert Director movies into Shockwave-compatible files, prior to the integration of the technology into Director itself. Movies converted with Afterburner display the suffix ".dcr".

## Airbrush

A tool driven by compressed air that applies a very fine spray of color to artwork to produce various effects. Its effects are simulated in Director.

## Alert

A dialog box that appears on the screen. Usually has only one button for response: "OK".

## AIFF File

A sound file saved in Audio Interchange File Format, which is the preferred format for Director. Usually the file extension is ".aiff" or ".AIF".

## Anti-Aliasing

A graphics software feature that eliminates or softens the jaggedness of low-resolution curved edges.

## Apple Computer, Inc.

A computer manufacturer based in Cupertino, California. Apple was responsible for the development of the Macintosh computer and the graphic user interface.

## AVI

An abbreviation of Audio-Visual Interchange, a digital video format supported by Director on the Windows platform. The file extension is usually ".AVI".

## Background

A Sprite whose layer on the Stage in behind the layer of another Sprite. Since layering follows numeric order of visual channels in the Score, a Sprite in channel 1 would remain in the background of all other channels. Not to be confused with the Stage itself (which can be colorized).

## Background Color

In the Paint window, this refers to the color that is used to fill selected area, which is changed via the background paint chip. In the Stage window, it refers to the color of the Stage.

## Backing Up

The process of making copies of current work or work-in-progress as a safety measure against file corruption, drive or system failure, or accidental deletion. Backing up work-in-progress differs from creating an archive (see Archiving) for long-term storage or system restoration.

## Behavior

An "encapsulated" Lingo script, which can be applied to a Sprite via drag-and-drop.

## Behavior Inspector

A window that allows you to monitor the behaviors attached to a Sprite. You can also remove such attachments and change the order in which behavior scripting is executed.

## Bit (Binary Digit)

A computer's smallest unit of information. Bits can have only two values: 0 or 1. This can represent the black and white (1-bit) pixel values in a line art image. Or in combination with other bits, it can represent 16 tones or colors (4-bit), 256 tones or colors (8-bit), 16.8 million colors (24-bit), or a billion colors (30-bit). These numbers derive from counting all the possible combinations (permutations) of 0 or 1 settings of each bit: 2 x 2 x 2 = 16 colors; 2 x 2 x 2 x 2 x 2 x 2 x 2 x 2 = 256 colors; 2 x 2 x 2 x 2 x 2 x 2 x 2 x 2 x 2 x 2 x 2 x 2 x 2 x 2 x 2 x 2 x 2 x 2 x 2 x 2 x 2 x 2 x 2 x 2= 16.8 million colors.

## Bit Depth

A measure of how many colors can be contained in an image. 8-bit color is 256 colors, 16-bit is 32,768 colors, 32-bit, 16.7 million. Color images are imported into Director at the bit depth of the current monitor setting, independent of the true bit depth of the image.

## Bitmap image

An image constructed from individual dots or pixels set to a grid-like mosaic. Each pixel can be represented by more than one bit. A 1-bit image is black and white because each bit can have only two values (for example, 0 for white and 1 for black). For 256 colors, each pixel needs eight bits (2 8 ). A 24-bit image refers to an image with 24 bits per pixel (2 24 ), so it may contain as many as 16,777,216 colors. Because the file must contain information about the color and position of each pixel, the disk space needed for bitmap images is usually quite significant. Most digital photographs and screen captures are bitmap images.

## Bitmapped

Forming an image by a grid of pixels whose curved edges have discrete steps because of the approximation of the curve by a finite number of pixels.

## Bitmapped Type

Type that has been created as (or converted to) artwork rather than editable type, and thus occupies a graphic rather than a text Cast slot.

## Border

A continuous line that extends around text; or a rectangular, oval, or irregularly-shaped visual in an ad.

## Bounding Box

The rectangular area that appears around a Sprite when that Sprite is selected on the Stage. All Sprites, even irregularly shaped ones, are contained within such an area. Ink effects relate to the entire bounding box when applied.

### Brightness

1. A measure of the amount of light reflected from a surface. 2. A paper property, defined as the percentage reflection of 457-nanometer (nm) radiation. 3. The intensity of a light source. 4. The overall percentage of light in an image.

### Button

Any Cast Member or Sprite that performs a function when selected (i.e. clicked upon) by the user. There are specific tools for creating buttons, but any graphic Cast Member ( an image, shape, or line) can be turned into a button.

### Button Tools

The Tool Palette offers these so you can create three different types of custom buttons.

### Byte

A unit of measure equal to eight bits (decimal 256) of digital information, sufficient to represent one text character. It is the standard unit measure of file size. (See also Megabyte, Kilobyte, and Gigabyte).

### Caption

The line or lines of text that identify a picture or illustration, usually placed beneath it or otherwise in close proximity.

### Cast Slot

An individual unit in a cast database, each a potential "address" for a Cast Member. Cast slots are listed and displayed in numerical order in a Cast window.

### Cast

A database in which the elements of a movie are stored. Graphics, sounds, text fields, digital video, animations, color palettes, and Lingo scripts can all be placed in a cast file.

### Cast Member

Any multimedia element residing in its own slot in the Cast window.

### Cast Member Name

Imported Cast Members are automatically given the names of the files from which they are imported. Names can be added or modified by typing in the name fields of the Paint, Text, Script, Info, and Cast windows. Naming Cast Members is optional.

### Cast Member Number

This number reflects a Cast Member's position in a Cast window database, and is assigned automatically by the Cast in order of creation and/or importation. Cast Member numbers can be changed only by rearranging the order of Cast Members in the Cast.

### Cast Member Script

A Lingo script attached to a Cast Member, and by extension to all Sprites derived from that Cast Member. When a Cast Member has a script, its icon in a Cast changes to display a distinctive icon in the lower left-hand corner.

### Cast Type

The category of multimedia element to which the Cast Member belongs (graphic, script, text, sound, etc.)

### Cast Window

The window in which a cast file is displayed. A Cast window can have a different name than the Cast file it displays, and the cast shown within the window can be switched via Lingo.

### CD-ROM

A device used to store approximately 600MB of data. Files are permanently stored on the device and can be copied to a disk but not altered directly. ROM stands for Read-Only Memory. Equipment is now available on the consumer market for copying computer files to blank CD-ROMs.

### Cell

The box in the Score in which an individual Sprite, script or command is placed; the area created by the intersection of Frame and Channel.

### Channel

A horizontal row of cells in the Score window. There are 48 visual channels, two sound channels, a script channel, a transitional channel, a palette channel, and a tempo channel.

### Checkbox button

A button used in which users toggle an "X" mark on and off in a standardized box. Created with the custom button tool in the Tool Palette.

### Child Object

An entity residing in RAM that was created with reference to a parent script. A child object may control physical objects on the stage as part of its scripting , but is not a physical object itself.

### Clipboard

The portion of computer memory that holds data that has been cut or copied. The next item cut or copied replaces the data already in the clipboard.

### Color Cycling

A special color palette effect. It changes the appearance of a display by rapidly showing each of a range of colors in a sequence. The sequence, and the order of cycling, can be set by the user.

### Color Depth

See *bit depth.*

### Color Model

The Web Color palette describing color, such as RGB, HLS, CIELAB, or CMYK.

### Color Picker

A function within a graphics application that assists in selecting a color.

### Comment

A line in a Lingo script that is intended to be read, not executed, by Director. These lines are preceded by a double dash ("- -").

### Commenting Out

The process of temporarily disabling Lingo script lines by adding double dash ("- -") to the beginning of each line. Director ignores these lines.

### Commercial Printing

Typically, printing on high-capacity, high-resolution presses. High-resolution commercial printing processes include offset lithography, flexography, gravure, and screen printing. Offset printing is the most widely used commercial printing process.

### Control Panel

The window that contains Director's playback controls.

### Copyright

Ownership of a work by the originator, such as an author, publisher, artist, or photographer. The right of copyright permits the originator of material to prevent its use without express permission or acknowledgment of the originator. Copyright may be sold, transferred, or given up contractually.

## Current Palette

The Color palette that is currently being used to determine colors displayed on the Stage. The default palette is the standard Macintosh or windows system palette.

## Custom Cursor

A cursor derived from a graphic Cast Member, as opposed to the cursors built into the operating system.

## Desktop

1. The area on a monitor screen on which the icons appear, before an application is launched. 2. A reference to the size of computer equipment (system unit, monitor, printer) that can fit on a normal desk; thus, desktop publishing.

## Digital

The use of a series of discrete electronic pulses to represent data. In digital imaging systems, 256 steps (8 bits, or 1 byte) are normally used to characterize the gray scale or the properties of one color. For text, see ASCII.

## Digital Camera

A camera which produces images directly into an electronic file format for transfer to a computer.

## Digital Video

A Cast Member category. On the Macintosh platform, digital video consists primarily of QuickTime files. On Windows, it may be QuickTime for Windows or AVI-formatted.

## Dithering

A process by which a range of colors or grays are simulated on-screen. Dithering creates the impression of third color by adjusting the colors of two adjacent pixels; the eye sees the two actual colors as a blend. Often used when a high-quality image (such as a 16-bit photo) is converted into a lower-quality one.

## Document

The general term for a computer file containing text and/or graphics.

## Editable Text

A text Cast Member in which the end user may enter or delete keystrokes. Sprites derived from such Cast Members display a text insertion cursor.

## Embedded Cast Member

A embedded Cast Member is one that resides entirely in the file space of the current Director movie (as opposed to a *linked Cast Member*, which appears in a Cast but is actually an external file.)

## End User

The hypothetical person or persons who will be using your multimedia production. When developing, it's important to make the distinction between options available to you (the creator) and the end user. For example, you can stop a Director movie at any time by clicking on the Control Panel. Unless you add a "Stop" button to the Stage, the end user of a *Projector* file made from that movie will not be able to stop it.

## Event

In Lingo, an event is an action that will automatically trigger a script known as an *event handler*.

## Event Handler

A script that is intended for execution when a Lingo event occurs. Each begins with the word on (on mouseup, on enterFrame, etc.)

## Execute

Lingo *executes* a script when it interprets and attempts to carry out the script's instructions. Therefore, to execute is to trigger a Lingo script.

## External Cast

A cast database that is saved as a file separate from the Director movie in which it is used (allowing it to be used in multiple movies). External casts are saved with the file extension suffix ".cst".

## Field

One of two types of text available in Director. Text saved as a field can be changed either "on the fly" –that is, modified in the end product by the end user-or by Lingo. *Rich Text* (the other kind of text) is converted into graphic artwork when a projector is created.

## File Extension

The three-character suffix used to identify file types under the DOS and Windows operating systems, separated from the rest of the file name by a period. The standard file extension for editable Director movies is ".dir".

## Film Loop

A Cast Member type consisting of a sequence of Sprites encapsulated into a single Cast Member. The Cast Members from which the film loop was derived must also be present in the Cast.

## Export

To save a file generated in one application in a format that is readable in another application.

## Flow Chart

A diagram sketching out the structure of an interactive production, documenting the relation that screens, scenes, and other discrete units bear to one another.

## Folder

1. The digital equivalent of a paper file folder, used to organize files in the Macintosh and Windows operating systems. The icon of a folder looks like a paper file folder. Double-clicking it opens it to reveal the files stored inside. 2. A mechanical device which folds preprinted pages into various formats, such as a tri-fold brochure.

## Font

A font is the complete collection of all the characters (numbers, uppercase and lowercase letters and, in some cases, small caps and symbols) of a given typeface in a specific style; for example, Helvetica Bold.

## Font Substitution

A process in which your computer uses a font similar to the one you used in your publication or presentation to display or print your publication or presentation. Although the substitute font may be similar to the original font, your publication will not look exactly as you intended; line breaks, column breaks, or page breaks may fall differently, which can affect the entire look and feel of the publication or presentation.

## Foreground

A Sprite whose layer on the Stage is in front of the layer of another Sprite. Since layering follows numerical order of visual channels in the Score, a Sprite in channel 1 would remain in the background; other channels would be in the foreground relative to that Sprite.

**Foreground Color**

The color designated in the left-most color chip in the color section of the Paint window's tool bar. Click and hold on this color chip to access a pop-up color menu from which a new color can be selected.

**Frame**

An individual column in the Score. Can be referred to by number (frame 15), or by the name attached to it with a marker (Frame "Central").

**Frame Script**

A Lingo script attached to an individual Frame by placement in the script channel cell for that Frame.

**Function**

A Lingo element that provides information on a particular state or condition. For example, the function the time will return the current time, and the function of the name of member (Cast Member) will return the name of the Cast Member residing at the given cast slot number. Lingo provides a number of functions that can be invoked from any script; you can also design and program custom functions.

**Gradient**

A type of fill found in the Paint window. The fill does not consist of a single color, but makes a gradual transition from one color (the foreground color) to another (the background). The shape of the gradient and the proportion of the two colors can be varied.

**Gradient fill**

See Graduated fill.

**Graduated fill**

An area in which two colors (or shades of gray or the same color) are blended to create a gradual change from one to the other. Graduated fills are also known as blends, gradations, gradient fills, and vignettes.

**Graphic Cast Member**

Any of the cast types that can be placed in the visual channels of the Score. The include: graphics (residing in the Paint window), Digital Video Cast Members, shapes and buttons (both created with the Tool Palette), film loops, and other Director movies (encapsulated and imported).

**Grid**

A division of a page by horizontal and vertical guides into areas into which text or graphics may be placed accurately.

**GUI**

Acronym for Graphical User Interface, the basis of the Macintosh and Windows operating systems.

**Handler**

A grouping of Lingo for execution as a unit, beginning with the keyword "on". A handler can be triggered by events (on mouseup, etc.).

**Hard Drive**

A disk sealed inside an airtight transport mechanism that is the basic storage mechanism in a computer. Information stored may be accessed more rapidly than on floppy disks and far greater amounts of data may be stored.

**Highlight**

A feature of all graphic Cast Members, accessed via the Cast Member's Properties dialog box. When the "Highlight when clicked" checkbox is selected, all Sprites derived from that Cast Member will reverse color when clicked upon. Often used when the Cast Member is a button.

**Host Computer**

The hypothetical computer (or computers) on which your multimedia production will run. The host computer may be configured differently than those you use for creation or troubleshooting.

**HTML**

An acronym for HyperText Markup Language. The language, written in plain (ASCII) text using simple tags, that is used to create Web pages, and which Web browsers are designed to read and display. HTML focuses more on the logical structure of a page than its appearance. HTML is used to mark, or code, the content of your design (text, graphics, sounds, and animation) so that it can be published on the Web and viewed with a browser.

**Hue**

The wavelength of light of a color in its purest state (without adding white or black).

**Hyperlink**

An HTML tag directs the computer to a different Anchor or URL (Uniform Resource Locator). The linked data may be on the same page, or on a computer anywhere in the world. A hyperlink can be a word, phrase, sentence, graphic, or icon. A hyperlink can also cause an action, such as opening or downloading a file.

**Icon**

A small graphic symbol used on the screen to indicate files or folders, activated by clicking with the mouse or pointing device.

**If/Then Statement**

An element of the Lingo scripting that specifies actions to be undertaken when certain conditions exist.

**Illustrator**

A vector graphic editing application owned by Adobe Systems, Inc.

**Import**

To bring a file generated within one application into another application.

**In-Betweening**

Also known as "tweening". The process of automatically "filling in the gaps" of a sequence. Director extrapolates the motion and position implied by the difference between two or more *keyframes*, and creates the appropriate intermediate Sprites. When only one key Frame is designated, in-betweening produces a series of exact duplicates.

**Ink Effect**

Any one of a series of effects that do not modify artwork so much as change the rules by which the artwork is displayed. They can be applied in both the Score and Paint windows.

**Inks**

The group of choices that modify an element's appearance and/or its display relative to other elements. In the Paint window, inks can be used for a variety of artistic effects. In the Score, inks dictate the Sprite's appearance on the Stage. Paint window inks are permanent, while Score inks can be changed at will.

**Internal Cast**

A Cast database that is saved as part of Director movie's file (as opposed to external casts, which are separate files.)

Director supports multiple casts within a single movie.

## Indexed Color Image

An image which uses a limited, predetermined number of colors; often used in Web images. See also GIF.

## Jaggies

Visible steps in the curved edge of a graphic or text character that results from enlarging a bitmapped image.

## JPG or JPEG

A compression algorithm that reduces the file size of bitmapped images, named for the Joint Photographic Experts Group, an industry organization that created the standard. JPEG is a "lossy" compression method, and image quality will be reduced in direct proportion to the amount of compression applied.

## Keyframe

An individual cell in a sequence of animation, from which other Frames are extrapolated. For instance, a linear movement can be extrapolated from two keyframes, one at the beginning and one at the end of the movement.

## Keyword

A Lingo term used to clarify or further define aspects of scripting. Terms like the, of, cast, field, and end are all keywords.

## Kiosk

A software/hardware unit, usually designed for public placement and general usage.

## Lasso

One of the selection tools in the Paint window. Used to make non-rectangular selections of artwork.

## Layer

A function of graphics applications in which elements may be isolated from each other, so that a group of elements may be hidden from view, reordered, or otherwise manipulated as a unit, without affecting other elements on the page.

## Layout

The arrangement of text and graphics on a page, usually produced in the preliminary design stage.

## Leading ("ledding")

Space added between lines of type. Usually measured in points or fractions of points. Named after the strips of lead which used to be inserted between lines of metal type. In specifying type, lines of 12-pt. type separated by a 14-pt. space is abbreviated "12/14," or "twelve over fourteen."

## Lingo

Director's custom control language.

## Linked Cast Member

A Cast Member that appears in the Cast window, but is not physically resident in the file space of the current Director movie; instead, it occupies an external file of its own.

## Looped Sound

A sound file with the "loop" option checked in its Properties dialog box. Unless overridden by the Score or scripting, it will play again and again.

## Looping

The process of continuously returning the playback head to a location until another action occurs, such as the movement of the mouse or the selection of a button.

## M, MB (Megabyte)

One million (1,048,576) bytes (220) or 1,024 Kilobytes.

## MacOS

An abbreviation for the Macintosh Operating System. Used in this book to refer to all Macintosh and Macintosh-compatible computer systems.

## Marker

The tabs at the top of the Score, used to indicate individual Frames. Once placed, markers may have names assigned to them as well. They can be relocated, renamed, and removed.

## Marquee

The blinking lines indicating the area selected with the lasso or selection rectangle in the Paint window.

## Medium

A physical carrier of data such as a CD-ROM, video cassette, or floppy disk, or a carrier of electronic data such as fiber optic cable or electric wires.

## Megabyte (MB)

A unit of measure of stored data equaling 1,024 kilobytes, or 1,048,576 bytes (1020).

## Megahertz

An analog signal frequency of one million cycles per second, or a data rate of one million bits per second. Used in specifying computer CPU speed.

## Memory Inspector

Window used to display information about Director's current RAM usage.

## Menu

A list of choices of functions, or of items such as fonts. In contemporary software design, there is often a fixed menu of basic functions at the top of the page that have pull-down menus associated with each of the fixed choices.

## Message Window

A diagnostic and "behind-the-scenes" window used in Lingo programming and debugging. Script lines entered in this window will be executed immediately (no need to place a script in the Score). If the "Trace" option is enabled, the Message window will keep a running text display of actions during movie playback.

## Moveable Sprite

A Sprite that can be moved by the end user. This option is achieved by enabling the Sprite's "Moveable" checkbox in the Score window.

## Movie

A Director file. Also used to refer to digital video (such as QuickTime) files.

## Movie In A Window (MIAW)

A Director movie running in a window of its own, separate from the Stage of the root movie running underneath. MIAWs can be fully interactive and even pass information (such as commands) to other opened movies.

## Movie Script

When a script Cast Member is designated a movie script via its Info Box, the scripting it contains can be accessed throughout playback of the movie. Movie-level operations (such as those in on startMovie and on stopMovie handlers) should be placed in a movie script.

**Multimedia**

The combination of sound, video images, and text to create a "moving" presentation.

**Noise**

Unwanted signals or data that may reduce the quality of the output.

**Nudge**

To move a graphic or text element in small, preset increments, usually with the arrow keys.

**Opacity**

1. The degree to which paper will show print through it. 2. Settings in certain graphics applications that allow images or text below the object whose opacity has been adjusted, to show through.

**Operator**

A symbol or term in Lingo used to perform a specific operation. For example, the asterisk ("*") will multiply two values; the greater-than symbol (">") will compare the first value against the second and decide which one is larger.

**Optical Disks**

Video disks that store large amounts of data used primarily for reference works such as dictionaries and encyclopedias.

**Palette**

A collection of colors for displaying artwork on the Stage. There are several palettes to choose from in Director, and you can create custom palettes as well. A palette is applied not to an individual piece of artwork, but to all graphic elements on the Stage in a given Frame of the Score.

**Palette Channel**

The channel in the Score in which palettes can be applied. Also used for embedding palette-related special effects such as color cycling.

**Palette Window**

The window in which the color palettes can be copied and/or modified.

**Parent**

A script from which child objects are derived. A parent script can contain instructions for behaviors common to all objects derived from it. When each child object is created, additional instructions can be given concerning the behavior of that individual object.

**Passed Event**

The notice of an event, which travels down the event hierarchy until it encounters an event handler linked to it. For example, if a Score script does not contain a mouseDown handler, it passes the mouseDown message to the Cast Member script level.

**Paste Relative**

This command copies a selected segment of Sprites-but rather than repeat the Sprite positioning exactly, it uses the last Sprite of the selection as a keyframe for the new Sprites. Thus, the animation is repeated, but at a point relative to where it last ended.

**Photoshop**

The Adobe Systems image editing program commonly used for color correction and special effects on both the Macintosh and PC platforms.

**PICT/PICT2**

A common format for defining bitmapped images on the Macintosh. The more recent PICT2 format supports 24-bit color.

**Pixel**

The individual units of display, each corresponding to a color, black or white, or grayscale dot on your monitor. Typical Stage dimensions for a 14-inch monitor are 640 pixels by 480 pixels.

**Playback**

The process of running a Director movie. For the movie to operate, it must be played, even if the display on Stage is static.

**Playback Head**

The cursor at the top of the Score window, which travels through the Score during playback to indicate the currently active Frame. In Director's interface, the Playback Head is made easier to trace by the addition of a thin line extending from the bottom of the Score channels.

**Plug-In**

A standard software architecture used to create special effects modules. Director can incorporate plug-ins written to Photoshop standards; they'll appear as menu options in the Paint window.

**Pop-Up Menu**

A menu of choices accessed by clicking and dragging on the current choice. Seen in many Director dialog boxes, and in the Paint window.

**PPI**

Pixels per inch; used to denote the resolution of an image.

**Primary Event Handler**

A handler script intended to trigger actions when the given event occurs. There are four types of primary event handlers, indicated by keydownScript, mousedownScript, mouseupScript, and time-outScript. When you set each of these scripts to a specific handler, that handler will execute whenever the event occurs. Unlike other stops on the event hierarchy, primary event handlers will automatically pass on the event message unless directed not to with the dontPassEvent command.

**Projector**

A self-contained, self-running version of a Director movie. Once created, a Projector file can run on host systems without a copy of Director installed.

**Properties Dialog**

The dialog box in which information about an individual Cast Member is stored. It is accessible by selecting the Cast Member, then clicking the "i" button. Also referred to as the Information icon.

**Property**

An aspect or quality of an element controllable by Lingo. For example, the ink of Sprite, the height of Sprite, and the color of Sprite are all properties of a given Sprite.

**Prototype**

An early version of a multimedia production designed to demonstrate the structure and/or design projected for the final project. In Director, prototypes are often used as structures upon which the final product is superimposed.

**Pt.**

Abbreviation for point.

**Pushbutton**

A button created with the Tool Palette. It is highlighted when selected, and selected by being directly clicked upon.

### QuickTime
A standard for digital video. In order to operate QuickTime videos in conjunction with Director, a copy of QuickTime (or QuickTime for Windows) must be installed.

### RAM
Random Access Memory, the "working" memory of a computer that holds files in process. Files in RAM are lost when the computer is turned off, whereas files stored on the hard drive or floppy disks remain available.

### Radio Button
A button created within Cast Member Properties by changing the "Type" pop-up menu.

### Raster
A bitmapped representation of graphic data.

### Raster Graphics
A class of graphics created and organized in a rectangular array of bitmaps. Often created by paint software, fax machines, or scanners for display and printing.

### Rasterize
The process of converting digital information into pixels at a specified resolution.

### Real Time
A method of recording animation. When recorded in real time, any movements of Sprites on the Stage will be played back with the same speed and sequence.

### Recording Light
A red light in the leftmost part of the visual channel, which indicates that movements in the channel are currently being retained by Director.

### Registration Point
The location that Director considers to be the physical center of Sprites derived from a Cast Member. The registration point can be moved in the Paint window; it does not have to be the actual center of the artwork.

### Resolution
The density of graphic information expressed in dots per inch (dpi) or pixels per inch (ppi).

### RGB
Acronym for red, green, blue, the colors of projected light from a computer monitor that, when combined, simulate a subset of the visual spectrum. When a color image is scanned, RGB data is collected by the scanner and then converted to CMYK data at some later step in the process. Also refers to the color model of most digital artwork. See also CMYK.

### Rich Text Format (RTF)
One of two types of text available in Director. Text saved in this format can be automatically anti-aliased and subjected to a number of typographical controls (such as kerning and leading), but is converted to graphic artwork when a projector is created. Field text (the other kind of text) does not have as many display options, and its display is dependent upon the fonts installed in the host computer.

### Rollover
The act of rolling the cursor over a given element on the screen. It's possible to write Lingo scripts that perform certain actions when the cursor rolls over individual Sprites.

### ROM
Read Only Memory, a semiconductor chip in the computer that retains startup information for use the next time the computer is turned on.

### Rotation
Turning an object at some angle to its original axis.

### RTF
Rich Text Format, a text format that retains formatting information lost in pure ASCII text.

### Scaling
The means within a program to reduce or enlarge the amount of space an image will occupy by multiplying the data by a scale factor. Scaling can be proportional, or in one dimension only.

### Score, Score Window
The spreadsheet-like database in which instructions and information about a Director movie are placed. In order to appear on the Stage during playback, a Cast Member must first be placed in a location in the Score.

### Score Display Mode
Any of several formats for viewing information in the Score window. For instance, the Extended mode displayed detailed information about individual Sprites.

### Screen Shot
A printed output or saved file that represents data from a computer monitor.

### Script Window
The window in which script Cast Members (and scripts attached to Cast Members) can be viewed and edited.

### Serif
A line or curve projecting from the end of a letterform. Typefaces designed with such projections are called serif faces.

### Shockwave
The technology used to compress, encapsulate, and embed Director movies in HTML (HyperText Markup Language) documents, the sort used on the World Wide Web. Also used to refer to the plug-in necessary to view such movies in on-line browsers such as Netscape Navigator.

### Shockwave Audio (SWA)
The sound compression format used by both Director and Macromedia SoundEdit 16. It can be used independently of the Shockwave playback technology.

### Skew
A transformation command that slants an object at an angle to the side from its initial fixed base.

### Slot
See *Cast Slot.*

### Small caps
A type style in which lowercase letters are replaced by uppercase letters set in a smaller point size.

### Snap-to (guides or rulers)
An optional feature in page layout programs that drives objects to line up with guides or margins if they are within a pixel range that can be set. This eliminates the need for very precise, manual placement of an object with the mouse.

**Sound File**

A Cast Member containing either a digital sound or a link to a digital sound file.

**Sound Channel**

Either of the two channels in the Score devoted to sound playback. Can also be applied to "virtual" sound channels, which can be directed by Lingo to play additional sounds.

**Source Cast Member**

The Cast Member from which a given Sprite (in the Score) was derived.

**Sprite**

An individual instance of a Cast Member on the Stage, as documented by the placement of the Cast Member in the Score. Sprites can display several qualities not shared by the source Cast Member, but changes to the Cast Member are immediately reflected in all Sprites derived from that Cast Member.

**Sprite Options**

The Sprite options in the Source are those that can be set by the checkmarks and pull-down menus on the left side of the Score window. They are: Ink effects, Trails, Moveable, and Editable.

**Sprite Script**

A Lingo script that is attached to an individual Sprite in the Score. This is done by selecting the Sprite, then selecting a script in the Score's pop-up script menu.

**Stage Window**

The window in Director that represents the action transpiring during playback. When a projector is created from a Director movie, the Stage window becomes the only visible window.

**Stage Color**

The color of the Stage window, which can vary from movie to movie. It is set in the Control Panel and remains constant throughout the movie, but can be changed with Lingo scripting.

**Step Recording**

The process of recording animation (Stage movement) on a Frame-by-Frame basis, as opposed to real-time recording.

**Streaming Shockwave**

The compression technology that allows playback of Shockwave movies to begin quickly in Internet browsers. Previously, the end user had to wait until the entire movie was downloaded before playback could begin.

**Tempo**

The rate at which the playback head moves from Frame to Frame in the movie. It can be set from a minimum of one Frame per second to a maximum of 500 Frames per second.

**Tempo Channel**

The Score channel where time-related controls are placed. It can be used to set the tempo, but also to introduce pauses (from one second to two minutes) and strategic delays (i.e. waiting for another channel to finish playing).

**Text**

The characters and words that form the main body of a publication.

**Text Attribute**

A characteristic applied directly to a letter or letters in text, such as bold, italic, or underline.

**Text Effects**

Means by which the display of non-bitmapped text can be modified, such as bolding, underlining, and italicizing.

**Text Window**

The window in which the non-bitmapped text Cast Members are stored, displayed, and edited.

**Thumbnails**

1. The preliminary sketches of a design.
2. Small images used to indicate the content of a computer file.

**Tool Palette**

The palette from which certain tools (pertaining to buttons, fields, text, shapes, and lines) are selected in Director. Sometimes called a "windoid" as it is not resizable by the user.

**Tracking**

Adjusting the spacing of letters in a line of text to achieve proper justification or general appearance. You may want to squeeze letters closer together to fit into a Frame, or spread them apart for a special effect.

**Trailing Sprites**

Sprites in the Score that have the "Trails" option enabled. With Trails, the images of earlier Sprites are retained on the Stage, creating the sense of a chain of Sprites rather than of motion over time.

**Trails**

The evidence of earlier Sprites, retained on the Stage even though other Sprites occupy the channels in the Score.

**Transition**

A special effect triggered when playback moves from one Frame to the next in the Score.

**Transition Channel**

The channel dedicated to containing transitional effects in the Score.

**Tweak Window**

The window in which individual Sprites on the Stage can be moved by a small distance (corresponding to a mouse movement or pixel value).

**Tweening**

See In-betweening.

**Type Family**

A set of typefaces created from the same basic design but in different weights, such as bold, light, italic, book, and heavy.

**Typesetting**

The arrangement of individual characters of text into words, sentences, and paragraphs.

**Typo**

An abbreviation for typographical error. A keystroke error in the typeset copy.

**Uppercase**

The capital letters of a typeface as opposed to the lowercase, or small, letters. When type was hand composited, the capital letters resided in the upper part of the type case.

**User**

See end user.

**Variable**

A container for data generated by Director. For example, the statement put 2 + 2 into myVar would create a variable named myVar, containing the value 4. Variables can be either local (existing only in the context of the script) or global (containing values which can be accessed by other scripts throughout the movie.

## Vector Graphics

Graphics defined using coordinate points, and mathematically drawn lines and curves, which may be freely scaled and rotated without image degradation in the final output. Fonts (such as PostScript and TrueType), and illustrations from drawing applications are common examples of vector objects. Vector graphics can be created in Director's Vector Shape window.

## Visual Channels

The channels in the Score designed to contain graphic Cast Members, such as bitmapped artwork, text fields, digital video, buttons and shapes.

## WYSIWYG

An acronym for "What You See Is What You Get," (pronounced "wizzywig") meaning that what you see on your computer screen bears a strong resemblance to what the job will look like when it is printed.

## X-height

The height of the letter "x" in a given typeface, which represents the basic size of the bodies of all of the lowercase letters (excluding ascenders and descenders).

## Xtra

A software module that adds enhanced capabilities to Director. These can be purchased separately from a variety of vendors and integrated into the Director authoring environment by placing them in the Xtras folder adjacent to the application. When thus installed, they will appear under the Xtras menu when Director is launched (except in the case of transitional Xtras, which will show up in the Frame Properties: Transitions dialog box).

## Zip

1. To compress a file on a Windows-based system using a popular compression utility (PKZIP). 2. A removable disk made by Iomega (a Zip disk) or the device that reads and writes such disks (a Zip drive).

## Zooming

The process of electronically enlarging or reducing an image on a monitor to facilitate detailed design or editing and navigation.

# Notes

# Index

# Notes